Practical Wisdom in the Age of Technology

The dramatic recent advances and emergent trends in technologies have brought to the fore many vital and challenging questions and dilemmas for leaders and organizations. These are issues that call for a critical, insightful examination of key questions such as: are modern technologies beneficial or problematic for the well-being of individuals, organizations, and societies at large; why do we seem to feel more disconnected in an age of technological connectivity; can organizations reduce technology-induced stresses and find ways to enable the mindful use of technologies; and how can organizations, governments, and societies manage the use of technologies wisely?

Such questions, when explored from various perspectives of wisdom, can yield significant insights, increase awareness of the issues, deepen the dialogue, and help redesign an increasingly technology-driven future. However, there is little researched published material available on such questions and issues. *Practical Wisdom in the Age of Technology: Insights, issues and questions for a new millennium* provides thought-provoking dialogue and critical reflection on a variety of themes linking technology and practical wisdom.

This text offers a foundation for exploration, inquiry, engagement, and discussion among organizational, political and social leaders, technology professionals, information systems academicians, wisdom researchers, managers, philosophers of technology, and other practitioners.

Nikunj Dalal is Professor of Information Systems in the Spears School of Business at Oklahoma State University, Stillwater, USA. His research relates to technology and its relationship to: wisdom, mindfulness, learning, dialogue, and philosophy, as elements of an integral inquiry of the human condition.

Ali Intezari is a Lecturer of Management and Leadership in the UQ Business School at The University of Queensland, Brisbane, Australia. His current research includes wisdom theory, management decision-making, and knowledge management. He has published in the fields of management and information systems.

Marty H. Heitz is Associate Professor of Philosophy at Oklahoma State University, Stillwater, USA. His research includes Chinese and Indian Philosophy, non-duality, existential phenomenology (especially the thought of Martin Heidegger), and the thought of David Bohm.

The Practical Wisdom in Leadership and Organization Series
Series Editors
Wendelin M. Küpers, Massey University, New Zealand
David J. Pauleen, Massey University, New Zealand

The *Practical Wisdom in Leadership and Organization Series* provides a platform for authors to articulate wiser ways of managing and leading and of reassessing both practice within organisational setting and organisational research.

Books in this series focus on the art and practice of inquiry and reflexivity and explicitly connect with challenges and issues of 'praxis' in the field of organisation and management, be that academic research or in situ management practice. Rather than offering closure and final answers, contributions to this series invite further critical inquiry, interdisciplinary conversations and exploration. The aim is to engage authors and readers – students, academics and practitioners alike – in reflexive and critical dialogue.

By thus engaging readers, these books play an important role in teaching, learning and informing in university classrooms, management boardrooms and public policy forums.

Titles in the series include:

A Handbook of Practical Wisdom
Leadership, Organization and Integral Business Practice
Edited by Wendelin Küpers and David Pauleen

Practical Wisdom in the Age of Technology
Insights, issues, and questions for a new millennium
Edited by Nikunj Dalal, Ali Intezari and Marty Heitz

Practical Wisdom in the Age of Technology

Insights, issues, and questions for a new millennium

Edited by
Nikunj Dalal, Ali Intezari, and Marty H. Heitz

Routledge
Taylor & Francis Group

LONDON AND NEW YORK

First published 2016 by Routledge

2 Park Square, Milton Park, Abingdon, Oxon, OX14 4RN
605 Third Avenue, New York, NY 10017

Routledge is an imprint of the Taylor & Francis Group, an informa business

First issued in paperback 2020

British Library Cataloguing in Publication Data
A catalogue record for this book is available from the British
Library

Library of Congress Cataloging-in-Publication Data
A catalog record for this book has been requested

ISBN: 978-1-4724-4222-2 (hbk)
ISBN: 978-0-367-73725-2 (pbk)

Typeset in Sabon
by Apex CoVantage, LLC

Contents

Illustrations

Editors

Nikunj Dalal inquiries into practical questions of humanity that call for wisdom. As Professor of Information Systems at Oklahoma State University, Stillwater, his research involves exploring the relationships between wisdom, technologies, and learning. He has chaired or co-chaired minitracks and moderated panels on transdisciplinary wisdom at international conferences. His work has been published in a number of international journals.

Marty H. Heitz received his PhD from the University of Hawaii at Manoa in 1999 in Comparative Philosophy, focusing on a comparative study of the early thought of Martin Heidegger and the *Zhuangzi*, and is currently Associate Professor of Philosophy at Oklahoma State University, where he teaches Asian and comparative philosophy as well as existential phenomenology. A student of the late Zen teacher, Maurine Stuart Roshi, he also practices Taiji, Qigong and Traditional Chinese Medicine, as well as forms of both Jnana and Bhakti Yoga. But through it all, he is seriously committed to the notion that no practice or belief should be taken all that seriously.

Ali Intezari is a Lecturer of Management and Leadership in the UQ Business School at The University of Queensland, Brisbane, Australia. His current research includes wisdom theory, management decision-making, and knowledge management. His PhD focused on the relationship between practical wisdom and managerial decision making. His works have appeared in such journals as *Communications of the Association for Information Systems, Journal of Business Ethics and Business Strategy*, and the *Environment Journal*. He is the co-author of the book *Wisdom, Analytics and Wicked Problems: Integral Decision-Making in and beyond the Information*. He also regularly (co-)authors papers presented at conferences, most notably: the Academy of Management (AoM), the Australia and New Zealand Academy of Management (ANZAM), the Australasian Conference on Information Systems (ACIS), and the American Conference on Information Systems (AMCIS).

Contributors

Jon W. Beard is Associate Professor in Information Systems and Operations Management at the School of Business at George Mason University. He has been on the faculty in the Krannert School of Management at Purdue University and the Mays Business School at Texas A&M University. He also worked as a Lead Systems Engineer for the MITRE Corporation. His research and consulting work has focused on strategic technology management, systems analysis and design, workspace design, and the social and behavioral impacts of technology change. He has published in a variety of journals, presented research at over 50 conferences, and is the editor of two books on Impression Management and IT.

Roberto Biloslavo is Professor of Management at the University of Primorska, Faculty of Management Koper, Slovenia. His research focuses on management and leadership, knowledge management, strategic management, and sustainable development. From 2008 to 2011, he was Vice-Rector for Academic Affairs at the University of Primorska. Besides teaching and researching, he consults with various domestic and international companies about vision and mission statement development, knowledge management, and leadership development. He has published extensively in respected national and international journals, and has participated in several international research teams.

Philip D. Carter is a psychodramatist. He has brought adventure and heart to the teaching of research methods to postgraduate students, the establishment of a system usability laboratory, and the researching of the human–computer relationship. He has developed experiential and participatory approaches to leadership training and working in domestic violence.

Caterina Desiato studies sociocritical aspects and empowering possibilities of the Internet, having completed a thesis in Philosophy at the Università degli Studi, Milan, Italy and currently within the interdisciplinary PhD program in Communication and Information Sciences at the University of Hawaii at Mānoa. As Instructional Designer for the Distance Course Design & Consulting group at the College of Education, she is committed to empowering diverse learners and challenging stereotypes. She has held an international Fulbright scholarship and studied technology and society in France on an Erasmus scholarship. Her current research investigates what mediational means facilitate empathy among diverse participants in online deliberation in order to foster wisdom in mediated political discourse. Her publications in the area of technology and empathy include: Virtualizing the past: Re-connecting on Facebook and emerging social relationships (*46th Hawaii International Conference on System Sciences*, pp. 3363–3372, 2013).

Michael A. Erskine is the Director of the Educational Technology Center at the Metropolitan State University of Denver. He is a graduate of the Computer Science and Information Systems PhD program at the University of Colorado Denver. His research interests include educational technology, disaster management, and spatial decision support systems. His research has been presented at the Americas Conference on Information Systems (AMCIS), the International Conference on Information Resources Management (ConfIRM), the IEEE Digital Ecosystems and Technologies Conference (DEST), and the International Conference on Project Management (ProjMAN). In addition, his work has been published in *Axioms* and the *Journal of Computer Information Systems* (forthcoming). He is a member of the Association for Information Systems and serves on the Board of Directors of Developing Minds Software.

Stefan Klein is Professor for Inter-organizational Systems at the University of Münster, Germany. Previously he held teaching or research positions at University College Dublin, Ireland; the University of Linz, Austria; the University of Koblenz-Landau, Germany; the University of St. Gallen, Switzerland; Harvard University; the German Research Center for Computer Science (GMD); and the University of Cologne. His current research areas are information infrastructures, network economy, information management, social media, and the transformation of work. He studies practices of technology use and organizational transformation from a group to an industry level. He has published widely and is a member of the editorial board of several international IS journals.

Nicholas Maxwell has devoted much of his working life to arguing that we need to bring about a revolution in academia so that it seeks and promotes wisdom and does not just acquire knowledge. He has published eight books on this theme, including: *From Knowledge to Wisdom* (Blackwell, 1984), *The Comprehensibility of the Universe* (Oxford University Press, 1998), and *Global Philosophy: What Philosophy Ought to Be* (Imprint Academic, 2014). For a book about his work, see L. McHenry (ed.), *Science and the Pursuit of Wisdom: Studies in the Philosophy of Nicholas Maxwell* (Ontos Verlag, 2009). For nearly 30 years, he taught philosophy of science at University College London, where he is now Emeritus Reader. In 2003 he founded Friends of Wisdom, an international group of academics and educationalists concerned that universities should seek wisdom and not just acquire knowledge (see www.knowledgetowisdom.org). For more about his work, see http://www.ucl.ac.uk/from-knowledge-to-wisdom and http://discovery.ucl.ac.uk/view/people/ANMAX22.date.html.

Alex E. McDaniel, a former US Army Military Intelligence Noncommissioned Officer, earned his BS in Organizational Communication from Metropolitan State University of Denver and his MA in Instructional Design and Adult Learning from the University of Colorado Denver. He has presented on the importance of a balanced academic ethos in a wide variety of academic venues and currently supports MSU Denver as the

Senior Instructional Designer and Interactive Applications Developer at the Educational Technology Center.

Bernard McKenna is Associate Professor at the University of Queensland Business School. His major areas of research interest are critical discourse studies and wisdom in management (*Wisdom and Management in the Knowledge Economy*, Routledge, 2010). He has published in a wide range of leading journals, including *Leadership Quarterly*, *Applied Linguistics*, *Social Epistemology*, *Public Administration Review*, and *Management Communication Quarterly*. He is on several editorial boards, including those for *Management Communication Quarterly*, *Journal of Management and Organization*, and *Journal of Technical Writing and Communication*.

Mara Miller earned a BA from Cornell, an MA from the Center for Japanese Studies at the University of Michigan, and a PhD from Yale University; she was a Mellon Post-Doctoral Fellow in East Asian Art and Religion at Emory University. An invited member of the first International Workshops on Comparative Informatics held at Copenhagen Business School (2010, 2012), she is a former USWEST enterprise web editor and graphics designer for USWESTNet (ISP) and tractor-trailer driver; she has taught computer literacy at the college and middle-school levels. She has lectured about the atomic bombings at the Hiroshima Peace Studies Institute, Drexel University, the University of Hawaii's Numata Conference in Buddhist Studies and Center for Japanese Studies, and the Canterbury Historical Society (Christchurch, New Zealand), and has published related articles and chapters in the *Journal of Aesthetics and Art Criticism*, *The Clearing House: A Journal of Educational Strategies, Issues and Ideas*, *Philosophy and Literature*; M. Mohr (ed.), *Violence, Nonviolence, and Japanese Religions: Past, Present, and Future*; N. Minh (ed.), *New Essays in Japanese Aesthetics*, and K. Davis-Hayes and R. Chapman (eds), *Hiroshima, Nagasaki and Memory*; and an editorial in the *Honolulu Star-Advertiser* (August 8, 2012). A lifelong student of Buddhism, Confucianism, Shinto, and other wisdom traditions, which she has taught, along with meditation, to her university and middle-school classes, she lived in Nagasaki for two years. She is currently writing a book on the atomic bombings: *Terrible Knowledge and Tertiary Trauma*.

Stefan Schellhammer is a faculty member of the Department of Information Systems at the University of Münster, Germany. He received his PhD from the University of Münster in the subject area of inter-organizational information systems. Currently he is working in Professor Stefan Klein's research group. His present research interests include studying the emergence of information infrastructures and IT-related stress.

Cindy Scheopner studies the intersection of law and religion, with specializations in ethics and Islamic philosophy, as a philosophy PhD candidate at the University of Hawaii at Mānoa. As a senior researcher, she directs education and communications for the Office of Research Compliance. She spent two decades in broadcast news after receiving a BS (Journalism) from the University of Kansas. She also holds a JD (law) from Baylor University and an MA (philosophy) from the University of Colorado. She co-edited *Cross-currents: Comparative Responses to Global Interdependence* (2013); has written several articles in *Multicultural America: A Multimedia Encyclopedia*;

an essay on Santa as cross-cultural connection in *Christmas: Better than a Lump of Coal*; and is managing editor of the *Sage Encyclopedia of Business, Ethics, and Society* (forthcoming). Her wisdom interests are in the role of empathy in motivating ethical behavior through group interaction.

Anita Trnavcevic is a full professor and former Dean of the Faculty of Management at the University of Primorska. Her research interests include qualitative methodology, sustainable development, education policy analysis, and marketization of public education. Her publications appear in national and international journals and as monographs.

Diane R. Watkins serves as the IT Services Communications Coordinator at the Metropolitan State University of Denver. She holds a BS in Technical Communications and an AAS in Computer Information Systems. The highlights of her professional experience include working as an instructional technologist and designer, developing computer-based training for the US Air Force, exploring how military training can be enhanced and learner motivation increased by adding gaming aspects to computer-based training, and leading projects investigating the use of inquiry-based learning and the use of the Structured Content Development Model.

Series editors' preface from *The Practical Wisdom in Leadership and Organization* series

It gives us great pleasure to see the publication of the second book in The Practical Wisdom in Leadership and Organization Series. *Practical Wisdom in the Age of Technology: Insights, issues, and questions for a new millennium* is a book for our time. The editors, Nikunj Dalal, Ali Intezari, and Marty H. Heitz, have succeeded in assembling an excellent collection of thoughtful and insightful commentary and hard-nosed practice-based analysis. This book gives focus to the challenges faced by society, organizations, and individuals as we attempt to make wise use of the science and technology that increasingly dominate our lives.

Since the first book of this series, *The Handbook of Practical Wisdom: Leadership, Organization, and Integral Business Practice*, came out in 2013, interest in the research and practice of wisdom in management has continued to attract increasing notice. This series and other recent books, journal articles, academic research, PhD dissertations, and empirical studies as well as practice-based industry conferences like Wisdom 2.0 are evidence of a growing interest in a basic re-ordering of management priorities in sustainable, more equitable ways.

The alternative pathway, the regression of reason, insight, and ethics, will inevitably lead to societies and economies dominated by greed, materialism, stupidity, and madness. We so often appear to be situated under the reign of forces (including technological forces) that show a lack of wisdom while facing ecological, social, and economic crises of global proportions. Wisdom is in ever-greater demand to temper these auto-destructive hyper-systems and may help us to re-orient ourselves to a more mindful re-articulation of psychic individuation, collective individuation, and technical individuation that makes life worth living (Stiegler, 2013, 2014) and to enact an ethics of technology (Verbeek, 2008).

This becomes more and more relevant as it is becoming increasingly evident that technology requires wisdom in its design and use, as the misuse of technology can lead to not only foolish but also dangerous outcomes. The passive seduction of technology requires thoughtful resistance (Pauleen et al., 2015). As ancient as wisdom is as a concept and practice, it needs updating and new translations for our technology-driven times and circumstances marked as the digital age.

Wisdom in this digital age or "digital wisdom" is called for in order to integrate reason and observation, insight, ethical skill, and praxis. As such, it can become particularly a drive to create positive and sustainable outcomes to the conditions of life (Pauleen et al., 2015). Digital wisdom not only refers to the wise design and use of technology, but also to the possibility of wisdom arising from the use and effects of modern and postmodern forms of technologies.

Along with Prensky (2013), we think that wisdom today and its development in the future need to be seen in connection of humans and technology:

> While future wisdom seekers will likely still be able to achieve today's level of wisdom without the cognitive enhancements offered by our increasingly sophisticated digital technology, that level of wisdom will not be sufficient, either in quality or in nature, to navigate the complex, technologically advanced world of our future. For that we require the cognitive enhancements and extensions of technology, and the digital wisdom to use them well . . . Our new, rapidly expanding technology means a changing environment, and our success as humans means adapting, as quickly and completely as possible, to that environment. Whether we are comfortable with or discomfited by this new technology, all of us, if we are going to succeed, need to learn to use it wisely. We all need digital wisdom.
>
> (Prensky, 2013, p. 78)

In this digital age, as networked technologies are becoming ever more interwoven into embodied subjectivities, the possibility of dwelling outside of technology-mediated worlds is shrinking. This goes beyond the active uses of media, such as making calls, sending messages, or taking pictures, to include the sensors that now inhabit our lived space and "passively register massive amounts of behavioral and environmental data without any active involvement, decision to initiate, or even awareness on our part" (Hansen, 2012, p. 53). Facing an increasing technologization of life, mobile technologies and networked connectivities afford an accelerated life in motion in a globally enframed world (Heidegger, 1977) that seems to be somewhere between everywhere and *now*here (Küpers and, 2015).

Today, under the "techno-human condition" (Allenby and Sarewitz, 2011), human-induced environmental change and domination of the earth's ecosystems have reached a global scale and an accelerated speed, all part of the dramatic pursuit and increase of economic growth, the spread of global markets, and commodity production and consumption since World War Two. These human activities could inadvertently drive the earth system into a much less hospitable state, damaging efforts to reduce poverty and leading to a deterioration of human wellbeing in many parts of the world, including wealthy countries (Steffen et al., 2015).

In addition to these global effects, on a more personal level, contemporary organizations and their members are facing constant change in many areas of daily work related to technology and technocratic regimes. Various forms of technological transformation affect the realities and management of workplaces in a challenging and demanding manner (Bersin et al., 2015). Being nearly continuously connected to their jobs by pervasive mobile and other technologies overwhelmed employees and managers, who today work under increasingly demanding conditions and constraints which they struggle to handle (Hodson et al., 2014). Likewise, these developments call for digital wisdom to make the make the best use of technology and to mitigate the worst. This book responds to this call.

We hope to see this book not only read by organizational leaders, managers, and academics but also by philosophers, technology and information systems professionals, and students in business, engineering, and technology. We have been especially heartened to see growing interest in the ways in which wisdom can be incorporated into management education both as a subject and a pedagogy. Indeed, the next book on wisdom learning in The Practical Wisdom in Leadership and Organization series is scheduled for publication in the near future.

As the editors of this series, we look forward to increasing the dialogue and the practice of practical wisdom and invite those who are interested in editing a book for this series to contact us.

With a joining of head, heart, and hands,

Wendelin Küpers and David J. Pauleen

Editors, *The Practical Wisdom in Leadership and Organization Series*

References

Allenby, B.R. and D. Sarewitz. (2011). *The Techno-Human Condition*. Cambridge, MA: MIT Press.

Bersin, J., Agarwal, D., Pelster, B., and Schwartz, B. (2015). Introduction: Leading in the new world of work. *Global Human Capital Trends 2015*. Retrieved from http://dupress.com/periodical/trends/human-capital-trends-2015 (accessed September 21, 2015).

Hansen, M. (2012). Ubiquitous sensation or the autonomy of the peripheral: Towards an atmospheric, impersonal and microtemporal media. In U. Ekman (ed.), *Throughout: Art and Culture Emerging with Ubiquitous Computing* (pp. 63–88). Boston: MIT Press.

Heidegger, M. (1977). *The Question Concerning Technology and Other Essays*. New York: Harper. (Original work published 1954.)

Hodson, T. Schwartz, J., van Berkel, A., and Winstrom-Otten, I. (2014). The overwhelmed employee. Retrieved from http://dupress.com/articles/hc-trends-2014-overwhelmed-employee (accessed September 21, 2015).

Küpers, W., and Howard, C. (2015, forthcoming). Inter-placed mobility in the age of "digital gestell." *Transfers: Interdisciplinary Journal of Mobility Studies*.

Pauleen, D., Dalal, N., Rooney, D., Intezari, A., and Wang, W. (2015, forthcoming). In bed with technology? Peril, promise, and prudence. *Communications of the AIS*.

Prensky, M. (2013). *Brain Gain: Technology and the Quest for Digital Wisdom*. New York: Palgrave Macmillan.

Steffen, W. et al. (2015). Planetary boundaries: Guiding human development on a changing planet. *Science*, 347(6223), DOI: 10.1126/science.1259855.

Stiegler, B. (2013). *What Makes Life Worth Living*. Cambridge: Polity Press.

——. (2014). *States of Shock: Stupidity and Knowledge in the 21st Century*. Cambridge: Polity Press.

Verbeek, P.P. (2008). Cultivating humanity: Toward a non-humanist ethics of technology. In J.K. Berg Olsen, E. Selinger, and S. Riis (eds), *New Waves in Philosophy of Technology* (pp. 241–266). Basingstoke: Palgrave Macmillan.

Editors' preface introducing *Practical Wisdom in the Age of Technology: Insights, issues, and questions for a new millennium*

Nikunj Dalal, Ali Intezari, and Marty H. Heitz

"The important thing is not to stop questioning."
Albert Einstein

Modern technologies have empowered individuals and organizations in unprecedented ways and have seemingly made living easier, better, cheaper, and more effective, and yet those very same technologies appear to be causing dissatisfaction, unhappiness, violence, isolation, and stresses. In the midst of overwhelming material abundance stemming from extraordinary scientific and technological advances, why is the world still grasping for answers to existential and societal problems? How do we begin to understand the complex relationships between modern technology and humanity? This book aims to stimulate thought-provoking dialogue and critical reflection on a variety of sociotechnological themes from the standpoint of practical wisdom. It is based on a judicious peer-reviewed selection from several proposals and manuscripts that were received in response to a wide call for papers in various interdisciplinary outlets. In keeping with the intrinsic complexity and subtlety of themes that resist a simple characterization, this book has an interdisciplinary flavor, a mix of research approaches, and a desirable diversity of collective wisdom, which we hope has a broader appeal that extends beyond academia and organizational leadership to practitioners of all hues as well as the general populace.

It must be understood that the intent of this book is *not* to provide simple answers to what are clearly complex issues that technologies have raised. A wise person (anon) has remarked: "It is the questions in life that move us forward, not the answers." We suggest that the chapters in this book be read as a means of sustaining a living inquiry of the impact of technologies on the world, in keeping with a spirit of questioning the status quo and critically evaluating the "answers" given to us by popular media and interested or vested forces.

Technology is now omnipresent and has become in no small measure the main determinant of how we live and work. We have created revolutionary technological tools that can either be significant enablers of human potential or can devastate the planet in more ways than one. While there are fundamental questions about the nature of technology in shaping the human mind and the institutions it creates, there are also issues around "technology-in-practice," that is, the design, development, and use of technologies, that require urgent and meticulous attention. Such questions and dilemmas include the following: are modern technologies largely beneficial or problematic for the wellbeing of individuals, organizations, and societies? Why do we seem to feel more disconnected in an age of techno-logical connectivity? How can organizations reduce technology-induced stresses and find ways to enable the mindful use of technologies? How can individuals, organizations, governments, and societies manage the use of technologies wisely? We believe that the attempt to respond to such critical questions from the stand-point of practical wisdom can yield significant insights, increase awareness of the issues, deepen dialogue, and help redesign what is increasingly a technology-driven future.

Looking through the lens of practical wisdom

Why practical wisdom? In recent times, we have seen financial crises, wars, political instabilities, unsustainable ecological calamities, and societal problems of all kinds, some of them unprecedented in terms of their scale and complexity, all calling for wise and responsive leadership. A central premise of this book is that our existing solution approaches based on knowledge, science, and technologies may be necessary, but are not sufficient. There is a clear need for wisdom. Specifically, there is a need for improved transdisciplinary understanding of the role of wisdom in a technology-driven world, and the design and impact of technologies in a world crying out for wisdom.

Wisdom has many definitions, perspectives, and facets. Rather than argue and intel-lectualize about which perspective is appropriate, practical wisdom is concerned with responding to modern individual, organizational, and societal challenges creatively, mindfully, and proactively, and thus looks to draw from all sources of wisdom, includ-ing scientific knowledge, organizational practices, and the wisdom traditions. We see practical wisdom as very relevant to the future of humanity, possibly its single most important determinant.

As a focal area of study, wisdom research is increasingly attracting interdisci-plinary interest from other academic fields and disciplines, such as management, leadership, psychology, sociology, gerontology, biology, neurosciences, market-ing, and medicine. Scholars and practitioners are exploring many attributes of practical wisdom, such as intelligence, compassion, mindfulness, authenticity, leadership, creativity, problem-solving pragmatics, ethics, and awareness. Practical wisdom research can shed light on the isolating effects and stresses associated with technology use, or suggest mindfulness practices that are increasingly used by tech-nology companies, or generate Internet-based efforts to tap into the wisdom of the crowd (crowd-sourcing). A focus on practical wisdom has led to the emergence of conferences led by well-known technology companies such as the fast-growing Wisdom 2.0, described on its website (http://www.wisdom2summit.com) as "a global community of people dedicated to living with deeper wisdom, compassion, and awareness in the digital age" as well as projects such as the scholarly wisdom project at the University of Chicago (http://wisdomresearch.org), which tackles interdisciplinary work relating to wisdom.

Moreover, practical wisdom is intricately connected to many needs of contemporary organizations in areas such as knowledge management, problem finding and problem solving in the face of uncertainty, systems thinking, judgment and decision making, group support, analytics, modeling, social networks, cyber-crimes, and artificial intelligence among others. Many technology leaders and academics have called for a real need to progress from our current focus on data, information, and knowledge toward understanding, intelligence, and ultimately wisdom. Wisdom is seen as the pinnacle of the data-information-knowledge-wisdom (DIKW) pyramid and other similar models, but such a categorization is only one aspect of what seems to be a multi-faceted relationship with technology.

Wisdom and technology intersection: critical issues

What follows is a sampling of critical issues that lie at the intersection of practical wisdom and technology. This is an initial limited set and is by no means meant to be exhaustive. The chapters in this book by necessity (given the sheer scope and diversity of the terrain) address an even smaller subset of the universe of topics in this domain.

The promise and the folly of technological solutionism

- Can we critically question the implicit belief that technologies are a panacea for societal problems?
- Is our understanding of technology narrow-minded, instrumentalist, and primarily driven by utilitarian ends?
- What sorts of problems can technologies best address and for what issues may technological solutions be limited or limiting in significant ways?
- What kinds of new issues do technological solutions create?

Wisdom management

- How can we design, build, implement, and use technologies for consciously discovering, creating, sharing, and supporting wisdom in individuals, organizations, and societies?
- What are the implications of such systems in practice?
- To what extent can existing research on decision support systems and knowledge management be leveraged for wisdom management?
- Is wisdom the culminating point of a progression of data, information, knowledge, and wisdom?
- Can technologies enable deeper dialogues between and among individuals and groups?

Interdisciplinary, transdisciplinary and integral understanding of the nature of wisdom in a technology-driven world

- What are the practical implications of wisdom theories and perspectives in a technological context?
- How do Western and Eastern wisdom traditions, theologies, and spiritual approaches affect our relationship with and use of technologies?
- Can we live mindfully with and connected by technologies, for personal, professional, and societal wellbeing?

- How can we critically understand technology-induced stresses, job displacement, work–life balance and technology addiction?
- Do technologies have a role to play in mediating practical wisdom, reducing technology-induced stresses, and improving mindfulness?

Organizations and technologies

- How do we understand emerging leadership practices and paradigms such as learning organizations, inquiring organizations, communities of practice, and personal knowledge management?
- How can we go beyond mere ethical frameworks to include wisdom?
- What new organizational forms may be needed in a technology-driven world?
- How may leadership integrate knowledge, truth, and reality?
- How can technology facilitate reflexivity and praxis in leadership?

Philosophy of technology and applications of philosophies to a technology-based world

- Is it possible to do more and more (with the help of technologies), yet actually do less and less existentially? How do we understand such implicit paradoxes and ironies of a technological life?
- How does the phenomenology of technology and Heidegger's or post-phenomenological critiques of enframing technology apply in this context?
- What is the status of *technē* in relation to phronesis?
- How can technologies be developed and implemented through an integrative contribution of phronesis, *sophia*, and episteme? How can organizations and professional leaders benefit from the technology?
- What are technological wisdom and the ethics of technology?
- What does it mean to be human in a world of computer artifacts such as cyborgs and robots?

Understanding new and emergent phenomena

- How can we critically understand new phenomena emerging in a technology-driven world? This may include Internet addiction, technological biases, virtual communities and cyberspaces, self-image and social media, cultural anxieties, crowd-sourcing, excessive gaming, mobile phone obsession, cyber-crimes, cyber-cultures, humanoid robots, crypto-technologies, and digital currencies, among others.

Technology, wisdom, and learning

- Can wisdom be taught (as we teach ethics) in management schools?
- How can issues dealing with wisdom and technology be discussed and incorporated into educational curricula?
- What materials (theories, contemplative practices, case studies, exercises) should be included in wisdom pedagogies? How can technology play a pedagogic role?

- Whose responsibility is it to develop wisdom-based pedagogies?
- Who is eligible to teach wisdom?

The chapters

The diversity of the material in this book makes it difficult to sequence the chapters in a straightforward logical scheme. Although the meanings of "practical wisdom" and "technology" might seem self-evident, Chapters 1 and 2 respectively provide details and highlight subtleties. The subsequent chapters explore various issues at the intersection of practical wisdom and technology, particularly from perspectives that include the philosophical (Chapter 3), organizational (Chapters 4 and 5), design and engineering (Chapters 6 and 7), societal (Chapters 8 and 9), and educational (Chapters 10 and 11).

This introductory chapter is followed by the following chapters.

Chapter 1, "Conceptualizing wisdom: theoretical perspectives" by Ali Intezari, presents an overview of the theoretical perspectives for conceptualizing wisdom. It sets the stage for an opening understanding of the concept of wisdom. Intezari addresses the fundamental questions that are central to the themes tackled in other chapters in this book: what is wisdom? And how do we perceive, recognize, and operationalize wisdom? The chapter provides a brief review of the philosophical discourses and psychological studies of wisdom. The author introduces a cross-disciplinary conceptualization of wisdom and proposes an integrated theory of practical wisdom. Five key qualities are argued to be associated with wisdom and to be central to the manifestation of wisdom in practice. The chapter concludes that wisdom – rather than merely being a state of mind or a set of behavioral characteristics and personality traits – is an integrative process of being and practicing.

In Chapter 2, "Toward a wisdom-based understanding of technology," Nikunj Dalal examines the notion of technology in the broader sense of the term, from its historical origins to its modern context, and suggests that a paradigm shift, a new kind of understanding of the relationship of humans to technologies is necessary, which must be based on perennial universal insights of wisdom viewed in a modern, practical, and scientific context. He defines "technologies" in the broader sense to include all technological artifacts – contrivances, machines, methods, practices, techniques, media, instruments, and systems – designed by humans to meet human ends. The approach he proposes in the chapter is an open-ended holistic multi-dimensional inquiry, not caught in simplistic conclusions, and focused on understanding the problem using a subtle experiential art of looking and listening. The intent of this approach is to not only understand and recognize the partial truths evident in current perspectives on the human–technology relationship, but to also transcend them in a deeper inclusive integral manner.

In Chapter 3, "The screening of reality: a phenomenological perspective on the computer screen," Marty H. Heitz reflects on the phenomenology of the ever-more prominent use of screens in our daily lives. In particular, he describes the phenomenon of giving attention to the various technological screens we encounter in our work and leisure time by way of three main perspectives: Martin Heidegger's account of being-in-the-world and how his understanding of phronesis is critical to this account; Iain McGilchrist's recent research on the lateralization of the brain (that is, the differing functions of the right and left hemispheres of the brain) and what is cognitively happening when we give attention to the screen; and the practice of mindfulness or meditation, and how this practice may be used while screen-gazing. He thereby not only provides a phenomenological account of what is happening while we are absorbed in paying attention to the screen, but also provides some indications of how we might more mindfully mitigate against the reductionist and alienating effects that such screen-gazing may engender.

In Chapter 4, "The anatomy of wisdom in an era of ubiquitous technology," Jon W. Beard takes an organizational vantage point to pose a key question: can ever-present technologies demonstrate wisdom or make us wiser? Approaching this question from a DIKW framework central to the information systems literature, he explores the general anatomy of wisdom in modern technology-rich environments, drawing on concepts of organizational learning and knowledge management as frames for information technology and wisdom.

In Chapter 5, "Benefits and perils of virtual modes of organizing: a call for practical wisdom," Stefan Schellhammer and Stefan Klein examine the role of practical wisdom in dealing with the opportunities and demands of technology-driven work and life. The authors open their discussion focusing on the inseparable links between organizations and technology. They then proceed to discuss the transformation of the traditional workplace into the virtual workplace, highlighting how virtual workplaces have caused paradoxes and tensions for employees. Klein and Schellhammer propose that practical wisdom in the workplace can help employees handle and/or eliminate work stresses resulting from over-connectivity.

Chapter 6, "Empathy by design: enhancing diversity in online participation" by Caterina Desiato and Cindy Scheopner, provides an interesting discussion on "deliberation systems," "deliberation interaction," and "empathetic collaboration" in e-democracies and online participation. The authors argue that empathetic engagement through which both intellect and emotions are involved is essential to deliberative democracies. Empathy allows diverse perspectives to be heard by others involved in group decision making. The authors argue that although information technologies can facilitate group decision making, empathy is not available through technology. They offer suggestions on designing collaborative technologies in order to enhance diverging online participation by taking empathy into consideration.

Chapter 7, "Wisdom in praxis: how engineers use practical wisdom in their decision making," sheds light on the contribution of practical wisdom to engineering. In this chapter, Bernard McKenna, Roberto Biloslavo, and Anita Trnavcevic draw on a techno-societal theoretical basis which provides an integrative approach to wisdom. This approach proposes a theoretical framework to blend and integrate wisdom into the rather dry, rigid, and highly ruled field of engineering. The chapter begins with the assumption that wise engineers adopt a phronetic approach to their work. Then the authors consider the nature of the cognitive complexity involved in engineering decision making and argue that it is intricately involved with intuition and the capacity for metacognition.

In Chapter 8, "Atomic/nuclear weapons and energy technologies (ANWETs): the need for wisdom," Mara Miller addresses issues beyond information technologies and helps us appreciate that there is more than IT-based disruption and stresses in the big question; human survival itself is at stake. The chapter argues for the need for wisdom in dealing with ANWETs and nuclear disasters in terms of the dangers and challenges that these technologies present. Miller suggests that wisdom is not just about increasing our safety and security associated with these technologies; it is also a matter of developing ourselves at the individual and communal levels. She advocates incorporating wisdom in every stage of consideration and action regarding atomic and nuclear weapons and energy technologies.

In Chapter 9, "The human–computer relationship: who shall survive?," Philip D. Carter takes an optimistic look at technology, decoupling it from domination by utilitarian needs and other ideological perspectives. Using the psychodramatic method, he identifies the common dynamics of relationship and reciprocity in people's stories about "the machine." Not knowing the future, he suggests being open to a spirit of spontaneity, collegiality, and learning to moderate our fears about the threats posed by technology.

In Chapter 10, "Academic ethos: embracing a culture of practical wisdom in higher education," Alex E. McDaniel, Michael A. Erskine, and Diane R. Watkins argue for imparting practical wisdom to learners in academia and other organizational contexts. They explore the academic ethos as higher education's commitment to implement and sustain a culture of practical wisdom. Technologies are disruptive and it is important to understand their historic and modern effects in order to harness their power to create pedagogies that foster practical wisdom; this can be a quite a balancing act.

Ending on a critical and cautionary note, in Chapter 11, "Can scientific method help us create a wiser world?", philosopher Nicholas Maxwell tackles the genesis of technologies – the scientific method itself – and asks whether it can focus on a new kind of inquiry rationally devoted to helping humanity make progress toward as good a world as possible.

We anticipate that these chapters, in their richness, diversity, and freshness, provide new ways of thinking about a complex subject. In a world of known and unknown unknowns, we hope the issues raised in this book can be a means of exploration, inquiry, engagement, reflection, dialogue, and discussion among organizational leaders, technology professionals, information systems academics, wisdom researchers, managers, philosophers of technology, and other practitioners. All must participate in this inquiry. Nothing less than the future of humanity is at stake!

Chapter 1

Conceptualizing wisdom
Theoretical perspectives

Ali Intezari

Introduction

The rapidly growing use of technology has decisively affected our life and work. Teaching the knowledge and skills that are required to use technology proficiently has become an inseparable part of any education system. Less attention, however, has been paid to teaching and learning how to use technology appropriately, as the right means toward the right ends. Developing and incorporating the knowledge of how to use technology wisely toward achieving the wellbeing of the self and others is just as vital as technical skills. The impact of technology on almost all aspects of our life and work emphasizes that the wise use of technology must be promoted as the main responsibility of the technology users. Without doubt, it is time for us to pause and think about how we can use technology wisely, not just proficiently.

In order to understand what "wise use of technology" means and to make sense of the arguments provided in the following chapters, it is critical to first examine the concept of "wisdom." Wisdom has recently become a buzzword in academia and industry. It appears in a diverse range of studies in various disciplines, including philosophy, psychology, neuroscience, organizations and management, engineering, and so forth. Some scholars have conceptualized wisdom, and some others have developed scales to measure wisdom. A quick review of the literature, however, reveals that there is little consensus among scholars on what wisdom means, how it can be measured, and, more challenging, how it can be developed. In our daily life, we all might have some sort of understanding of wisdom. We probably understand (or at least we assume that we understand) what others refer to when they describe someone or a decision as wise or unwise. However, if you were asked to articulate wisdom, it would be a very challenging task, let alone that it is highly likely that even you and your friends would have different understandings of the concept of wisdom. Looking at wisdom's articulation in the technology context would reveal more concerns. Technology designers and developers may have different concerns from users as to the appropriate or, more precisely, the "wise" use of technology. How would you describe "wise use of technology" in the first place? Whose responsibility is it to ensure that technology is used "wisely?"

These questions and many others are explored in more detail in the following chapters. Each chapter provides valuable insight into the relationship between wisdom and technology. Depending on the context and argument, an appropriate definition of wisdom is provided in each chapter. Nonetheless, providing a theoretical basis for the concept of wisdom at the beginning of this book would be helpful in order for the reader to gain an integrated understanding of the subject matter and the forthcoming arguments. This chapter addresses a very fundamental question: what is wisdom? In other words, how do we perceive, recognize, and operationalize wisdom with respect to the use of technology?

The first part of this chapter provides a brief review of the philosophical discourses and psychological studies of wisdom. Next, an integrated theory of wisdom, which is based on the findings of the author's empirical study of wisdom, is introduced. The chapter concludes that wisdom – rather than merely being a state of mind or a set of behavioral characteristics and personality traits – is an integrative process of being and practicing. The process engages five qualities: multi-perspective consideration, self–other awareness, cognitive–emotional mastery, reflexivity, and praxis. A list of critical questions about the conceptualization and operationalization of wisdom is also provided.

Wisdom from ancient discourses to modern studies

For centuries, wisdom was an important topic in philosophical discourse in the Western, Eastern, and Middle-Eastern traditions. Over the last three decades, however, the concept of wisdom has been extensively studied in psychology and now it has become an emerging topic in other fields such as leadership, education, organizations and management, neuroscience, and public policy. Psychological studies of wisdom pioneered the contemporary studies of wisdom. The following sections comprise an introductory discussion of the major philosophical and psychological approaches to the concept of wisdom. Following the discussion, an interdisciplinary and empirically driven conceptualization of wisdom will be presented.

Philosophical discourses

The early discourses on wisdom can be found in the Western, Eastern, and Middle-Eastern traditions. While many of the recent studies of wisdom draw on the works of the classical philosophers such as Plato (428–348 B.C.), Socrates (469–399 B.C.), and mainly Aristotle (384–322 B.C.), the Eastern traditions such as Confucianism and Buddhism have recently been considered in modern studies of wisdom (cf. Case, 2013; Harwood, 2011; Rowley and Slack, 2009; Yang, 2011). The ancient Middle-Eastern approaches to wisdom, unlike their Western and Eastern counterparts, do not yet appear in the modern studies of wisdom. Due to limited space, and also given the prominence of the Aristotelian approach in contemporary studies of wisdom, the philosophical discussion of wisdom in this chapter revolves mainly around the Aristotelian stance. However, in order to set the stage for further discussion of the contemporary investigations of wisdom, a brief review of some of the main Eastern and Western approaches to wisdom will also be provided.

In both Western and Eastern traditions, wisdom is concerned with moral conduct and governance. Some may argue that the Eastern tradition has a strong theist foundation compared to its Western counterpart (cf. Rowley and Slack, 2009). However, a mixture of both mundane/practical and non-mundane/spiritual contemplations of the nature of wisdom can be found in both the Western and Eastern traditions. For example, while Hinduism in the Eastern tradition appears to have a more theist foundation, other Eastern approaches such as Confucianism, Daoism, or Buddhism incline toward articulating wisdom as having a mundane/practical nature.[1] According to the latter, wisdom is an integrated form of mind and virtue (Baltes and Kunzmann, 2004), which is concerned with harmonizing the person with their environment (Bierly III, Kessler, and Christensen, 2000). A similar standpoint is seen in Daoism and Confucianism. In Daoism, wisdom is regarded as being more associated with the balance between *yin* (female) and *yang* (male) aspects, and in Confucianism, wisdom is concerned with right living, morality, and social order (Aldwin, 2009). Likewise, the Japanese traditions associate wisdom with the interrelationship between and among people and context. Wisdom in the Japanese tradition is identified by four aspects: sociability and interpersonal relationships, education and knowledge, introspective attitudes, as well as understanding and judgment (Takahashi and Overton, 2005). Some examples of Shinto teachings and sayings are "do not be sluggish in your work," "sincerity is the mother of knowledge," and "in governing, let us govern with true sincerity."

The non-mundane and spiritual nature of wisdom is also, arguably, reflected by the Western philosophers. In the pre-Socratic tradition of Heraclitus in particular, we see that the role of a person's ability to understand the contextual nature of their existence, and how various elements in the given context are interrelated, are regarded as central to wisdom (Holliday and Chandler, 1986). For Aristotle, as reflected by *The Nicomachean Ethics*, wisdom is a contemplation of what is good for living a good life. Western philosophical approaches to the study of wisdom emphasize that wisdom is associated with one's ability to reflect on paradox and uncertainty. In *War and Peace*, Tolstoy (2007) emphasizes that wisdom is developed based on a consideration of the whole and how one is related to that whole. Likewise, in Kant's *Critique of Practical Reason* (1996), wisdom is concerned with the practical end of humans' existence on earth (Rowley and Slack, 2009).

Eastern and Western approaches, however, seem to vary as to the emphasis that each puts on cognitive and practical aspects of wisdom. In their study, Takahashi and Bordia (2000) found that Westerners tend to put more emphasis on cognitive dimensions of wisdom, whereas Easterners' view of wisdom is more synthetic, stressing both cognitive and affective dimensions. Nevertheless, wisdom is among the core virtues in both traditions (Dahlsgaard et al., 2005), and serves as a means to achieve a good life for self and others (Yang, 2011). Other virtues identified by the two traditions include courage, justice, humanity, temperance, and transcendence (Dahlsgaard et al., 2005). As I have already mentioned earlier in this chapter, given that the Aristotelian perspective, compared to those of other classical philosophers, is more prominent in the contemporary studies of wisdom, I avoid a comparative study of the Eastern and Western traditions, and focus more on Aristotle's (*The Nicomachean Ethics*) conceptualization of wisdom.

There are two concepts that are critical in the philosophical discourses of wisdom: virtue (*arête, ἀρετή*) and happiness (*eudaimonía, εὐδαιμονία*). Virtue refers to excellence in quality (Begley, 2006) and, more specifically, to the socially valued character traits such as humility and graciousness (Beauchamp, 1991). Aristotle describes virtue as "the state of character which makes a man good and which makes him do his own work well" (2009, 1106a, 20–25). Virtues can be achieved through bringing together emotions, desires, passions (Baggini and Fosl, 2007), and cognition in an excellent way (Intezari, 2014). Virtues are considered as the paths toward achieving *eudaimonia*.

Eudaimonia (happiness or wellbeing) is the good end toward which human beings move. As Aristotle put it, happiness is "something final and self-sufficient [that] is the end of action" (2009, 1079b, 20). "Self-sufficient" refers to the main characteristic of happiness. It conveys the meaning that happiness is its own reward and is not chosen for the sake of something else (2009, 1079b, 1–5). *Eudaimonia* means flourishing and making a success of life (Beauchamp, 1991), which is achieved through the development of excellence in both character (moral virtue) and intelligence (intellectual virtue) (Intezari, 2014). Examples of the virtues are honor, pleasure, and reason, which we choose because they lead to happiness. Wisdom, courage, temperance, and justice are regarded as the cardinal virtues (Small, 2004).

Aristotle uses two main concepts to describe wisdom: *sophia* (σοφία) and phronesis (φρόνησις).[2] *Sophia* is concerned with eternal truth and can be interpreted as theoretical or philosophical wisdom, whilst phronesis is action-oriented and concerned with conduct, and is therefore referred to as practical wisdom (2009, 1143b, 15–20). The two types of wisdom are interrelated and the conceptual difference between them is somewhat blurred. However, they are not the same. Someone who is practically wise makes decisions based on theoretically wise contemplation, and puts theoretical wisdom into action by practicing and habituating moral and intellectual characteristics. On the other hand, one may have certain and theoretical wisdom (episteme, *sophia*), but can never have such certainty with the regard to practical wisdom (phronesis, *technē*) as that is context-dependent and cannot be universalized. While phronesis is concerned with the deliberation on practical decisions, judgment, and choices, *sophia* is love of knowledge for knowledge's sake (Aldwin, 2009). Both theoretical and practical wisdom lead toward achieving excellence. In theoretical matters, it is called (theoretical) wisdom, and in practical matters, practical wisdom (Urmson, 1998).

The psychological approach

Over the last three decades, wisdom has been extensively studied by psychologists. Although the work of more recent psychologists such as Baltes (Baltes and Freund, 2003; Baltes and Kunzmann, 2003; Kunzmann and Baltes, 2005) and Sternberg (Sternberg, 2000, 2001, 2003, 2013) is popular and well established, the psychological studies of wisdom were initially provoked by Erikson's (1959, 1963) life-span model as well as the emergence of developmental psychology (Sharma, 2005). For Erikson (1968), wisdom is intimately tied to age. He argues that wisdom emerges in the later years of life, when the aging individual reflects on his or her life, evaluates his or her impact on others and the world, and characterizes himself or herself as a person who has had positive impact on those around them and the world. The studies of wisdom were adopted and followed by other psychologists, such as Clayton (1975, 1976), who provides the same understanding of wisdom as Erikson. Clayton (1982) argues that wisdom increases with age, and provokes the person to critically evaluate how the way that he or she acted in the past has affected the self and others. In this sense, wisdom and intelligence can provide positive features of development in the later years of life (Clayton, 1975, 1982). In both pioneering approaches, wisdom is believed to develop over time through an insightful and sober reflection on, and a critical evaluation of, one's actions in relation to others.

In the 1990s, psychological studies investigating, conceptualizing, and operationalizing wisdom began to increase significantly. Wisdom was more systematically studied and considerable efforts were made to operationalize and, more importantly, measure wisdom. Two main schools are identifiable in the psychological studies of wisdom.[3] The first group includes the implicit studies that try to understand wisdom by examining people's perception of wisdom. Based on this approach, a group of participants are asked to identify the behavioral or personal characteristics of wise people. The list of characteristics is then rated by another group of participants in terms of their relation to wisdom. The researcher analyzes the rated characteristics to identify the main aspects and dimensions of wisdom (Staudinger, 2008). Examples of this type of research are Clayton and Birren (1980), Holliday and Chandler (1986), and Glück and Bluck (2011).

Conversely, explicit studies are concerned with the behavioral expressions and manifestations of wisdom (Baltes and Staudinger, 2000). This group of studies focuses on tasks rather than perception. In such studies the researcher produces a list of tasks that measure wisdom (Sternberg, 1985). The way that participants perform the tasks and address the provided issues is evaluated toward obtaining an understanding of the concept of wisdom. A review of the explicit theories indicates three main aspects of the nature of wisdom: 1) wisdom engages cognition and affect; 2) not necessarily all people can become wise; and 3) wisdom is practice-based and guides one's behavior toward optimizing one's own and others' potentials (Kunzmann, 2004). The work of McAdams and de St Aubin (1998), Baltes and Staudinger (2000), and Taylor et al. (2011) can be categorized under this group.

Regardless of the nature of the studies, two psychological conceptualizations of wisdom are prominent in the relevant literature: the Berlin school (Baltes and Kunzmann, 2003; Baltes et al., 1995; Pasupathi et al., 2001) and Sternberg's balance theory (Sternberg, 1990, 1998, 2001). Ardelt's (2004) critique of the Berlin school could arguably be identified as the third main approach to the conceptualization of wisdom. Ardelt's approach will be examined after a discussion of the Berlin school.

The Berlin school

The Berlin school defines wisdom as "an expertise" (Baltes and Staudinger, 2000) and "expert knowledge" (Baltes and Smith, 1990; Pasupathi and Staudinger, 2001). Wisdom is defined as "an expert knowledge system in the fundamental pragmatics of life permitting exceptional insight, judgment, and advice involving complex and uncertain matters of the human condition" (Baltes and Staudinger, 1993, p. 76). According to this school, wisdom is not, however, a purely cognitive matter, but requires a coalition between experiences and understanding. The knowledge is not for knowledge's sake; rather, it plays a central role in the development of one's self and others in dealing with the fundamental pragmatics of life (Baltes and Kunzmann, 2004). In this sense, wisdom is a utopia of mind and virtue that has individual and collective representations (Baltes and Kunzmann, 2004).

Baltes and Staudinger (1993) argue that wisdom-related knowledge can be assessed by five criteria:

1   factual knowledge regarding fundamental pragmatics of life (for example, specific knowledge, examples, variations, general knowledge of emotions, vulnerability, and multiple options);
2   procedural knowledge about life problems (for example, strategies of information searching, decision making and advice giving, monitoring of emotional reactions, and heuristics of cost–benefit analysis);
3   life-span contextualism, which refers to the knowledge that considers the contexts of life and societal change (sociohistorical and idiosyncratic context, coordination of life themes – family, education, and work – and temporal changes);
4   relativism or the knowledge that considers relativism of values and life goals (personal preferences, current/future values, goals, motives, and cultural relativism); and
5   uncertainty (the knowledge which considers the uncertainties of life).

The criteria are regarded as the necessary conditions for wisdom (Gugerell and Riffert, 2011), as they present, according to Baltes and Smith (1990, p. 96), "a set of characteristics that should be evident in a given body of knowledge about the fundamental pragmatics of life in order to approximate wisdom" as expert knowledge.

Wisdom as an inherent characteristic of wise people

Ardelt (2004) challenges the Berlin school's methodological stance as to measuring and conceptualizing wisdom. Baltes and colleagues (Baltes and Smith, 1990; Kunzmann and Baltes, 2005) use the maximal performance approach, which requires a person to solve a challenging problem in order to measure wisdom. The challenging problems include hypothetical questions about fundamental issues and pragmatics of life. As in explicit studies, the answers to the questions are analyzed by the researcher based on a set of criteria. Ardelt (2004) argues that the measurement that the Berlin school uses to conceptualize wisdom assesses intellectual knowledge, not wisdom per se. The criticism questions the assumption that *hypothetical* scenarios facilitate gaining an understanding of how people actually perform in the same but *real* circumstances. In contrast, Ardelt (2004) suggests that personality testing, which focuses on one's description of how one typically responds to a given situation (Sternberg, 2004a), offers a more accurate and realistic indication of wisdom. She further emphasizes that wisdom must be measured on a basis of people's individual assessments of their typical reactions to their own real situations.

The second criticism that Ardelt expresses is that conceptualizing wisdom as expert knowledge and expertise implies that wisdom is a quality that exists independently of the person and therefore can be acquired by everyone. Ardelt (2004) would strongly argue that wisdom – being associated with personality characteristics and emotions – cannot exist independently of the wise person. Wisdom is instead a characteristic inherent in and reserved for wise people. The characteristic encompasses a combination of cognitive, reflective, and affective qualities (Ardelt, 2004). Ardelt's conceptualization of wisdom in terms of reflection and affect is represented by a more comprehensive concept, reflexivity, which will be discussed later on in this chapter.

Accordingly, in order for a person to be wise, he or she must have a true understanding of life, a desire to know the truth, and acknowledge the inherent limits of knowledge and of life's uncertainties (cognitive). The wise person must be also capable of perceiving phenomena from multiple perspectives through self-examination, self-awareness, and self-insight (reflective). He or she should feel sympathetic love for others (affective) (Ardelt, 2005). As far as knowledge is concerned, Ardelt and the Berlin school share the same presumption: that wisdom engages knowledge. The same understanding is offered by Sternberg's balance theory too. According to this theory, wisdom is rooted in tacit knowledge which underlies practical intelligence.

Balance theory

Sternberg's (1998) theory of wisdom mediates the Berlin and Ardelt perspectives. With regard to measuring wisdom, Sternberg argues that a more effective approach to the assessment of wisdom in individuals is to apply a combination of both hypothetical and real scenarios. People's reactions to hypothetical scenarios would provide a more comprehensive understanding of wisdom if accompanied by an assessment of their reaction to the real-life scenarios. For Sternberg, wisdom is a quality that exists independently of the context. The comprehension that articulates wisdom in terms of expert knowledge, as argued by Baltes and Smith (1990) and Baltes and Staudinger (1993, 2000), or a property of a person, as suggested by Ardelt (2004), neglects the context. To address this issue, Sternberg (1998, 2000, 2004b) suggests that wisdom is inherent in the interactions among person, situation, and task.

Balance theory proposes that wisdom is the use of intelligence toward achieving a common good:

> the use of one's intelligence and experience as mediated by values toward the achievement of a common good through a balance among (1) intrapersonal, (2) interpersonal, and (3) extra personal interests, over the (1) short and (2) long terms, to achieve a balance among (1) adaptation to existing environments, (2) shaping of existing environments, and (3) selection of new environment.
>
> (Sternberg, 2004a, p. 164)

According to the theory, wisdom – rather than being an internal system of functioning such as cognition and affect – is the outcome of a balanced interaction between the person and his or her context (Sternberg, 1998). Another important aspect of the theory is that wisdom and values are seen as interwoven. The balance that the person achieves between multiple interests, as well as multiple responses to the environment, is mediated by values.

The psychological perspectives have greatly influenced studies of wisdom in other disciplines. Without delving into an extensive review of all other disciplines that have studied wisdom, I will just provide two examples: one from leadership and one from organization studies. The examples show the influence of the psychological perspective on studies of wisdom in other disciplines. In the leadership field, Biloslavo and McKenna (2013) identify four interdependent dimensions that they argue are the indicators of wisdom: cognitive, conative, affective, and moral. Likewise, Edwards (2013) proposes a wisdom typology from an organizational perspective. He argues that wisdom is contextual and that, depending on the level of environmental stability and turbulence, organizations' wise responses may vary from innovative and conformative wisdom, to transitive and transformative wisdom, and then to adaptive wisdom. For instance, when the environment is highly stable and the conventional modes of managing dominate, organizations may move toward nurturing innovative ideas and scanning the environment, and focusing on conventional contingencies that form strategic goals.

Although there is no universally agreed-upon list of such qualities, understanding the human characteristics associated with wisdom can help one gain a better understanding of why some people are considered as being wise or acting wisely, while others are not. Based on a review of the relevant literature and in order to provide an overall perspective, the qualities that are regarded as associated with wisdom are listed below (Clayton, 1975, 1982; Dahlsgaard et al., 2005; Holliday and Chandler, 1986; Kramer, 1990; Liew, 2013; Opdebeeck and Habisch, 2011; www.wisdompage. com). Having specific characteristics by no means implies that one is necessarily wise. Incorporating the wisdom-related characteristics into one's decisions and practices is central to the development and manifestation of wisdom.

To sum up, whether we define wisdom as a quality that is independent of the person, or as a combination of personality characteristics, or a balanced behavioral response to the surrounding environment, wisdom resides in the person's capacity for judgment and decision making in dealing with extremely complex problems. Wisdom engages various qualities that enable one to make more effective decisions and take more effective actions. In the following paragraphs, the qualities that are critical to consider in the decision-making process when the outcome must be wise are discussed.[4]

Table 1.1 Qualities associated with wisdom

Acceptance	Desiring the good	Intelligence	Respect
Adopting multiple	of the whole	Interpersonal skills	Responsibility
perspectives	Detached concern	Intuition	Self-acceptance
Aliveness	Discernment	Joy	Self-actualization
Appreciating	Emotional reasoning	Judgment and	Self-investigation
ramifications	Empathy	communication	Self-knowledge
Appreciating	Equanimity	skills	Self-sufficiency
significance	Exceptional	Justice	Serenity
Attentiveness	understanding	Kindness	Social
Breadth of	Experience	Knowledgeable	unobtrusiveness
considerations	Fairness	Magnificence	Sound judgment
Caring	Friendliness	Mindfulness	Temperance
Commitment	Generosity	Nurturance	Truthfulness
Compassion	Gratitude	Openness	Understanding
Cooperation	Greatness of soul	Patience	Vision
Creative cognition	Hopefulness	Peacefulness	Willingness to risk
Curiosity	Humility	Perspicacious	Wit
Dedication	Insight	Positive attitude	Wonder
Deep understanding	Integrity	Reflective thinking	

Wisdom as an integrated decision-making process and practice

It is challenging, if not impossible, to assuredly predict all the consequences of a particular decision before the decision is made, particularly in an inextricably interlinked social, environmental, economic, and technological environment. It would be even more challenging to determine whether the consequences of the decision would turn out to be wise or unwise (Intezari and Pauleen, 2014). With these presumptions in mind, there are five qualities that, when integrally incorporated into the decision-making process, lead the decision toward consequences that are more likely to be considered as wise.

The qualities that will be explored below are interrelated and form an integral process of decision making that incorporates wisdom into decisions.

Multi-perspective consideration (MPC)

Wisdom draws more than anything else on a true understanding of the bigger picture of the problem at hand and the decision situation. The overarching understanding is achieved through a careful consideration of alternative points of view and the respected values and beliefs of the decision maker and the wider community, including industry and society. In this sense, wisdom can be articulated as the ability to see beyond the horizon (Awad and Ghaziri, 2004), whereby the far-reaching consequences of a decision as well as its immediate impacts are all seen together (Hays, 2007). Considering a diverse range of expectations (a diverse range of stakeholders), as well as the short- and long-term impacts of the possible outcomes of a decision and a course of action, underlies wise decisions and actions. Achieving MPC requires a high level of awareness of the self and of the surrounding environment.

Self–other awareness (SOA)

The scope and the accuracy of the multi-dimensional understanding that MPC provides for wise decision making depends in no small degree on the level of awareness that the decision maker has of himself or herself and the surrounding environment. The awareness includes what one knows and what one does not know. One essential aspect of wisdom is the recognition of the limitations and fallibility of one's own knowledge (Hays, 2010; Sternberg, 1998), and how the limitations can be tackled in the real world, taking into account all inevitable constraints. The critical role that self- and other-awareness plays in the enhancement of one's growth and productivity is not something new to academics and practitioners. Wisdom theory, however, underlines the interrelatedness of the two types of awareness and brings these two types of awareness together in an integrated fashion. Put differently, a person would not be able to make wise decisions if he or she severely lacks either awareness of the self or the environment, or both. A person would also not be able to make a wise decision at a given time if he or she were not able or willing to integrally incorporate self–other awareness into the decision-making process.

Cognitive–emotional mastery (CEM)

Wisdom engages and develops a balance of cognition and feelings. In order for one to be able to make wise decisions, one needs to have a combination of cognitive and analytical abilities as well as the capacity to incorporate information and emotion into decision making as necessary. CEM is an integrated contribution of cognition and emotion throughout the decision-making process and the course of action. Mastery is not a state of mind; rather, it is a continual learning process (Senge, 1990). Cognitive mastery connotes that the decision maker not only has the required knowledge and information to make the decision, but also is able to acknowledge and identify the limitations of his or her knowledge, deal with the missing information and knowledge, and recognize the interconnectedness of various sources of knowledge and information. The decision maker must also be able to draw on and apply what has been learned through his or her own and/or others' experiences. Emotional mastery refers to the extent to which the decision maker is able to consider, yet not be overly influenced by, emotion when making decisions (Birren and Fisher, 1990).

Reflexivity

At the heart of wisdom is a critical (re-)evaluation of one's underlying assumptions about oneself and one's interrelationship with the surrounding environment. The reflection enhances one's wisdom. Reflection is an in-depth consideration of phenomena or events involved in the decision-making situation. Through the reflection, the decision maker attempts to understand the problem, context, and his or her and others' thoughts and feelings about the subject matter. The effectiveness of a decision is more likely to be enhanced once the decision maker critically reflects on his or her personality, characteristics, behavior, experiences, feelings, and perceptions (reflection on the internal world), as well as on the surrounding environment, including the wider society and the environment (reflection on the external world). The latter includes the decision maker's reflections on others' experience and feelings about the impacts of the decisions. It also includes reflection on the values and beliefs that are prominent in society.

Reflexivity is "a *stance* of being able to locate oneself in the picture, to appreciate how one's own self influences [actions]" (Fook, 2002, p. 43). Reflexivity encompasses, yet goes beyond, a simple combination of the two types of reflection. Edwards and Küpers (2014, p. 3) argue that reflexivity is concerned with a critical evaluation of one's own underlying assumptions. As they put it, reflexivity:

> exposes and enables the questioning of ways of being and doing as well as its underlying structures. In so doing, reflexivity enables us to engage with the core assumptions and interpretative frames. Through this reflexive and critical re-turning the generation of alternatives and the emergence of deep change is made possible.

Wise decisions are made based on a constant reflexivity over time and during the decision-making process.

Praxis

Closely linked to the concept of reflexivity is "praxis." Praxis integrates reflexivity into practice. Praxis means *acting* based on prudent decisions toward improving the world (Kodish, 2006). In this sense, wisdom is defined as a "morally committed action" (Russell and Grootenboer, 2008, p. 109), which also engages practical reasoning (Kemmis, 2012), and thoughtful and mindful practices in a particular situation. Praxis is the action distinctive to phronesis. It is concerned with the rightness and properness of what is done in practice, in terms of the consequences of that particular action for all those who are involved in or affected by the action (Kemmis and Smith, 2008). Accordingly, a decision and action would be considered wise if they are concerned with doing the thing that is good for both the individual and humankind.

What is important to reiterate here as to the aforementioned qualities – MPC, SOA, CEM, reflexivity, and praxis – is that the qualities are interwoven. They are interrelated and enhance each other. A person who constantly reflects on his or her own underlying assumptions and practices and on what is going on around him or her is more likely to be able to acquire an accurate and overarching view of the decision-making situation. The integration of this overarching understanding with one's cognitive and emotional mastery leads the decision maker to be able to recognize not only the obvious (that is, those that are objectively understandable) but also the latent aspects of complex problems. Practicing the integration of MPC, SOA, CEM, reflexivity, and praxis in action can develop the person's wisdom over time. To sum up, wisdom is multi-dimensional in nature and provides an integrative framework for the individual, the surrounding environment, and the relationship between the two.

Conclusion

Wisdom has been the topic of numerous discourses in philosophy and psychology, and recently in many other disciplines including neuroscience, leadership, and education. The diverse range of approaches and the culturally sensitive and multi-dimensional nature of wisdom make it highly elusive in terms of definitional clarity. Accordingly, it would be challenging, if not impossible, to comprehensively articulate the meaning of wisdom in one single chapter or book. However, given that the notion of wisdom appears frequently throughout the book and that the following chapters refer to the concept of wisdom from slightly different angles, providing a review of the major trends in wisdom studies is helpful for gaining a better understanding of the respective arguments. This is particularly important because the theoretical bases discussed in this chapter provide a conceptual framework for the reader to avoid any confusion about the concept of wisdom and wisdom theory.

Following a review of the wisdom literature, this chapter has drawn on the findings of an empirical study of wisdom to provide a cross-disciplinary conceptualization of wisdom. Five key qualities are argued to be associated with wisdom and to be central to the manifestation of wisdom in practice. The manifestation of wisdom requires an integration of the qualities in decisions and actions. Practicing the qualities in an integral manner can help people develop their wisdom over time as they make decisions and reflect on their assumptions and actions. The chapter argues that wisdom is a process of practice and development, rather than just being a state of mind or a set of personality traits and behavioral characteristics. Moreover, wisdom engages, yet goes beyond, accumulated knowledge, experience, and ethics.

In this sense and with regard to the book's topic of wisdom and technology, I argue that the wise use of technology requires more than just the accumulation of technical skills and knowledge. Wise use of technology refers to a more effective use of technology while avoiding or minimizing unintended and negative impacts of the technological implications on the self and others. The role of technology in improving numerous aspects of our life is undeniable. However, any reckless and unscrupulous reliance on technology solutionism may be extremely dangerous. The technology user's responsibility goes beyond just the technical use of what technology offers. The interrelatedness of social, economic, environmental, and political concerns, as well as the omnipresence of technology requires an integrally overarching approach to the use of technology and how it affects humankind. Wisdom can provide such an approach by incorporating qualities including awareness, reflection, cognition, and emotion, as well as the consideration of multiple perspectives, into the use of technology toward the wellbeing of the self and others.

Reflection and critical thinking

- How would you define wisdom?
- How would you differentiate wisdom from knowledge, expertise, and intelligence?
- What is the evidence of wisdom? Successful and effective decisions/actions?
- What would lead you to characterize a person as wise or unwise?
- How do interpretations of wisdom vary depending on the geographic, political, and cultural boundaries?
- What abilities, skills, and competencies are associated with wisdom?
- How can people develop wisdom?
- How can we measure the level of wisdom?
- What would be the role of technology in developing and measuring wisdom?
- Is the level of wisdom different at the individual and communal levels?
- How can wisdom enhance individual, group, and organizational performance in life and the workplace?

Notes

1 This interpretation of Hinduism is a rather simplified presentation of this tradition. It must be noted that philosophies underlying Hinduism cover a vast and diverse ground, including Vedanta, Yoga, and Sankhya, which include numerous perspectives on wisdom including the practical notion of Dharma.
2 In addition to *sophia* and phronesis, Aristotle also uses another notion: episteme. For Aristotle, the concepts of *sophia*, phronesis, and episteme represent three states of mind. Here, I am not mentioning episteme, as the concept refers to a type of knowledge (scientific knowledge) rather than to wisdom.
3 Categorizing the psychological approaches into these two groups is a simplified presentation of the wisdom studies in the discipline. The number of perspectives on wisdom either in psychology or other disciplines is increasingly growing.
4 The discussion is based on the findings of an empirical study conducted by the author between 2010 and 2014 (Intezari, 2014).

References

Aldwin, C.M. (2009). Gender and wisdom: A brief overview. *Research in Human Development*, 6(1), 1–8.
Ardelt, M. (2004). Wisdom as expert knowledge system: A critical review of a contemporary operationalization of an ancient concept. *Human Development*, 47(5), 257–285.
——. (2005). How wise people cope with crises and obstacles in life. *Revision*, 28(1), 7–19.

Aristotle (2009). *The Nicomachean Ethics*, D. Ross (trans.). Oxford: Oxford University Press.

Awad, E.M. and Ghaziri, H.M. (2004). *Knowledge Management*. Upper Saddle River, NJ: Prentice Hall.

Baggini, J. and Fosl, P.S. (2007). *The Ethics Toolkit: A Compendium of Ethical Concepts and Methods*. Malden, MA: Blackwell Publishing.

Baltes, P.B. and Freund, A.M. (2003). Human strength as the orchestration of wisdom and SOC. In U.M. Staudinger and L. Aspinwall (Eds), *A Psychology of Human Strengths: Perspectives on an Amerging Field* (pp. 23–35). Washington, DC: APA Books.

Baltes, P.B. and Kunzmann, U. (2003). Wisdom: The peak of human excellence in the orchestration of mind and virtue. *The Psychologist*, 16(3), 131–133.

——. (2004). The two faces of wisdom: Wisdom as a general theory of knowledge and judgment about excellence in mind and virtue vs. wisdom as everyday realization in people and products. *Human Development*, 47(5), 290–299.

Baltes, P.B. and Smith, J. (1990). Toward a psychology of wisdom and its ontogenesis. In R.J. Sternberg (ed.), *Toward a Psychology of Wisdom and its Ontogenesis* (pp. 87–120). New York: Cambridge University Press.

Baltes, P.B. and Staudinger, U.M. (1993). The search for a psychology of wisdom. *Current Directions in Psychology Science*, 2(3), 75–80.

——. (2000). Wisdom: A metaheuristic (pragmatic) to orchestrate mind and virtue toward excellence. *American Psychologist*, 55(1), 122–136.

Baltes, P.B., Staudinger, U.M., Maerker, A., and Smith, J. (1995). People nominated as wise: A comparative study of wisdom-related knowledge. *Psychology and Aging*, 10(2), 155–166.

Beauchamp, T.L. (1991). *Philosophical Ethics: An Introduction to Moral Philosophy*, 2nd edn. New York: McGraw-Hill.

Begley, A.M. (2006). Facilitating the development of moral insight in practice: Teaching ethics and teaching virtue. *Nursing Philosophy: An International Journal for Healthcare Professionals*, 7(4), 257–265.

Bierly III, P.E., Kessler, E.H., and Christensen, E.W. (2000). Organizational learning, knowledge and wisdom. *Journal of Organizational Change Management*, 13(6), 595–618.

Biloslavo, R. and McKenna, B. (2013). Testing a 4-dimensional model of wisdom on wise political leaders. In W.M. Küpers and D.J. Pauleen (eds), *Handbook of Practical Wisdom: Leadership, Organization and Integral Business Practice* (pp. 111–132). Aldershot: Gower.

Birren, J.E. and Fisher, L.M. (1990). The elements of wisdom: Overview and integration. In R.J. Sternberg (ed.), *Wisdom: Its Nature, Origins, and Development* (pp. 317–332). Cambridge: Cambridge University Press.

Case, P. (2013). Cultivation of wisdom in the Theravada Buddhist tradition: Implications for contemporary leadership and organization (pp. 65–78). In W. Küpers and D.J. Pauleen (eds), *Handbook of Practical Wisdom: Leadership, Organization and Integral Business Practice*. Aldershot: Gower.

Clayton, V. (1975). Erikson's theory of human development as it applies to the aged: Wisdom as contradictory cognition. *Human Development*, 18(1–2), 119–128.

——. (1976). A multidimensional scaling analysis of the concept of wisdom. Dissertation, University of Southern California, Los Angeles, Graduate School, Psychology.

——. (1982). Wisdom and intelligence: The nature and function of knowledge in the later years. *International Journal of Aging and Human Development*, 15(4), 315–320.

Clayton, V. and Birren, J.E. (1980). The development of wisdom across the life-span: A re-examination of an ancient topic. In P.B. Baltes and O.G. Brim Jr. (eds), *Life-Span Development and Behavior* (Vol. 3, pp. 103–135). New York: Academic Press.

Dahlsgaard, K., Peterson, C., and Seligman, M.E.P. (2005). Shared virtue: The convergence of valued human strengths across culture and history. *Review of General Psychology*, 9(3), 203–213.

Edwards, M.G. (2013). Wisdom and integrity: Metatheoretical perspectives on integrative change in an age of turbulence. In W.M. Küpers and D.J. Pauleen (eds), *A Handbook of Practical Wisdom: Leadership, Organization and Integral Business Practice* (pp. 197–216). Aldershot: Gower.

Edwards, M.G. and Küpers, W.M. (2014). *Integral Science*. Albany, NY: State University of New York Press.

Erikson, E.H. (1959). *Identity in the Life Cycle*. New York: International Universities Press.

——. (1963). *Childhood and Society*. New York: Norton.

——. (1968). *Identity: Youth and Crisis*. New York: Norton.

Fook, J. (2002). *Social Work: Critical Theory and Practice*. London: Sage.

Glück, J. and Bluck, S. (2011). Laypeople's conceptions of wisdom and its development: Cognitive and integrative views. *Journals of Gerontology*, 66(3), 321–324.

Gugerell, S.H. and Riffert, F. (2011). On defining "wisdom": Baltes, Ardelt, Ryan, and Whitehead. *Interchange*, 42(3), 225–259.

Harwood, L.D. (2011). Sagely wisdom in Confucianism. *Analytic Teaching And Philosophical Praxis*, 31(1), 56–63.

Hays, J.M. (2007). Dynamics of organizational wisdom. *Business Renaissance Quarterly*, 2(4), 77–122.

——. (2010). The ecology of wisdom. *Management and Marketing*, 5(1), 71–92.

Holliday, S.G. and Chandler, M.J. (1986). *Wisdom: Explorations in Adult Competence*. Basel: Karger.

Intezari, A. (2014). Wisdom and decision making: Grounding theory in management practice. Doctoral dissertation. Auckland: Massey University.

Intezari, A. and Pauleen, D.J. (2014). Management wisdom in perspective: Are you virtuous enough to succeed in volatile times? *Journal of Business Ethics*, 120(3), 393–404.

Kant, I. (1996). *Critique of Practical Reason*, T.K. Abbott (trans.). Amherst, NY: Prometheus Books.

Kemmis, S. (2012). Phronēsis, experience, and the primacy of praxis. In E.A. Kinsella and A. Pitman (eds), *Phronesis as Professional Knowledge: Practical Wisdom in the Professions* (pp. 147–161). Rotterdam: Sense Publishers.

Kemmis, S. and Smith, T.J. (2008). Personal praxis: Learning through experience. In S. Kemmis and T.J. Smith (eds), *Enabling Praxis: Challenges for Education* (pp. 15–35). Rotterdam: Sense Publishers.

Kodish, S. (2006). The paradoxes of leadership: The contribution of Aristotle. *Leadership*, 2(4), 451–468.

Kramer, D.A. (1990). Conceptualizing wisdom: The primacy of affect-cognition relations. In R.J. Sternberg (ed.), *Wisdom: Its Nature, Origins, and Development* (pp. 279–313). New York: Cambridge University Press.

Kunzmann, U. (2004). Approaches to a good life: The emotional-motivational side ot wisdom. In P.A. Linley, S. Joseph, and M.E.P. Seligman (eds), *Positive Psychology in Practice* (pp. 504–517). Hoboken, NJ: Wiley.

Kunzmann, U. and Baltes, P.B. (2005). The psychology of wisdom: Theoretical and empirical challenges. In R.J. Sternberg and J. Jordan (eds), *Handbook of Wisdom: Psychological Perspectives* (pp. 110–135). New York: Cambridge University Press.

Liew, A. (2013). DIKIW: Data, information, knowledge, intelligence, wisdom and their interrelationships. *Business Management Dynamics*, 2(10), 49–62.

McAdams, D.P. and de St Aubin, E. (eds) (1998). *Generativity and Adult Development: How and Why We Care for the Next Generation*. Washington, DC: American Psychological Association.

Opdebeeck, H. and Habisch, A. (2011). Compassion: Chinese and Western perspectives on practical wisdom in management. *Journal of Management Development*, 30(7/8), 778–788.

Pasupathi, M. and Staudinger, U.M. (2001). Do advanced moral reasoners also show wisdom? Linking moral reasoning and wisdom-related knowledge and judgement. *International Journal of Behavioral Development*, 25(5), 401–415.

Pasupathi, M., Staudinger, U.M., and Baltes, P.B. (2001). Seeds of wisdom: Adolescents' knowledge and judgment about different life problems. *Developmental Psychology*, 37(3), 351–361.

Rowley, J. and Slack, F. (2009). Conceptions of wisdom. *Journal of Information Science*, 35(1), 110–119.

Russell, H. and Grootenboer, P. (2008). Finding praxis? In S. Kemmis and T.J. Smith (eds), *Enabling Praxis: Challenges for Education* (pp. 109–126). Rotterdam: Sense Publishers.

Senge, P.M. (1990). *The Fifth Discipline: The Art and Practice of the Learning Organization*. New York: Currency Doubleday.

Sharma, R. (2005). Five factors of personality and wisdom. *Gyanodaya*, 2(2), 82–87.

Small, M.W. (2004). Wisdom and now managerial wisdom: Do they have a place in management development programs? *Journal of Management Development*, 23(8), 751–764.

Staudinger, U.M. (2008). A psychology of wisdom: History and recent developments. *Research in Human Development*, 5(2), 107–120.

Sternberg, R.J. (1985). Implicit theory of intelligence, creativity, and wisdom. *Journal of Personality and Social Psychology*, 49(3), 607–627.

——. (1990). Wisdom and its relations to intelligence and creativity. In R.J. Sternberg (ed.), *Wisdom: Its Nature, Origins, and Development* (pp. 142–159). New York: Cambridge University Press.

——. (1998). A balance theory of wisdom. *Review of General Psychology*, 2(4), 347–365.

——. (2000). Wisdom as a form of giftedness. *Gifted Child Quarterly*, 44(4), 252–260.

——. (2001). Why schools should teach for wisdom: The balance theory of wisdom in educational settings. *Educational Psychologist*, 36(4), 227–245.

——. (2003). *Wisdom, Intelligence, and Creativity Synthesized*. New York: Cambridge University Press.

——. (2004a). What is wisdom and how can we develop it? *Annals of the American Academy of Political and Social Science*, 591(1), 164–174.

——. (2004b). Words to the wise about wisdom? *Human Development*, 47(5), 286–289.

——. (2013). The WICS model of leadership. In M.G. Rumsey (ed.), *The Oxford Handbook of Leadership* (pp. 47–62). New York: Oxford University Press.

Takahashi, M. and Bordia, P. (2000). The concept of wisdom: A cross-cultural comparison. *International Journal of Psychology*, 35(1), 1–9.

Takahashi, M. and Overton, W. (2005). Cultural foundations of wisdom: An integrated developmental approach. In R.J. Sternberg and J. Jordan (eds), *A Handbook of Wisdom: Psychological Perspectives* (pp. 32–60). New York: Cambridge University Press.

Taylor, M., Bates, G., and Webster, J.D. (2011). Matthew Taylor Glen Bates. *Experimental Aging Research*, 37(2), 129–141.

Tolstoy, L. (2007). *War and Peace*, R. Pevear and L. Volokhonsky (trans.). London: Vintage Books.

Urmson, J.O. (1998). *Aristotle's Ethics*. Oxford: Basil Blackwell.

Yang, S. (2011). East meets West: Cross-cultural perspectives on wisdom and adult education. *New Directions for Adult and Continuing Education*, Fall (131), 45–54.

Chapter 2

Toward a wisdom-based understanding of the human–technology relationship

Nikunj Dalal

Introduction

Modern technologies, whether the latest consumer gizmo, a cutting-edge military application, or a genetic test, are revolutionizing our ways of living, our culture, our society, our education, our sports, our politics, and, more importantly, what and how we think. The forces may be bigger and more unconscious than we can see. The promise these technologies offer is undeniable: unfettered freedom, economic efficiencies, social conveniences, and incredible potential to change the world for the better. Simultaneously, the technologies threaten our jobs, security, privacy, relationships, and, going deeper, human survival and our very sense of self. And they are set to become exponentially more powerful in the future!

Are technologies good or bad overall? Perhaps this question itself needs to be examined. The prevailing mood about technology seems to be of exuberance. However, technologies have both positive and negative effects. Huesemann and Huesemann (2011, p. 7) observe that: "This character of technology creates a serious intellectual challenge for technological optimists who exclusively focus on the positive aspects of technology while ignoring the, often enormous, negatives." It is clear, perhaps more than ever before, that technologies are not neutral. They are game-changers, far more than mere contrivances, and it is no longer possible to contain the effects of technological change to a limited domain; they systemically touch all aspects of human endeavor. Technologies – current and those in the making – have the potential not only to revolutionize our lives for the better but also to destroy the world as we know it, both physically and psychologically. Unfortunately, in the name of technological "progress," technologists and scientists in industrialized nations are in a race to develop even faster, cheaper, and "better" technologies, unmindful of the potential consequences and looming disasters. In this chapter, instead of abstractly discussing the positives and negatives of technologies from the vantage points of exuberance or criticality, I choose to focus on understanding the human–technology relationship.

How do we as individuals, organizations, communities, nations, and societies relate to these engines of rapid growth? Are we uncritically enthusiastic? Are we disturbed, whether slightly or profoundly? Are we aware of the effects that technologies have on us? Are we personally addicted to particular technologies? How should we relate to them? Is it important that we ask such questions and conduct an inquiry?

In this chapter, I suggest that a different kind of understanding – a paradigm shift – is necessary in our understanding of the relationship of humans with technologies, and

I propose that this understanding be based on perennial universal insights of wisdom viewed in a modern, practical, and scientific context. Rather than settling on one conclusion or the other (of exuberance or condemnation or places in the middle), I suggest an open approach of deep critical inquiry founded on practical wisdom. I begin the chapter with the why question, which is to express the imperative for this kind of inquiry and understanding. Next, I examine the notion of technology in the broader sense of the term, looking at its historical origins and parallels with modern times. Then I sketch the outlines for what may be called a wisdom-based understanding, one that recognizes the partial truths in current perspectives of the human–technology relationship, but attempts to go beyond them. I conclude with the implications and limitations of this approach.

The need

How does one react to the following comment?

> The Industrial Revolution and its consequences have been a disaster for the human race. They have greatly increased the life-expectancy of those of us who live in "advanced" countries, but they have destabilized society, have made life unfulfilling, have subjected human beings to indignities, have led to widespread psychological suffering (in the Third World to physical suffering as well) and have inflicted severe damage on the natural world. The continued development of technology will worsen the situation. It will certainly subject human beings to greater indignities and inflict greater damage on the natural world, it will probably lead to greater social disruption and psychological suffering, and it may lead to increased physical suffering even in "advanced" countries.
>
> (Kaczynski, 2005, p. 1)

A technophile might react with vehement disagreement and summarily dismiss the above comment of the infamous Neo-Luddite (aka the Unabomber) as the rant of an ideologically deranged person. But when more or less similar concerns about the effects of technologies are echoed by discerning commentators as varied as historians, scientists, technologists, philosophers, and sociologists, one may be compelled to listen to the "other" side. For example, technology-induced stresses are leading to a variety of physical, emotional, psychological, and behavioral symptoms such as compulsive behaviors, insecurity, and anxiety that have become common in the workplace as a result of the rapid pace of technological change, ubiquity of devices, increased workload pressure, and fears of being replaced by technology (see for example, Ayyagari et al., 2011; Ragu-Nathan et al., 2008). A recent study on work–life balance (Pauleen et al., 2015) finds that although most cell phone users believed the technology was an enabler and gave them the freedom to choose how to integrate their work and private lives, this freedom was largely used to perform more work. Even outside the physical workplace, there is a sense of being always connected or "always-on," a phenomenon also observed with today's youngsters, who have been referred to as technology-tethered teens (Turkle, 2012).

Beyond the concerns of technology-induced stresses and strains and job displacement by intelligent technologies are questions that lie at the root of our identity as human beings. Inventor, author, and futurist Ray Kurzweil predicts that in the future, biology and technology will begin to merge in order to create newer forms of life that combine machine and human intelligence, thereby actualizing the cyborgs of science-fiction movies and novels. He further predicts in an audio commentary that by 2029, "we'll have reverse-engineered and modeled and simulated all the regions of the brain. And that will provide us the software/algorithmic methods to simulate all of the human brain's capabilities including our emotional intelligence. And computers at that time will be far more powerful than the human brain" (Honan, n.d.). Whether or not Kurzweil's prediction comes true, major advances almost certainly will further blur the distinction between human and technology. And beyond the question of identity lies the matter of human survival itself, stemming from the dangers posed by an uprising of super-intelligent robots in the future.

Bill Joy (2000, para. 1), co-founder of Sun Microsystems, asserts: "Our most powerful 21st-century technologies – robotics, genetic engineering, and nanotech – are threatening to make humans an endangered species." Both physicist Stephen Hawking and Elon Musk – inventor and founder of Tesla Motors and SpaceX – have strongly warned of the existential risks to humanity posed by artificial intelligence of the future. Bill Gates – philanthropist and co-founder of Microsoft – has joined Musk, Hawking, and many other leading voices urging the world to take the threat of super-robots seriously. Nick Bostrom – a philosopher at Oxford University – believes there is no reason to assume that radically superior artificial intelligence will be benevolent or wise:

> We cannot blithely assume that a superintelligence will necessarily share any of the final values stereotypically associated with wisdom and intellectual development in humans – scientific curiosity, benevolent concern for others, spiritual enlightenment and contemplation, renunciation of material acquisitiveness, a taste for refined culture or for the simple pleasures in life, humility and selflessness, and so forth.
>
> (Bostrom, 2014, p. 14)

The profound question – "What does it mean to be human in a technology-driven world?" – thus acquires new significance.

Even if we assume that none of the apocalyptic predictions about technology come to pass, there are good reasons to temper our enthusiasm for technologies. Kanner – a psychologist – laments:

> To be against technology is to deny a crucial part of human nature. Today, however, it has become extremely difficult to fully appreciate or ponder our ability to make things. Instead, we are caught in a tragically flawed philosophy called "technological progress" that blinds us to the numerous choices we have, the various ways open to us to become both wise and creative technological beings. It is as if we had decided that the only proper use of our legs is to run, and run as hard as we can, at every possible moment.
>
> (Kanner, n.d., para. 2)

According to Joy:

> The experiences of the atomic scientists clearly show the need to take personal responsibility, the danger that things will move too fast, and the way in which a process can take on a life of its own. We can, as they did, create insurmountable problems in almost no time flat. We must do more thinking up front if we are not to be similarly surprised and shocked by the consequences of our inventions.
>
> (Joy, 2000)

Hence, there is every reason now for scientists, technologists, managers, experts, and the general populace to tread the waters cautiously and to ask the right questions.

The nature of technology

When we normally think of technologies in today's world, we think of cell phones, tablets, computers, and gizmos of various kinds: in short, information technologies. But do we realize that writing is also a technology? Writing was transformational because it created a completely new modality: associating symbols with spoken words, which could then be inscribed on stone and read by someone else. And long before writing and reading came the revolutionary technologies of fire, which transformed our sources of food, and the wheel, which made mobility and trade possible on an unimaginable scale. This was to be followed in later years by the horseless carriage (automobile), the phone, the television, and more recently a wide variety of information technologies all connected via the Internet. Technologies that are expected to change the world now and in the future include, among others: virtual reality, drones, smarter smartphones, brain mapping, artificial intelligence, genome editing, 3D printing, and alternative energy.

So what is technology? The term "technology" has its origin from the Greek τέχνη, *technē*, which means art or skill, and λογία, *logia*, which implies science, knowledge, and study. The *Merriam-Webster Dictionary* (2015) defines technology as: "the practical application of knowledge especially in a particular area" and "the use of science in industry, engineering, etc., to invent useful things or to solve problems." The use of the term "technology" has changed significantly over the past two centuries, going from a study of useful arts to more modern notions of useful tools, techniques, methods, practices, and devices founded typically as applications of science and engineering. A common thread one can see in all definitions of technology is that of practicality and utilitarianism. Technologies, whether stone tools in the Paleolithic era or modern-day tablets, were created by humans to meet human needs. This chapter uses the term "technologies" to include all technological artifacts – contrivances, machines, methods, techniques, media, instruments, and systems – developed by people. (There is some evidence that other animals such as dolphins and chimpanzees can create and fashion technologies to suit their ends in limited ways, but we will not enter into that domain for the purposes of this chapter.)

Throughout all of human history, technologies, while meeting human needs and revolutionizing society in many ways, have also raised ethical, philosophical, and practical questions. For instance, the technology of writing raised profound questions about what it has done to alter the nature of thought, communication, and society. In contrast to pure observation and oral communication (the dominant "natural" technologies at the time that writing was invented), Ong (2012), in a widely cited book, has observed that writing can be seen as artificial and frozen, and divisive in that it creates abstractions separated from the contextual living present, alienating and destructive of the valuable social fabric of direct human-to-human interactions, separating the known from the knower by text, distancing the communicator from the recipient in time and space, imperiously dividing society into the literary haves and the illiterates, and so on. Further, Ong points to how the technology of writing has become inseparable from who we are:

> Functionally literate persons, those who regularly assimilate discourse such as this, are not simply thinking and speaking human beings but chirographically thinking and speaking human beings (latterly conditioned also by print and by electronics). The fact that we do not commonly feel the influence of writing on our thoughts shows that we have interiorized the technology of writing so deeply that without tremendous effort we cannot separate it from ourselves or even recognize its presence and influence.
>
> (Ong, 1986, p. 24)

At this juncture, we might ask whether we have interiorized modern technologies in a similar way. This is an issue that will be explored later.

Toward a wisdom-based understanding of the human–technology relationship

Looking back now at the technology of writing, despite the many criticisms leveled against it, few will deny the unparalleled transformative nature of writing as "utterly invaluable and indeed essential for the realization of fuller, interior, human potentials" (Ong, 1986, p. 32). In a similar vein, it would be arguably tempting to conclude that, on balance, just as writing as a technology has on the whole been undoubtedly beneficial for human good, the same may be said of most technologies now and in the future. I argue that such conclusions warrant hardheaded skepticism, as part of an inquiry that perhaps even the most ardent critical technophile might endorse, given the game-changing nature of new and yet-to-be-developed technologies. At the same time, it should be obvious that having a healthy skepticism is not necessarily about taking up an opposing position or an antagonistic stance to technology. The wisdom-based understanding described here implies that being for or against a specific technology or being positive or negative about technology in general is simplistic and can miss the larger point. For there is a recognition that understanding the human–technology relationship is a living inquiry that we must conduct, which may not end in one conclusion or the other because the object of inquiry itself – the nature and impact of technology – is in a state of flux and will affect the inquiry, the inquiry process, and also the inquirers themselves, and in turn the technologies will be shaped by inquiring minds in holistic interdependent and potentially undecipherable ways.

Hence, we increasingly have to ask, face, and explore fundamental questions far beyond the typical issues of the dark side of technology and risk their mitigation by changes in mindsets, of identity, of the blurring boundaries between human beings and their technological extensions, of the sustainability of the planet, and fundamentally of the manner and process of this inquiry itself.

How do we conduct such an inquiry and respond to urgent questions that affect the survival of the human species and the planet? First of all, let us understand that there is no place for simplistic answers. We first have to understand the issues at deeper levels before we go headlong into a search for answers. Perhaps in the active exploration of the issues lies the unfolding of potential approaches based on better and deeper understanding. The manner in which we respond is as important as the content of our responses. Ancient and modern wisdom offers frameworks and perspectives that may enable us to find the "right" ways to respond. When we explore such questions from various perspectives of timeless wisdom adapted for the modern age, we believe the process can yield significant insights, increase awareness of the issues, deepen dialogue, and help redesign an increasingly technology-driven future. Wisdom has been at the heart of practical, philosophical, and spiritual interest since antiquity. Over the past decade, wisdom as an academic area is increasingly attracting interdisciplinary interest from fields that include psychology, sociology, gerontology, biology, neurosciences, management, marketing, health, and medicine. The traditional and scholarly literature ascribes to wisdom important qualities and attributes that include values, compassion, love, truth, skillfulness, equanimity, kindness, goodness, insights, and mindfulness, among others (Sternberg and Jordan, 2005; see also Intezari, Chapter 1 and Heitz, Chapter 3 in this volume).

Recognizing that technological artifacts are created by human beings to suit their purposes, understanding of the human–technology relationship encompasses not only the fundamental assumptions we have about technology but also about us, our hopes, our despairs, our needs, and our deeper quest for meaning. To understand this relationship, we have to start with humans.

What are the key characteristics of a wisdom-based understanding?

1. It is focused on understanding the problem first

Before we rush headlong into responses and solutions (especially technological fixes), it is important to know whether we critically comprehend the questions so that we understand the severity and complexity of the underlying problems. Understanding allows us to pause, reflect, identify, examine, and articulate the multiple dimensions that underlie the technological complexity in which we are embedded. Understanding may also help us see that our technological solutions themselves are creating new problems, for which we seem to have to build more new technological artifacts.

2. It includes multiple perspectives but also transcends them

The impact of technology on society has been examined through many lenses and perspectives, including technological determinism, technological imperative, technological solutionism, techno-utopia, techno-dystopia, scientism, and others. There have been several movements created by adherents of various philosophies and beliefs, which have also led to conflict and violence. While this chapter does not attempt to survey various systems and movements, can we observe that any attempt to understand from a single lens will always lead to a partial, or distorted, or limited understanding? Yet, if we can recognize the partial truths that may lie in each perspective, our understanding can be non-simplistic, nuanced, multi-dimensional, and, to that extent, richer. In this sense, we can be closer to an integral vision (Wilber, 2011), wherein all partial truths in multiple perspectives are recognized, included, and ultimately transcended. Hence, a wisdom-based understanding attempts to go beyond mere notions of utopia, dystopia, and neutrality. Technologies are neither good nor bad. Nor are they neutral. What matters is how wisely we relate to them.

3. It recognizes the holistic nature of understanding

Understanding is not just based on a cognitive process. If one has read and studied different types of video games, but has never experienced the "flow" feeling of losing oneself in a game, one's understanding of the effect of video games on the mind is limited and possibly quite superficial. Observing videos of babies experiencing their first rain or first snow (on YouTube and elsewhere), it can be noticed that they seem to be not just making sense of the new phenomenon, but are also experiencing and visibly displaying joy, awe, fear, and other emotions. Their understanding seems to have a holistic flavor that is not reducible into parts in their present consciousness at the time. Hence, the holistic nature of understanding is based not only on the cognitive dimension of knowledge, that is, of knowing what, how and why, but also feeling and experiential dimensions in that one has actually experienced the very thing or activity.

Besides the experiential aspect of understanding, there is also an art of looking (Krishnamurti, 2013). Typically, when we look at something, say a tree or a river or a computer, we look at it with eyes of the past, eyes that have already labeled the river as a river. So we do not "feel" the river in any given moment as a perpetually changing body of water that has fluidity, beauty, and magnificence. Or when we view a computer with the eyes of the specialist, we might see an instrumental device understood in terms of inputs, outputs, and processes. If one has been brought up on technology as a digital native, one might understand it quickly and easily figure out the icons on a screen, whereas for the older person who grew up on an older technology (say reading books), seeing an operating system message such as "Fatal error: System shutdown" might shock them into a state of worry. The techno-savvy kid under these circumstances will simply reboot the device. The point is that we view the world through various lenses shaped by our past, our experiences, our specialization, and our background. This can be helpful, but it can also limit, distort, and color our vision. Is there a way to look at phenomena of the human–technology relationship in a fresh way, unconditioned by training, worldviews, backgrounds, and specialized expertise? This is an important challenge for humanity if we are to look for creative solutions raised by the complex problems of the human–technology relationship.

An inquiry-based approach for understanding the personal human–technology relationship

Returning to the question of whether we have interiorized modern technologies, in his insightful book *Technology Matters* (2006), historian David Nye concludes that technology has been interiorized to the point that it is inseparable from being human.

In his book, he explores 10 central questions about our relationship to technology, suggesting that the answers will evolve over time:

> Can we define technology? Does technology shape us, or do we shape it? Is technology inevitable or unpredictable? (Why do experts often fail to get it right?)? How do historians understand it? Are we using modern technology to create cultural uniformity, or diversity? To create abundance, or an ecological crisis? To destroy jobs or create new opportunities? Should "the market" choose our technologies? Do advanced technologies make us more secure, or escalate dangers? Does ubiquitous technology expand our mental horizons, or encapsulate us in artifice?
>
> (Nye, 2006, p. vii)

Instead of attempting to give final answers to these questions, with the help of historical, scientific, and socio-cultural perspectives, Nye analyzes the issues embedded in each of the questions, and observes the paradoxes and dilemmas they create. For example, he points out how complex military technologies can increase national security on the one hand by intimidating and deterring enemies, but are increasingly prone to potential inadvertent malfunctions and disasters on the other hand.

If technology is inseparable from being human, as Nye argues, an inquiry of the *personal* human–technology relationship should raise further new questions. Here, I will attempt to explore the human relationship to technology, posing four progressively deeper questions relating to the knowledge of individual technologies, the knowledge of systemic effects of technology, awareness of one's relationship with and attitude to technology, and self-knowing. Consistent with the wisdom-based understanding described in the previous section, I state the questions using the personal pronoun "I" to emphasize the direct personal relationship of human and technology. The ordering of the questions does not suppose or imply any progression from one question to another in practice because understanding itself is an organic, multi-layered, integral, and multi-dimensional process.

1. How knowledgeable am I about the promise and perils of individual technologies I use in a personal or work context?

At a basic level, most entities (individuals and organizations) acquire knowledge about specific technologies by experiencing their benefits, which would be the case particularly with consumer technologies such as television, personal computers, cell phones, and the Internet. However, there may be relatively less knowledge of the perils of specific technologies, which typically can be acquired by way of exposure to horror stories in the news or unfortunate occurrences and experiences with those technologies. Examples of perils abound: a credit card company database gets hacked, compromising private and personal information; or an individual becomes a victim of identity fraud; or a teenager suffers from addiction to a particular video game; or an individual becomes extremely dependent on television-watching.

When it comes to newer emerging technologies, there is likely to be much less knowledge, let alone experience, because the technology is not yet widely available in the mainstream. As an example, consider the policy issues raised by robot swarms as listed in the 2015 list of emerging ethical dilemmas and policy issues in science and technology by the John. J. Reilly Center:

> Researchers at Harvard University recently created a swarm of over 1000 robots, capable of communicating with each other to perform simple tasks such as arranging themselves into shapes and patterns . . . The concept of driverless cars also relies on this system, where the cars themselves (without human intervention, ideally) would communicate with each other to obey traffic laws and deliver people safely to their destinations. But should we be worried about the ethical and policy implications of letting robots work together without humans running interference? What happens if a bot malfunctions and causes harm? Who would be blamed for such an accident? What if tiny swarms of robots could be set up to spy or sabotage?

It is important to have knowledge of the promise and perils of specific technologies, especially the ones that are being used regularly, but understanding is enhanced if it is informed by knowledge of systemic effects of technology.

2. How knowledgeable am I about the systemic effects of technology as a whole?

Having knowledge, more or less, about specific dangers of a few technologies that one employs is quite different from an understanding of the systemic effects of technology in general. This type of understanding comes from knowledge of general attitudes to technology and perhaps some familiarity with underlying theories about the human–technology relationship. A broader discussion about attitudes or theories of technology is beyond the scope of this chapter. However, it may be pertinent to introduce a few ideas at this point.

Technological determinism is a theory that posits that technological developments are the prime driver of social structure and cultural values (Smith and Marx, 1994). Social commentator and communications theorist Neil Postman (2011, p. 71) has coined the term "technopoly" to describe a state of mind that "consists in the deification of technology, which means that the culture seeks its authorization in technology, finds its satisfactions in technology, and takes it orders from technology." Postman believes that modern society has become a technopoly, a view more recently echoed by Morozov (2013), a self-proclaimed digital heretic who in his acerbic and acclaimed critique of digital technologies, *To Save Everything, Click Here: The Folly of Technological Solutionism*, assails our gullibility in the solutionistic belief that technology can or will provide answers to all our complex problems. These critics and many others have pointed out the naiveté in our subconscious reliance on technologies, which in turn fosters a belief in experts, who rely on measurement and data provided by even more technologies. The proliferation and glut of data and information has also led to a tendency to measurement reductionism, which suggests in practice that data is all-important and what cannot be measured does not exist or is unimportant. Moreover, the fact that technologies have steadily replaced human capabilities and recent advances in robotics have led to the fear that robots and intelligent systems (for example, IBM's Watson) will replace knowledge workers. Over a sufficiently long period, in the opinion of many discerning observers, there is a risk of total annihilation from the follies of our own making.

3. How aware am I of my personal relationship and attitude to technology?

SO far, we have discussed knowledge about particular technologies and holistic understanding about the systemic effects of technology in general. A progression to greater wisdom calls for this learning to be taken to a yet deeper plane so that individuals become personally aware of their own individual responses to these issues. Awareness goes beyond information, knowledge, and intellectual understanding to encompass how one individually and existentially relates to technologies. It includes not just knowledge but also awareness of beliefs, attitudes, emotions, assumptions, and behaviors that underlie technologies and technological change. This awareness is beneficial because it can be the seed for change. So, for example, awareness in the case of a technophobe may provide clues for the reasons for his or her fear. Does it stem from ignorance, bias, or past experiences? Is the fear emotional or does it have a rational basis? How does fear affect the potential for the individual's growth? How do one's assumptions and beliefs play into the fear?

Awareness of one's relationship to technologies may also bring to light how technology may redefine or change the meanings of words, which may happen almost imperceptibly, insidiously, or subconsciously. A case in point is the term "memory," originally defined as a faculty by which the mind stores information, which later came to include RAM and secondary storage. With recent technological advances, one may well ask what human memory is when digital photos can define what is remembered later or when spatial memory is replaced and/or augmented by GPS systems. Postman (2011, p. 8) observes that "technology redefines 'freedom,' 'truth,' 'intelligence,' 'fact,' 'wisdom,' 'memory,' 'history' – all the words we live by. And it does not pause to tell us. And we do not pause to ask." Perhaps we need to pause to ask so that new contextual meanings come to light.

Awareness of an individual's relationship to technologies may help in determining their personal happy balance, where technologies find their right place in the bigger scheme of things, where the distinction between cyberspace and physical space is felt and understood, where "presence" is not just a virtual phenomenon, where mindfulness is at the center, and where technology-related behaviors stem from true understanding rather than unconscious reactions.

4. Who am I?

The preceding discussion makes clear that to understand in a deeper way, a quality of awareness is necessary: an experiential aspect that is not always crystallized into a lens from which one views the world, but is rooted in the here and the now, and has a quality of freshness and mindfulness, which is informed but not necessarily distorted by various perspectives. The "who am I?" question takes personal awareness to its deepest level: one of identity.

In the ultimate sense, humankind cannot understand its relationship to technologies if we do not understand ourselves first. "Know thyself" – the ancient aphorism attributed to Socrates and other sages from the East and the West – is as relevant today as it was in the past, perhaps more so in a world dominated by technologies where it is easy to confuse the real and the virtual. When "avatars" are seen as representations of the "I" and virtual identities have become aspects of the real identities, the "who am I?" self-inquiry is critical in understanding the nature of reality and oneself. This inquiry may lead one to a deep understanding of identification and attachment to all material things, including technologies, which marks the beginning of freedom from human suffering. As educator and philosopher Krishnamurti observed:

> Technological progress does solve certain kinds of problems for some people at one level, but it introduces wider and deeper issues too. To live at one level, disregarding the total process of life, is to invite misery and destruction. The greatest need and most pressing problem for every individual is to have an integrated comprehension of life, which will enable him to meet its ever-increasing complexities . . . The man who knows how to split the atom but has no love in his heart becomes a monster.
>
> (Krishnamurti, 2001, pp. 155–6)

Responding to the "who am I?" question may enable us to ask whether technology with all its good intent is being developed by a clever thought-based utilitarian optimizing instrumental materialistic mind, a mind which is so caught up in its intellect and measurement that it is ever harder to realize truth (or transcendence) and freedom from the burdens of thought, culture, knowledge, and systems.

What has been attempted here is an exploration of fundamental issues of the human relationship to technology via a set of deep interpenetrating questions. This overall approach of inquiry is not meant to be prescriptive or normative lest it too will fall into the trap of solutionism. However, responding to these questions from depth and practice may provide valuable insights for individuals in order to meet challenges wisely in their personal and work contexts.

Conclusions

Humankind has used technologies for many thousands of years. But there are good reasons to believe that current and future technologies are game-changing in an unpredictable sense and can affect humanity in potentially disastrous ways. As technologies seemingly take over the world, how we relate to technology matters greatly. We have to ask, face, and explore fundamental questions raised by technology. The manner in which we conduct this inquiry is as important as the content of our responses. In this chapter, I have proposed an inquiry into the human–technology relationship based on perennial universal insights of wisdom viewed in a modern, practical, and scientific context. Instead of taking technology-driven change as a given and accepting its effects as inevitable, the central thesis of this chapter is that a paradigm shift is necessary in our understanding of our relationship to technologies, and that a new understanding rooted in practical wisdom may help us ask the right questions and find creative responses to proactively shape the future.

Einstein is believed to have said that a problem cannot be solved from the same level of consciousness or thinking that created it in the first place. The obvious implication is that we, individually, have to dig deeper into our consciousness. In trying to understand the depths of the human–technology relationship, we must reiterate that attempts to jump to simplistic solutions or to take up hard intellectual positions may be missing the point. The right responses to burning issues raised by technology are not purely canned, pre-determined, formulaic, or fixed, but emerge from a process of wise questioning and transcending of perspectives and ideologies. In this chapter, I have sketched the beginnings of what a wisdom-based understanding in a technology-driven world may look like. This attempt is not meant to be exhaustive or conclusive; rather, it is meant to start a different kind of conversation on this critical subject. An understanding based on practical wisdom may include many facets such as consideration of multiple perspectives, responsibility, self-knowing, sensitivity, empathy, mindfulness, attentiveness, inquiry, compassion, reflectiveness, insight, depth of vision, fairness, goodness, and objectivity, among others. Our deeper responses to reflective questions raised in this chapter may enable us to see the traps of technological solutionism and measurement reductionism, and to help us go beyond all kinds of solutionism to mindfully and creatively understand the problems we face as individuals, organizations, and societies.

Wisdom-based understanding is founded not on valueless science alone, but on science working in concert with timeless wisdom adapted for our times. The understanding is not just about knowing the promise and perils of technologies, but is also about prudence regarding the holistic effects of technology and awareness of one's relationship to it in practical, intellectual, and existential spheres. Realizing that the world is largely gushing about the latest technologies, a wisdom-based understanding may lead us to be cautiously and healthily skeptical. And it may simultaneously fill us with awe, wonder, and optimism. The hope is that we, individually and collectively, personally and professionally, will wisely create, design, use, and manage technological artifacts for the betterment of individuals, society, and the planet.

Reflection and critical thinking

1   What is "wise" use of technology?
2   How can science work in concert with practical wisdom? How can scientists and technologists proactively and wisely consider the effects of their inventions?
3   How can we transcend our backgrounds and conditioning to better understand the human relationship to technologies and to develop intelligent responses?
4   While analytical abilities are critical in dealing with ubiquitous information and big data, how can such abilities be complemented by wisdom-related qualities such as awareness, mindfulness, consideration of multiple perspectives, reflexivity, and compassion?
5   How may technology designers incorporate wisdom in the artifacts they create?
6   How knowledgeable am I about the promise and perils of individual technologies I use in a personal or work context?
7   How knowledgeable am I about the systemic effects of technology as a whole?
8   How aware am I of my personal relationship and attitude to technology?
9   Who am I?

References

Ayyagari, R., Grover, V., and Purvis, R. (2011). Technostress: Technological antecedents and implications. *MIS Quarterly*, 35(4), 831–58.

Bostrom, N. (2014). *Superintelligence: Paths, Dangers, Strategies*. Oxford: Oxford University Press.

Honan, D. (n.d.). Ray Kurzweil: The six epochs of technology evolution. Retrieved from http://bigthink.com/the-nantucket-project/ray-kurzweil-the-six-epochs-of-technology-evolution (accessed September 4, 2015).

Huesemann, M., and Huesemann, J. (2011). *Techno-fix: Why Technology Won't Save Us or the Environment*. Gabriola Island, BC: New Society Publishers.

John. J. Reilly Center (2015). 2015 list of emerging ethical dilemmas and policy issues in science and technology. Retrieved from http://reilly.nd.edu/outreach/emerging-ethical-dilemmas-and-policy-issues-in-science-and-technology-2015 (accessed September 4, 2015).

Joy, B. (2000). Why the future doesn't need us. *Wired*, April.

Kaczynski, T. (2005). *The Unabomber Manifesto: Industrial Society and its Future*. Minneapolis, MN: Filiquarian Publishing.

Kanner, A. (n.d.). Technological wisdom, *Tikkun*. Retrieved from http://www.tikkun.org/nextgen/technological-wisdom (accessed September 4, 2015).

Krishnamurti, J. (2001). *What are You Doing with Your Life?* Ojai, CA: Krishnamurti Foundation.

——. (2013). *The First and Last Freedom*. London: Rider Books.

Merriam-Webster Dictionary (2015). Technology. Retrieved from http://www.merriam-webster.com/dictionary/technology (accessed September 4, 2015).

Morozov, E. (2013). *To Save Everything, Click Here: The Folly of Technological Solutionism*. New York: PublicAffairs.

Nye, D.E. (2006). *Technology Matters: Questions to Live with*. Cambridge, MA: MIT Press.

Ong, W.J. (1986). Writing is a technology that restructures thought. In G. Baumann (ed.), *The Written Word: Literacy in Transition* (Wolfson College Lectures 1985), (pp. 23–50). Oxford: Clarendon Press.

——. (2012). *Orality and Literacy: The Technologizing of the Word*. New York: Methuen.

Pauleen, D.J., Campbell, J., Harmer, B., and Intezari, A. (2015). Making sense of mobile technology: The integration of work and private life. *SAGE Open*, April/June, 1–10.

Postman, N. (2011). *Technopoly: The surrender of culture to technology*. New York: Random House.

Ragu-Nathan, T.S., Tarafdar, M., Ragu-Nathan, B.S., and Tu, Q. (2008). The consequences of technostress for end users in organizations: Conceptual development and empirical validation. *Information Systems Research*, 19(4), 417–433.

Smith, M.R. and Marx, L. (eds) (1994). *Does Technology Drive History?: The Dilemma of Technological Determinism*. Cambridge, MA: MIT Press.

Sternberg, R.J. and Jordan, J. (eds) (2005). *Handbook of Wisdom: Psychological Perspectives*. New York: Cambridge University Press.

Turkle, S. (2012). *Alone Together: Why We Expect More from Technology and Less from Each Other*. New York: Basic Books.

Wilber, K. (2011). *The Marriage of Sense and Soul: Integrating Science and Religion*. New York: Random House.

Chapter 3

The screening of reality

A phenomenological perspective on the computer screen

Marty H. Heitz

Introduction

Perhaps no other single sign of the entanglement of our lives with technology is reflected as much as by the predominance of various "screens" – from computer screens to television, movie, tablet, and smartphone screens – in our daily lives. The screen is called an "interface" as it allows us to control our environment, to find information, to communicate with others, to do our work, to play our games, to watch films, and so many other things that have become staples of human life today. The first screens, movie and television screens, were essentially flat surfaces that merely allowed for the viewing of images, but now screens have become interactive as well, allowing for much greater versatility and complexity of use as they have become active conduits and not merely passive displays. With the advent of the Internet and wireless communication, our screened devices are active players in the management and enjoyment of our lives, to the extent that many of us spend literally hours every day giving our attention to screens. This much seems plain. But what is the significance of this phenomenon? What impact, if any, does this have on our lives? And, most especially, how might the use of practical wisdom apply to such a phenomenon?

In light of the fact that our lives are dominated ever more by the ubiquitous use of various computerized screens, I would like to offer something of a phenomenology of attending to the computer screen. In other words, I would like offer a preliminary, descriptive account of what is happening when we give our attention to a screen as well as how this reflects a certain understanding of what it means to be human. I assume that such attending is an *active* engagement on our part and not merely one of passive reception, but also that this attending represents fundamental features of what it means to be a human being in the age of technology. I will offer this account in light of the following three areas of concern: first, Heidegger's ideas on being-in-the-world and the environmental aspect of phronesis (a form of practical wisdom), as well as his take on "representational" versus "meditative" thinking (*vorstellendes* and *besinnendes Denken*); second, the recent work of psychiatrist Iain McGilchrist on the lateralization of the human brain (that is, the differing functions of the right and left hemispheres of the brain); and, third, the practice of meditation and mindfulness, and how and why it might be wise to utilize an active awareness while attending to a screen of any kind.

Heidegger

Among the many contributions to Western philosophy made by Martin Heidegger, perhaps none is more important than his description of the basic ground of human existence as "being-in-the-world." Fully aware of the predominance of substantive metaphysics in the West, he pushed the envelope of serious, philosophical inquiry beyond the limits of what can be rationally comprehended by deconstructing the notion of being as having the nature of *a being*. In other words, what we ordinarily perceive as individual things existing separately in a world – a world usually thought of as the vast collection of all things – are themselves grounded in a more primordial openness or field, *out of which* individual things come to stand, or to exist. As a "field," one cannot reduce this openness to some "thing" that in any way exists in itself, delimitable from other likewise self-standing things. To the Western mind, this makes little (if any) sense, as the Western paradigm is itself substantive, meaning that we tend to think of all that is as being some-*thing*, the greatest of all somethings being God, the ultimate entity. This reflects the ancient Greek attitude that something *cannot* come from nothing, and so the ancient Greeks consistently postulated a "that" from which all things come, whether that be one of the natural elements, Plato's Demiurge or Aristotle's Prime Mover, or the "forms" or "actualities" that shape all dumb matter. However, consistent with most philosophies of ancient India and China, Heidegger's non-dualistic philosophy promotes the basic concept that what pervades *all* things cannot itself be *a* thing.

This idea, while not unique, was certainly revolutionary in Western thought and demands an expansion of our predominant paradigm, lest we mistake Heidegger's neologisms as mere wordplay. Being-in-the-world itself announces as much, for we are to understand this as a holistic phenomenon irreducible to any single "part." Crudely put, we might say that "we are the world and the world is us," so long as we are careful not to think of being-in-the-world as the *composition* of the parts, human being and world. This means that "I" and "world" arise *mutually*, that "my" life, no matter how private or secluded, is an inseparable facet of the world. For Heidegger, it makes no sense to say "I came into this world," as self and world never *actually* exist separately. Hence, the non-dual, mutual interplay of all beings is the fundamental ground *out* of which our lives run their course, though more strictly we must say it is the ground*less* ground, as it is empty of any substantive thingness. The importance of this non-dual ground for our lives is immense, as it literally frames our entire existence with meaning and significance (though, again, strictly as a "frameless frame"); it is the existential referent for all human comportment and understanding, for all "building, dwelling, and thinking." As such, it is likewise the referent for all language or, as Heidegger (2008, p. 217) famously put it in his *Letter on Humanism*, "language is the house of being."

In terms of our individual lives, this means that we do not, fundamentally, deal with a world "outside" of us, or introspectively turn to an "inner" world, such that either exists separately from the other. Instead, we find ourselves always and ever *situated* in an interpersonal world, whereby we take our fundamental cues for our activity and thought *from* this world, and whereby all our activity and thought refers ultimately *back to* this world; that is, we are-in-the-world. This also means that the subject–object mode of thinking and relating, to ourselves as much as to things or others in the world, is itself only possible on the basis of this holistic phenomenon and thus is not reflective of our basic being. Of course, this subject–object mode seems to be our "default" mode, and our contemporary culture virtually demands that we assume such a posture. Yet we readily recognize that the world and ourselves appear "as a whole" and are "given at once," and are not, so to speak, assembled piece-by-piece. But we often fail to realize that this holistic sphere or field is the first, primordial fact, and instead place chief importance on *this* or *that*, on *me* and on *you*, on *him* or *her* or *us* and *them*. We fragment the whole of being-in-the-world and compartmentalize our lives accordingly, concerned only with narrowed interests, and thus ever more in conflict with others.

But insofar as we are always situated through being-in-the-world, all fragmentation arises from a more primordial "sighting" of the whole situation or an inclusive vision and understanding that frames our comportment; this is what Heidegger termed *Umsicht*, literally meaning "around sight" and translated as "circumspection" by Macquarrie and Robinson in the first English translation of *Being and Time* (1962). However, I would like to translate this term as "peripheral vision," as it is a kind of attention that, while not usually noticed and never completely held in focus, is insepa-rable from what we might call the focus of our activity and thought. For example, when we enter a restaurant or public dining room, we do not need to count heads to know that the restaurant is crowded or, conversely, empty. We likewise pick up other hints and signals that indicate the atmosphere of the room and the mood of the patrons. This process is always ongoing and critically helps orient us in whatever situ-ation we find ourselves. As individuated, this "background understanding" includes, mostly subconsciously, our entire past experiences and the sum of our knowledge, while still being constantly molded by present experience. This, for Heidegger, is the essence of the practical wisdom Aristotle termed "phronesis," the habituated skill to readily size up a situation and know how to best respond or act or behave, and it is thoroughly *contextualized*. Even when concentrating on a particular task, as I am now in this chapter, we intuitively comprehend our situation; I know that it is late after-noon without having to consciously attend to the time, that the house is quiet, that the air warm and fresh, that I am not moving or being moved. All this lies in "peripheral vision" whenever we maintain focus on *this* or *that*.

To sum up, this means that the subject–object mode of attending to things can-not occur without the support and backdrop of our "peripheral vision," a perceptive and intuitive understanding of our current situation (and *as* current is the only way it operates). When we focus attention, then, we "lift out" a feature of the whole, contextualized situation and grasp it in its individuality, and this is essentially what Heidegger means by "representational thinking" (*vorstellendes Denken*). But it is pos-sible to attend, in a way, to the peripheral by allowing our attention to expand and thereby notice what else is happening in our immediate environment. Visual attention is a useful example of this and can serve as a model for other modes of perception and thought, in that whenever we look at something, there is both a focus (what we are looking at) and a periphery (what lies around that focus), and while one cannot look *at* the periphery (for it thereby becomes the new focus), one can attend to it by noticing what lies around the focal point. Likewise, while we cannot "grasp" our peripheral understanding or all that existentially informs our current situation, we *can* be attentive to it in a more open way, as happens when we contemplate our situation as opposed to directly thinking *about* it. This other mode of attending Heidegger refers to as *besinnendes Denken*, often rendered as "meditative thinking" (and often also contrasted with "calculative thinking," or *rechnendes Denken*). When Heidegger said that the most thought-provoking thing is that we have not even begun to think, he was, in part at least, gesturing toward this more holistic, contextualized manner of attending to the periphery of the center of our thinking and strongly felt that such a way of attending was crucial for an understanding of technology. In what follows I will show that such a manner is especially crucial for understanding of, and dealing with, "screen gazing."

Iain McGilchrist

This distinction between two dominant modes of giving attention in the present moment, as well as many other versions of the same, reflects the polar nature of human cognition and that in turn as specifically rooted in the lateralization of the brain. Thanks to Iain McGilchrist's recent work, outlined in *The Master and His Emissary: The Divided Brain and the Making of the Western World* (2012), this issue is receiving renewed interest and research, and the results are quite interesting. Here I wish only to present the directly relevant aspects, but McGilchrist's work reaches far beyond what I can depict here. Although the majority of brain activity occurs in both hemispheres, some 7–9 percent of cognitive activity is centered in one or the other hemisphere, the functional differentiation known as lateralization, and this phenomenon is explored in depth in his book. Besides being a player in the differing ways we give attention, this hemispheric specialization is further enhanced by increased inhibition of communication between the hemispheres via the corpus collosum which, while connecting the two, also acts to inhibit cross-communication, and this combined with asymmetrical growth in the frontal cortex has led to huge advances in our cognitive abilities. Briefly, research shows that the two hemispheres have quite different "personalities," meaning that while they work together to yield a unitive consciousness, they each add unique qualities that are not found in the other. Thus, whereas the functioning of the left hemisphere is similar to a computer's serial processor, the right hemisphere acts as a parallel processor, meaning that the left is used chiefly for understanding events in series, like causality, while the right is used chiefly for understanding the given, contextualized whole. Whereas the left is mechanically adroit, able to make useful associations and execute fine manipulation through the right hand (and, if left-handed, the coding for such manipulation arises from the left hemisphere and passes through the right to operate the left hand), the right is more sensitive to the organic, living, immediately present reality. In fact, the left not only literally grasps things through the hands, it also metaphorically "grasps" things conceptually, as it is responsible for "lifting out" relevant features of the given, perceptual whole and identifying them. The right hemisphere, on the other hand, presents the given, holistic moment *to* the left, such that without this presentation, the left would not be able to execute its more familiar cognitive functions such as through concept formation and a rational, sequential thought process.

What is of special importance here is the fact that attention literally spans the two on a continuum from the fine, detailed, grasping "focus" of the left to the broadly open, holistic and contextualized "peripheral" awareness of the right hemisphere. In reference to the example given above, this means that as I write, attending to this computer and screen, my left hemisphere is chiefly in play as I think about these issues and focus on the keyboard and screen, while my right hemisphere is chiefly responsible for the "peripheral awareness" of my surroundings, or for what Heidegger called *Umsicht*. Given our tendency, especially in this contemporary culture, to operate through the "subject–object" mode – a mode that is essentially centered in the left hemisphere – we most often neglect what is provided by the right hemisphere to such an extent that, at one time, scientists even thought that the right hemisphere was largely redundant. In fact, however, we "sight" our situation and orient our understanding through this "silent" hemisphere, and could not even begin to think without it. But we can attune ourselves to its functioning through practice with peripheral awareness, as we will see shortly in the section on meditation below.

To put all this another way, the right hemisphere (or, recognizing that *phenomenologically* these functions are mutually physical and mental, what I shall henceforth call the "right mind") *presents* the immediate, holistic reality, while the left hemisphere (henceforth the "left mind") *re-presents* this reality. This means that in our actual experience, we fluidly and fluently shift our attention from the specific and focal to the broad and peripheral, thereby activating lateralized functions as the present situation calls for, such that the "presented" arises mutually with the "re-presented." Only in the dualistic mindset of subject–object is this idea depicted as if the left mind were a "controller" and the right mind the "input" of sensory information, a model strongly reminiscent of the Cartesian "ghost in the machine." And yet there is an operant *polarity* present in giving attention, a polarity that gives rise to our ability to "stand back" from the world and entertain events, things and possibilities *not* immediately given; that is, a polarity that allows for *imagination* and, with that, thought.

In the attempt to design a machine that can mimic human thought, there has been great success in modeling the left mind, but, as of yet, little success in creating a truly "thinking" machine, and this undoubtedly lies in the difficulty of programming a "right minded" machine. As Hubert Dreyfus (1990) has argued, utilizing Heidegger's concept of being-in-the-world, we cannot *detail* or otherwise *program* what is provided by peripheral awareness, or the right mind, as the ultimate referent is nothing other than the world itself in its "worlding" (*Welten*, a term Heidegger first used in his *Kriegsnotsemester* of 1919, a full seven years prior to his writing *Being and Time*). Still, the computer screen "re-presents" reality for us virtually, and it may seem as though the screen metaphorically acts as the left mind; certainly, insofar as we attend not to the *screen* itself, but rather the content presented on the screen, the computer acts as the "whole" out of which we retrieve data and can slip into the background when we are involved in the re-presentations on the screen. But of course this "mirroring" of the nature of the mind is overtly dualistic as it maintains the apparent distance between the "agent-I" and the "given data," or in other words as it re-affirms the subject–object distinction. The significance of this continual re-positing of the subject–object modality will be treated below.

Mindfulness

The practice of meditation is commonly understood to yield a variety of benefits, from relaxation and stress reduction to enhanced concentration and transformative insights. Given what has already been said about the nature of attention, however, it can be readily seen that meditation and mindfulness activate a deeper awareness than we maintain in our daily activities by first activating the "right mind." Indeed, the simple shift of attention from focal to peripheral – or, as I like to call it, the "step to the right mind" – is at the heart of the Buddhist practice of mindfulness, as it requires that one be aware of more than what is "in focus." In other words, to be able to "watch" the mind, the breath, our body, feelings, and emotions requires that we "stand back" and observe with a more broadly open mind.

Beginning meditation practice is mainly concerned with remembering to bring our attention back to the present, environmental moment when we get drawn into the stream of thinking, as there is an inverse relationship between involved, "representational" thinking and broadly open awareness. One cannot, then, be *both* intensely thinking *and* broadly attentive to what is happening within and around oneself at the same time, though the polar opposite is never completely absent (so when I am completely absorbed in thought, I will still notice someone shaking me to get my attention, though perhaps not immediately!). Such meditation practice requires that we "perch" the focus of attention on some feeling or perception that is happening now *while not giving total attention to it* (such exclusive attention is a technique utilized in certain practices of concentration, but is not used as frequently in Buddhist practice). Rather, with the focus perched on, say, our breathing, we peripherally attend to whatever is happening in our body, mind, and surroundings, bringing the focus back to the perch when our attention is caught by thought. Mindfulness, by extension, means practicing this more global awareness in all of our activities, thereby keeping us anchored in the present without becoming consumed by what is happening in this moment.

For Buddhists, the real aim of meditation and mindfulness is to see things as they are, as they purely and simply *present* themselves or, to put this the other way around, to realize the extent to which we *re-present* reality in terms of our own past experiences, judgments, fears, and desires. This also means to transform our life through such realization, and this does not happen if we merely know this intellectually (that is, if it is merely re-presented). The process of awakening is a transformation of our entire being-in-the-world, whereby we literally "see" things differently *from the ground up* and not from the conscious, re-presented virtual reality down. What is required is not an action of the "agent," not a decision willfully undertaken by the "subject," but rather a transformative "seeing" that arises holistically and integrally, a "vision" that is itself action as it transforms the ground from which we arise as individuals. From what has been said above, this deep understanding is not subject to the grasping of the left mind and must occur through our "stepping to the right" by utilizing the non-grasping, broadly open, peripheral awareness that is always available. The meditative mind is not "formed" through technique, but is naturally found when we relax the focus of our attention and "attend" peripherally to whatever is happening now, an awareness whose depths no one can plumb.

In peripheral awareness, the "thingliness" of things dissolves, in part because when being aware without grasping, what is there to grasp? Yet the persistent sense of self, the "I" that in subject–object mode feels "in control," continues to attempt to grab hold of something. Perhaps this is because this supposed ego is in fact empty itself, being nothing more than the *re-presented*, mental body that can only exist in the left mind. In other words, perhaps the egoic self is but the *re-presentation* of the body in the left mind, itself lacking all but conceptual reality, or how we "see" ourselves *in* a situation, a *re-presentation* that arises mutually with the *presented*, actual situation. In any case, there is general agreement among many Hindus and Buddhists that we are deeply confused about our nature, mistaking the *re-presented* ego for a really existing self, made particularly troublesome by the fact that they arise mutually. And I believe it is no stretch of the imagination to say that this confusion is literally kill-ing us, as we vie and contend and compete with one another all on the basis of this supposed "individuality," a personalized individuality that is literally *sustained* by the focal attention of the left mind when in ignorance of vastly greater depths of being-in-the-world accessible through the right mind. This is *not* to say that the left mind is in any way "bad," but only that when we live in ignorance of the nature of our minds, we run terrible risks, as we live more in a virtual world than the real one. And the ubiquitous use of screens, this "interface" with technology, reinforces this imbalance in ever-increasing ways.

Toward a phenomenology of screen gazing

Returning now to the simple phenomenon of gazing at a screen, of whatever kind, it is apparent that the screen is an objective piece of technology that *re-presents* infor-mation for our consumption, utilization, and enjoyment in just the same way as the left-mind *re-presents* our lived experience. Of course, I am limited in my own con-sciousness to re-presenting only what is in my knowledge and past experience or what is currently presented to me, while on the other hand the computerized screen puts me in *re-presented* connection with nothing short of the entirety of information available on the World Wide Web. Screen gazing, as the screen itself, represents the epitome of left-minded cognition and functioning, vastly extending the ability of the mind to comprehend the world as well as to grasp specific information ("information" taken in the broadest possible sense here, including visual images as well as auditory sounds and music). Thus, when I am actively gazing at a screen, I am engaging in an objecti-fication of what I do when I give attention to thought or when I narrow my attention to something in my perceptual field, and this is the phenomenological basis I wish to highlight in this chapter.

This is also to say that our ability to interact through the computerized screen reflects the dominant, inherent practicality of the functioning of the left-mind, for all that is "practical" *is only possible on the basis of re-presentation*. Screen gazing thus mirrors for us this aspect of human cognition and consciousness that lies at the heart of all technology and without which there would simply be no technology, at least of the sort we know. Of course, this only describes one aspect of the holistic phenomenon that I am calling screen gazing, for this ability to re-present is thoroughly dependent upon the prior givenness of the whole, lived situation, meaning that technology and all that is "practical" *also* rests upon what is immediately *presented*. But when awareness of the immediate whole is lost in absorption in the mind (or in gazing at the screen), then we are existentially off-balance, becoming shortsighted and giving free rein to the fragmentary and virtual nature of such *re-presentation*.

To alter our relationship with screen gazing (or with representational thinking) requires that we take some conscious steps, that we both realize that there *is* a greater whole of which I am not specifically, narrowly capable of focusing on as well as to actively shift my awareness to include *more* than what I am *re-presenting*. In other words, this requires a kind of practical wisdom that is knowingly based on an understanding of our nature as being-in-the-world as well as the nature of our lateralized cognition and that actively extends awareness from being merely fixated upon something *re-presented* to include what is tacitly, peripherally *present*. Given the ubiquitous dominance of the computerized screen, I would suggest that altering *how* we attend to the screen has the capacity to radically alter *how* we relate to technology writ large. Simply by expanding one's awareness to include the feeling of one's body, to have an ear open to the sounds around us as we gaze at the screen, to maintain some sense of presence in our current environment, we can practice a subtle but powerful form of phronesis that can literally keep us grounded in reality, even as we gaze upon a *re-presented*, virtualized one.

It is also worth mentioning that this more mindful form of practical wisdom can be seen as rooted in a greater sense of wisdom, one that supersedes all that has been depicted here so far. In other words, as "practical," practical wisdom always has an end in view, an objective, and can thus be measured as to its efficacy. As such, I see all forms of practical wisdom as species of knowledge, but reserve the singular use of the term "wisdom" for what goes beyond all knowledge and therefore all that is practical, efficacious, or measurable. For Eastern spiritual traditions, especially Hinduism, Buddhism, and Daoism, reality in itself *is* truth, and the *seeing* of this reality – as it is – is what constitutes wisdom. Such wisdom differs profoundly from Western notions of wisdom, particularly conceived as "practical wisdom," as this does not involve knowledge and fits no "in-order-to" process, for the seeing of truth (or, reality in itself) is beyond the mind and serves no auxiliary purpose. Likewise, genuine wisdom cannot be defined, for that would reduce such truth to a species of intellectual knowledge; at best, however, it can be "pointed" to, and such pointing is what constitutes the core texts of the Eastern traditions. Thus, while the kind of practical wisdom outlined here, with specific reference to screen gazing, does not and *cannot* directly bring about genuine wisdom, it *can* help put one in a better position for such wisdom to arise, for as long as we remain fixated on the *re-presented* (what might be referred to as *maya* in an Eastern context), we likewise remained turned away from the greater whole that *is* reality.

Conclusion

I have endeavored to show that while the computerized screen mirrors an aspect of our cognition and is reflective of the cultural paradigm in which we live, it is a reflection that demands our attention, our *right-minded* attention. I do not contest the value of computers or screens, but given the predominance of such "mirrors" in our daily lives, given that the "screen" is the primary interface we have with current technology, we need to bring the practical wisdom that can be found in peripheral awareness to bear on all our comportment with regard to them. In other words, when we sit down and open our laptop, we can be aware not only of what engages our direct attention on the screen but also of the environing present moment, in just the same way as we meditate with the use of a perch. We can, then, allow a broader understanding to arise to balance, as it were, the incessant demands on our left minds. We can realize that, as being-in-the-world, we are far more than what we can *re-present*, no matter how powerful such representations may be. We can remember what the Daoist philosopher Chuang-Tzu (1968) said so long ago: be aware in your use of things lest you be thinged by things!

Reflection and critical thinking

1   How would you characterize your state of mind when using a computer? Are you aware of your surroundings? How does your body feel?
2   After working at a computer for an extended period of time, how would you characterize your state of mind? How does your body feel? What might you do differently while using your computer that could alleviate any negative qualities that you discover after extended use?
3   Practice utilizing peripheral attention for short periods while taking a break from your computer work. Begin by simply sitting up straight, take a deep breath and relax; then give some focal attention to the feeling of the chair beneath you (or, alternatively, the floor beneath your feet). While maintaining some awareness of this sensation, notice any other sensations or perceptions or thoughts that are happening in the periphery, so to speak, and just note them. Continue this for several minutes at least, returning the focus of your attention to the feeling of the seat or floor whenever it wanders away. Before returning to work, note any differences in the state of your mind, body, and/or emotions.
4   How much of your life is built around what occupies your attention? In other words, reflect on what captures your attention, and what you give most of your attention to, in relation to your overall life situation. Also, what is excluded from your life by being relegated to the periphery?
5   Practice utilizing peripheral attention while engaged in conversation with another person through listening more intently and allowing more than just the other person's words to be the center of your attention. Listen more openly, with less expectation as to what they may say next or what you will say in response, feeling your own body and sensations while also noticing the other person's body language. Notice, too, how anxious the mind is to comment on everything the other is saying, how eager it is to interject or give its interpretation, but just note it and continue listening and feeling. Listening more earnestly to another person is a powerful practice, one that can easily lead to deep insights about oneself as well as the other, and can teach us valuable, practical wisdom in how to be more present, whether that be with another person or ourselves while we are engaged in screen gazing.
6   What changes do you notice when practicing mindfulness? How does your relationship with the computer change? Do you feel any physical or emotional changes? Does your engagement with other people change? Do you feel any differently about yourself?

References

Chuang-Tzu (1968). *The Complete Works of Chuang Tzu*, B. Watson (trans.). New York: Columbia University Press.
Dreyfus, H. (1990). *Being-in-the-World: A Commentary on Heidegger's Being and Time, Division I*. Cambridge, MA: MIT Press.

Heidegger, M. (1962). *Being and Time*, J. Macquarrie and E. Robinson (trans.). New York: Harper & Row. (Original work published 1927.)

——. (2008). *Basic Writings*, D.F. Krell (ed.). New York: Harper Perennial. (Original work published 1929.)

McGilchrist, I. (2012). *The Master and His Emissary: The Divided Brain and the Making of the Western World*. Providence, RI: Yale University Press.

Chapter 4

The anatomy of wisdom in an era of ubiquitous technology

Jon W. Beard

Introduction

It has become a foregone conclusion that information technology (IT), including hardware, software, and networks, has become ubiquitous. Individually we have smartphones with us at all hours of the day and night, along with tablets and/or laptop computers. Internet connectivity is often an assumed resource; we feel disconnected without it. We can search for almost anything through our various search engines, stream movies and shows, play games, map where we are or need to be, and can easily (and seemingly constantly) communicate with one another through various social media sites and online tools.

Our organizations, too, increasingly rely on ever-increasing IT infrastructure and connectivity to acquire expanding sets of data about us as customers, users, and workers. In addition to email communication, organizations have been developing and integrating company-wide enterprise resource planning (ERP), customer relationship management (CRM), and supply chain management (SCM) systems, and launching broad Internet-based environments spanning the value chain, including suppliers and customers, all with the goal of capturing massive amounts of data. And this wealth of data, sometimes called "big data," is processed and mined to attempt to glean comprehension about wants and needs.

But has this ever-present technology made us wiser, that is, has it contributed to our wisdom? Fundamentally, can IT demonstrate, or exhibit, wisdom? As an initial step to consider this question, we will explore the DIKW (Data-Information-Knowledge-Wisdom) framework, followed by an exploration of the general anatomy of wisdom in this technology-rich environment. Then, we will briefly explore the concepts of organizational learning and knowledge management as frames for IT and wisdom. Finally, we will consider the implications of wisdom and IT.

The DIKW framework

As part of a general hierarchical framework, wisdom is often considered as the logical next, and perhaps final, sequential step in the progression from data to information to knowledge to wisdom (DIKW). The model is often portrayed as a pyramid structure, with data at the base and wisdom at the peak, or as a two-dimensional flow diagram with data at the left flowing ultimately to wisdom on the right (Bierly et al., 2000; Rowley, 2007; Wallace, 2007). Interestingly, Rowley (2007) has suggested that there has been limited systematic examination of this framework.

It is beyond the scope of this chapter to explore in great depth the variety and complexity of the detailed definitions of data and information; knowledge and wisdom are explored in more depth below. There is still disagreement on the basic definitions for each of the components of the DIKW framework, with Liew (2013, p. 49) describing the multitude of descriptions as a "definition fallacy" due to circular referencing between the concepts. An extensive set of definitions of each of these concepts from the published literature is provided by Liew (2013) and Rowley and Slack (2009).

In general, data is conceived as the raw material consisting of disorganized symbols or signals. Information is characterized as data that has been processed and given meaning and context (Zins, 2007).[1] Knowledge is a "mental structure" (Boulding, 1955). Further, knowledge is derived through the "synthesis of information over time" (Rowley and Hartley, 2006, pp. 5–6), including context, individual values, and experience, and can become embedded in situational rules and routines, and organizational norms, practices, and processes (Davenport and Prusak, 1998). According to Rowley and Slack (2009), information and knowledge are the foundation for wisdom (cf. Baltes and Staudinger, 2000; Beck, 1999). And, it should be noted that the terms "data" and "information," as well as "information" and "knowledge," are sometimes used interchangeably, creating circular interrelationships between them instead of what the DIKW framework would consider a sequential relationship (Liew, 2013). While data and information are relatively tangible, and are often objective or explicit, knowledge is less so, and wisdom is even less tangible.

Liew (2013) has recently suggested that the DIKW paradigm should be revised and expanded to be the progression of data to information to knowledge to intelligence to wisdom (DIKIW). Sternberg (2003) describes intelligence as consisting of the ability to solve practical problems, verbal ability, a balance between intellectual actions and integration, goal orientation and attainment, intelligence in context, and fluid thought. The addition of intelligence between knowledge and wisdom is to specifically recognize that knowledge must be properly organized and assembled, and this requires the changing or restructuring of mental processes to achieve, and ultimately demonstrate, wisdom (Liew, 2013). But what is wisdom?

The anatomy of wisdom

Anatomy is the scientific study of the structure, most often of living things, including their systems, organs, and tissues (Oxford, 2014a). Anatomical study typically includes the materials or things from which they are composed, their relationship(s) to other materials, concepts, or parts, and even their appearance (cf. *Gray's Anatomy* (1974)). For our purposes, let us briefly consider the anatomy of wisdom.

Wisdom has been studied and explored since the earliest periods of recorded history; the writings and teachings of Plato, Socrates, Aristotle, and Confucius, among others, are replete with consideration of wisdom (Hall, 2010; Kane, 2010; Robinson, 1990; Rowley and Slack, 2009). Some of the earliest writings containing the concept of wisdom date to soon after 3000 BC (Birren and Fisher, 1990). Csikszentmihalyi and Rathunde (1990, p. 26) observe that "the meme[2] of wisdom . . . contains a nucleus of meaning that has been transmitted relatively unchanged for at least 80 generations, providing directions for human thought and behavior." In spite of this long time horizon, the concept of wisdom can be difficult to articulate. For example, wisdom does not necessarily correlate with high intelligence. However, we do often think of wisdom as something that is most commonly found among those who are older and who have more experience with a situation or domain of activity, that is, those who have the "authority of experience" (Robinson, 1990, p. 21).

More specifically, *wisdom* has been defined as "the quality of experience, knowledge, and good judgment; the quality of being wise" (Oxford, 2014b). A second part of this definition focuses on "the soundness of action or decision with regard to the application of experience, knowledge, and good judgment." Finally, wisdom can include a developed "body of knowledge." Interestingly, it has been noted that "there is limited reference to wisdom" in much of the research on the DIKW model (Rowley, 2007; Wallace, 2007). Yet, according to Rowley and Slack (2009), there has been recent renewed interest in wisdom.

From the research literature, wisdom has been described as the reasoned application of the perception of a situation, judgment on how and why to respond, and directed action toward an optimal course of action, while retaining control of one's emotional response; it is the thoughtful application of knowledge. Wisdom requires rational judgment, but also includes the capability for counterintuitive thought, abstract thinking, an ability to detect fine nuances, demonstrate foresight, and act with humanity (Rowley and Slack, 2009). *Webster's New World Dictionary* (1997), as cited in Sternberg (2003, p. 147), defines wisdom as the "power of judging rightly the soundest course of action, based on knowledge, experience, and understanding." In one study, Sternberg (2003) suggests that common characterizations of wisdom as selected by a set of subjects include reasoning ability, sagacity (that is, being keen in perception and judgment), learning from ideas and the environment, judgment, expeditious use of information, and perspicacity (that is, being able to understand things that are not obvious).

Wisdom is also characterized as possessing additional qualities. Arlin (1990, p. 230) suggests that a part of wisdom is not just what you do know, but also "knowing what one does not know." Kitchener and Brenner (1990) echo this perspective by proposing that wisdom also consists of an awareness of the unknown and the implications for solving real-world problems and making real-world judgments. The ultimate goal of wisdom is to understand the causes and consequences of events in relation to one another (Csikszentmihalyi and Rathunde, 1990). Yet, Dixon and Baltes (1986, as cited in Kitchener and Brenner, 1990) suggest that wisdom is required when working on difficult problems, sometimes called decisions in the face of uncertainty, ill-structured problems, or wicked problems,[3] that do not have clear-cut solutions; in other words, wisdom may become more important where clear, definitive decisions are difficult or impossible to achieve. Given the imprecise and varied depictions of wisdom, perhaps our recognition of wisdom may be similar to Supreme Court Justice Stewart Potter's characterization of pornography as something that "I know when I see it";[4] that is, we know wisdom when we see it.

We typically think of wisdom as being more than just learning and intelligence. As an example of the concept of wisdom, in his book *The Best and the Brightest* (1992), David Halberstam recounts how the Kennedy and Johnson administrations consisted of many "whiz kid" advisors, that is, young intellectuals who were very smart, but may have lacked real-world experience and application of their theories and ideas. In reflections for the 20th anniversary edition of the book, Halberstam notes that his favorite passage of the book relates to where an excited Vice President Johnson has a quick conversation with his mentor, Speaker of the House Sam Rayburn. After the first Kennedy Cabinet meeting, Johnson is bragging about all of the President's brilliant men. Rayburn responds: "You may be right, and they may be every bit as intelligent as you say, but I'd feel a whole lot better about them if just one of them had run for sheriff once" (Halberstam, 1992, p. 41). As noted by Rich (2008), this story suggests a significant weakness of the Kennedy team, that is, "the difference between intelligence and wisdom, between the abstract quickness and verbal facility which the team exuded, and true wisdom, which is the product of hard-won, often bitter experience." Their lack of understanding of the application of theory in the real world, that is, their lack of wisdom, at least in part, led the decision makers toward increasing engagement in Vietnam and the Vietnam War in spite of strong evidence of the foolhardiness of their approach.

Due to rapid advances in both hardware and software, we are data rich. For example, according to one study (as of 2007), we collectively generated 276 exabytes[5] of digital information every eight weeks (although not all of it is permanently stored) (Vastag, 2011). Further, according to another report, as of May 2012, users were uploading 72 hours of video onto YouTube every minute (Tsukayama, 2012); the volume of uploads is even greater in the present day. As reported by Duhigg (2012), retailers possess a wealth of data about their customers and can very specifically target ads and coupons based on those customer purchase histories. And Coke, in managing its orange juice business, has developed an algorithm that uses up to one quintillion[6] decision variables (Stanford, 2013).

Yet, some would suggest that, in spite of the technical advances, we too often remain information poor (Drucker, 1999) and, by extension, lacking in knowledge. By "information poor," Drucker is suggesting that we lack a detailed understanding of what the information could be telling us. If this is an accurate conclusion, how can we expect technology to help us achieve and use wisdom?

Concepts from organizational learning, the way an organization learns and adapts (Vasenska, 2013), and knowledge management, the process of effectively using organizational knowledge (Davenport, 1994), may provide some insight into the anatomy of wisdom and how wisdom might relate to and be supported by IT. Following this exploration, some implications for where and how technology can help achieve wisdom may be derived, as well as some consideration of the limitations of technology in achieving wisdom.

Organizational learning and wisdom

Organizational learning became a popular topic of organizational study in the 1980s following Argyris and Schön's (1978) seminal work. Learning is about changing behavior. At a basic level, organizations alter their actions based on a mismatch between expected and realized outcomes, that is, single-loop learning. This type of learning, or behavioral change, is typically a series of incremental changes and might be considered as "adaptive learning," but it does not include a change in the organization's core values and norms (Bierly et al., 2000). Double-loop learning is a more complex form of behavioral change, where people in the organization reexamine the policies, values, and assumptions, and then incorporate the appropriate changes from these assessments; that is, they change the framework of organizational norms and assumptions (Bierly et al., 2000). Double-loop learning is learning about single-loop learning and often involves more radical changes, or "proactive learning."

While organizations do not have an individual brain, it would be an oversight to suggest that they are just the sum of the cognitive parts of their members (Hedberg, 1981). Instead, "organizations develop world views and ideologies. Members come and go, and leadership changes, but organizations' memories preserve certain behaviors, mental maps, norms, and values" (1981, p. 6). From this, Fiol and Lyles (1985) have described organizational learning as a process of using better knowledge and understanding to improve organizational decisions and actions. As a contrast, Huber (1991) has noted that a person's effectiveness, or even potential effectiveness, and by extension an organization's, does not always increase with learning.

As described by Bierly et al. (2000), the resource-based view of the firm suggests that knowledge is, or has become, one of the most important strategic resources. A firm's ability to create, process, integrate, and use knowledge can lead to a sustainable competitive advantage (Barney, 1991; Mata et al., 1995). However, the variety of information available, particularly the need to acquire and understand external information, presents the need for organizations to develop an "absorptive capacity" for organizational knowledge (Cohen and Levinthal, 1990). Huber (1990) notes that there is a strong belief that advanced IT should generate more effective intelligence leading to higher-quality decisions, yet Brynjolfsson (1993) reports that confirmation of that perspective is equivocal and idiosyncratic.

Senge (1990) provided a popular capstone to the organizational learning literature. His work emphasized a systems thinking approach to integrate our personal mastery, mental models, shared vision, and team learning to achieve organizational learning for understanding and managing complexity. In sum, organizational learning has some explanatory power for what happens to and in organizations. However, based on the typical descriptions of the models of organizational learning, it is focused on the better use of information and embedding knowledge in the organization so that it can be directed toward improved decision making; wisdom is not an explicit part of organizational learning. Organizational learning can support wisdom through an increased emphasis on capturing data, deriving worthwhile information, and ultimately generating and making available knowledge. Further, organizational learning that leads to improved or refined approaches to decision making through double-loop learning processes, that is, learning that dramatically changes the norms and behaviors of the organization, should contribute to wisdom through the enhanced generation of knowledge and knowledge management. Unfortunately, for our purposes at least, organizational learning may fail to provide guidance on how to generate wisdom.

Organizational learning and knowledge management are closely linked (Bierly et al., 2000). Knowledge management can be considered as the more recent (and more applied) incarnation of organizational learning.

Knowledge management and wisdom

According to Drucker (1999), in the mid-1950s, the US economy crossed the threshold from being primarily a manufacturing-centered economy (that is, an economy focused on building things) to being one that focused increasingly on the importance of correctly applying knowledge toward work-related tasks or services (that is, the generation and application of information and knowledge). Extending this idea, Bell (1973) articulated the concept of a post-industrial society that relies on the application of the abstract knowledge and principles of theoretical knowledge, that is, "the importance of intellectual work" (Hislop, 2013, p. 2) and the accompanying social and economic transformations that were contributing to this shift (Spender and Scherer, 2007). The concept of knowledge management has grown from this early foundation. As noted in Hislop (2013), there was a substantial increase in interest in knowledge management during the late 1990s, as suggested by the growth in published research. And, more recently, the role of Chief Knowledge Officer (CKO) has become common in many organizations, with the CKO being responsible for ensuring that the organization gets the full benefit from its intellectual capital (that is, knowledge) and overseeing the organization's knowledge management efforts (Dalkir, 2005). The CKO also functions as an evangelist who preaches and exemplifies the important skills required to leverage the knowledge embedded in every person and system within the organization (Bontis, 2001).

While far more complex than can be completely described here, knowledge management is built on the ideas of both knowledge creation (cf. Bogner and Bansal, 2007) and the effective application of that knowledge being a source of an organization's competitive advantage (Swart, 2011). The ultimate goal is knowledge sharing, followed by knowledge use. Most knowledge is initially tacit in nature; it is laboriously developed over a long period of time through trial and error, and it is under-utilized because "the organization does not know what it knows" (O'Dell and Grayson, 1998, p. 154). But these early concepts suggested that tacit knowledge – knowledge that people possess, but that is difficult to fully articulate and codify because it is subjective and personal – could be captured (or codified) and converted into explicit knowledge that is objective, impersonal, and independent of its context (Hislop, 2013; Serenko and Bontis, 2004). Once made explicit, the information could be easily disseminated and used. This perspective was recognized as being overly simplistic; instead, a more nuanced approach suggested that the tacit-to-explicit evolution was cyclical, with the extraction and capture of the implicit knowledge making it explicit and the subsequent re-internalization of knowledge making it implicit or tacit, with the cycle repeating from tacit-to-explicit-to-tacit-to-explicit, and so on (Nonaka and Takeuchi, 1995; Nonaka and von Krogh, 2009). In other words, this assumes that knowledge can be captured and transferred, and then correctly used. Finally, Earl (2001) identified seven separate "schools" of knowledge management grouped into three broad categories or approaches – technographic, economic, and behavioral.

As the concept of knowledge management has matured, it has come to be recognized that knowledge is an inseparable part of work activities and is often embedded in the work, the artifacts of the work, or the design of the system itself (Cook and Brown, 1999; Hislop, 2013). Some knowledge is embedded in business processes, activities, and relationships that have been created over time through the implementation of a continuing series of improvements (Nonaka, 1994). To the extent that knowledge is embedded in the work and is derived from experience, it becomes more difficult or time-consuming to acquire wisdom related to this set of knowledge.

Wisdom in an era of ubiquitous technology

The question remains: can IT demonstrate wisdom? The challenge of the concept of wisdom is, at least in part, due to its less-than-precise definition.

If by wisdom we mean the application of "knowledge" and "good judgment" (Oxford, 2014a), then the answer should be a solid "Yes" in favor of technology being able to support and demonstrate wisdom. As is well recognized, IT is excellent at the rapid processing of data to generate useful information, and perhaps even evolving that information into knowledge. IT can be most easily applied to problems that are explicit, that is, problems that are objective or structured and can therefore be codified, that can easily be shared, and that are impersonal. These characteristics allow data to be easily captured and processed (converting it to information), stored, and disseminated to many potential users. IT works exceptionally well at tasks that can be quantified and for decision environments, even exceptionally complex ones, where the information can be structured. We can probably go even further in acknowledging that through the capabilities of IT to provide access to and search through a vast amount of material, the technology can demonstrate one aspect of wisdom through the consolidation and construction of a "body of knowledge" that can be both broad and deep in content.

For more structured, or objective, decisions, algorithmic processing of the data and information can yield good decisions in even complex, data-intensive environments.

An algorithm is one method for embedding knowledge in an organization or a system. An algorithm is "a precise recipe that specifies the exact sequence of steps required to solve a problem" (MacCormack, 2012, p. 3). The *Oxford Dictionary* (Oxford, 2014c) defines it as: "A process or set of rules to be followed in calculations or other problem-solving operations, especially by a computer." It is a mechanical recipe that always works, regardless of the inputs. Each step must be precise, with no human intuition or guesswork required. However, an algorithm falls short of the full concept of wisdom, that is, it can be applied, but is lacking in the larger understanding and experience represented by wisdom.

For example, like many retail enterprises, Target has been collecting sales transaction data about its customers for a number of years (Duhigg, 2012). One effort toward data analysis was focused on whether Target's data analysis could accurately determine whether a woman was pregnant based on the combination and pattern of items purchased. If an accurate determination could be made, Target could direct focused advertising and coupons toward that individual and her family. A relatively high level of accuracy was achieved. Unfortunately, on at least one occasion, the pregnancy-focused ads and coupons were sent to a teenage girl who had not yet told her parents that she was pregnant (Duhigg, 2012). This represents an excellent example of deriving useful customer profile information, but also suggests a lapse in good judgment (that is, wisdom) in not considering the age of the identified customers, or at least in not recognizing the perils inherent in this approach. The technology does an excellent job in performing the algorithms, but the algorithms were not designed to consider whether or not the results should be acted upon.

However, less well-structured situations are still often lacking in the requisite clarity and organization of the decision-making environment. Further, if wisdom must also consist of or be derived from "experience," it is much less obvious that wisdom can be exhibited by IT. We appear to still have a substantial distance to travel to achieve wisdom in our IT.

A less well-structured situation also portrays the challenge of embedding wisdom in IT. Christensen (1997) has articulated the concept of "disruptive technologies," where well-managed, successful companies fail to anticipate market shifts due to new, evolving (that is, disruptive) technologies and lose their dominance in the marketplace. In this situation, the successful companies are paying close attention to their customers; it is logical for organizational decision makers to continue to pay close attention to their best customers, especially as profits and margins continue to increase. This is what a typical business education would suggest. Yet, these same successful companies often find themselves missing important (subtle) market shifts from initially cheaper, often low-quality substitutes. It is difficult for organizations to anticipate when, and often how, their industries will be disrupted and by whom, especially when these shifts are led by new entrants to the marketplace. Instead, normal data analysis will rarely yield a clear indicator of the changing marketplace, that is, it requires more than just information and knowledge to decide when to consider a revised product approach; it requires wisdom.

An apprenticeship is one method where individuals can gain both broad and deep knowledge of a trade or profession. Skills are developed over several years – three to six years, or longer, for many formal apprenticeship programs – through on-the-job training and education in the trade or profession. Information is communicated, understanding is gained through practice, knowledge is acquired, and wisdom can be developed through work and hands-on experience with the domain of work. Ironically, in an era of rapidly evolving technology – both hardware and software – experience with a particular domain of knowledge may be difficult to acquire.

Perhaps suggesting that IT can provide wisdom should currently be characterized as "a bridge too far." Stated differently, given our understanding of wisdom and the current limitations of hardware and software, perhaps it is too much to expect wisdom to be embedded in, or even heavily supported by, IT beyond the more-or-less typical processing of the vast pools of collected data. It is difficult to model something, such as wisdom, that cannot be precisely defined and articulated. Although our technology is growing substantially more powerful in terms of raw processing capabilities every year (cf. "Moore's Law"), we cannot embed the capabilities in the hardware if we do not fully understand what is to be embedded. And we cannot create algorithms to encode in our software if we cannot unambiguously describe what is to be put into code.

Yet, opportunities exist to continue to develop and refine our IT capabilities in relation to wisdom. A number of decision-making domains have been automated, or at least more fully supported, by IT as we have come to understand that what at one time appeared to be expertise and wisdom that had to be acquired over many years was something that was in fact well structured, if very complex. The challenge, in part, was to capture the tacit expertise and recognize what was routine and procedural from that knowledge base and could therefore be integrated with and supported by IT. For example, automated robots now help on assembly lines and do thorough fault checking and quality control; autopilots can fly aircraft from initial runway alignment for take-off through to landing at the destination; medical expert systems can diagnose (or assist in the diagnosis of) less common, but difficult-to-identify ailments; surgical robots can assist with some types of surgery (for example, hip and knee replacement) requiring high levels of precision; systems perform high-speed trading of investments, and so on. Many other examples could be listed.

Therefore, what may have traditionally been thought of as wisdom – the learned application of knowledge toward the solution of complex problem situations – has yielded to increased support by IT. As we have learned more about the problems (that is, how to structure them), as we have learned more about how people and organizations solve problems, and as we have come to better understand and apply the capabilities of IT, we have been able to capture and share information and knowledge, and perhaps wisdom, through systematic approaches to organizational learning and knowledge management.

Conclusion

Having wisdom embedded within the IT infrastructure may not be a requirement in many situations. For well-structured decision-making situations, even those that may be complex, where the goals can be clearly articulated and algorithms can be developed to support the situation, wisdom may not be an immediate requirement. At a minimum, decisions can be derived from the algorithms. Then, assuming that the algorithms and models accurately portray the decision situation, it is relatively straightforward to implement the "decisions" generated.

For less well-structured situations, or ill-structured, or even wicked problem environments, the application of IT capabilities toward the solution of these situations may be of limited utility. The IT can support decision makers by providing analysis of potentially vast quantities of data. Unless or until these situations can be better understood and modeled, it will be difficult to develop useful algorithms to make final recommendations. Therefore, for the foreseeable future, the final decision must still be made by the practitioner based on his or her knowledge, experience, and wisdom.

IT may demonstrate wisdom at some point in the future. It now performs many tasks that were once considered too complex or requiring too much breadth and depth of knowledge. For example, IBM's Deep Blue chess-playing computer defeated Gary Kasparov, a Grand Master and the World Chess Champion, and IBM's Watson, a computer that defeated two champions at the game of Jeopardy, have both succeeded at tasks that were once considered beyond the capabilities of computer technology. New developments in computer hardware and increasingly sophisticated software suggest that IT will continue to exhibit capabilities that move further into the realm of what we have typically called wisdom.

Reflection and critical thinking

1   Do you think that IT can ever demonstrate wisdom? Why or why not?
2   What would be necessary for IT to demonstrate wisdom?
3   Are there any examples of where IT does demonstrate wisdom? How were these systems developed? What are their capabilities? What are their limitations?
4   Does it matter whether or not IT can demonstrate wisdom?
5   Do you think examples such as IBM's Deep Blue chess-playing program or IBM's Watson (the Jeopardy-playing program) demonstrate wisdom? Why? How? If not, what is lacking?

Notes

1 See Gleick (2011) for a more extensive and thorough exploration of the history and theory of the concept of information.
2 A "meme" is an idea, symbol, or practice that can be transmitted or sustained over time through imitation or repetition via writing, speech, gestures, rituals, and so on.
3 "Wicked problems" have several common features, including the following: it is extremely difficult to actually define the problem that needs to be solved; there are too many possible solutions, making it difficult to enumerate potential alternatives; it is problematic in determining when to stop, that is, when a solution has been achieved; they tend to be unique, one-shot situations; they are often symptoms of other problems; and solutions tend to be good or bad, not right or wrong (Rittel and Webber, 1973, 1984).
4 This quote is taken from the Supreme Court decision *Jacobellis v. Ohio* 378 U.S. 184 (1964).
5 An exabyte is a billion gigabytes.
6 One quintillion is 10^{18}, or 1 followed by 18 zeros.

References

Argyris, C. and Schön, D. (1978). *Organizational Learning: A Theory of Action Perspective.* Reading, MA: Addison-Wesley.

Arlin, P.K. (1990). Wisdom: The art of problem finding. In R.J. Sternberg (ed.), *Wisdom: Its Nature, Origins, and Development* (pp. 230–243). New York: Cambridge University Press.

Baltes, P.B. and Staudinger, U.M. (2000). Wisdom: A meta-heuristic (pragmatic) to orchestrate mind and virtue toward excellence. *American Psychologist*, 55(1), 122–136.

Barney, J. (1991). Firm resources and sustained competitive advantage. *Journal of Management*, 17(1), 99–119.

Beck, S. (1999). Confucius and Socrates: Teaching wisdom. Retrieved from www.san.beck.org/C%26S-Contents.html (accessed September 7, 2015).

Bell, D. (1973). *The Coming of Post-industrial Society.* Harmondsworth: Penguin.

Bierly III, P.E., Kessler, E.H., and Christensen, E.W. (2000). Organizational learning, knowledge and wisdom. *Journal of Organizational Change Management*, 13(6), 595–618.

Birren, J.E. and Fisher, L.M. (1990). The elements of wisdom: Overview and integration. In R.J. Sternberg (ed.), *Wisdom: Its Nature, Origins, and Development* (pp. 317–332). New York: Cambridge University Press.

Bogner, W. and Bonsal, P. (2007). Knowledge management as the basis of sustained high performance. *Journal of Management Studies*, 44(1), 165–188.

Bontis, N. (2001). CKO wanted – Evangelical skills necessary: A review of the Chief Knowledge Officer position. *Knowledge and Process Management*, 8(1), 29–38.

Boulding, K. (1955). Notes on the information concept. *Exploration*, 6, 103–112.

Brynjolfsson, E. (1993). The productivity paradox of information technology. *Communications of the ACM*, 35(1), 66–77.

Christensen, C.M. (1997). *The Innovator's Dilemma: When New Technologies Cause Great Firms to Fail.* Boston: Harvard Business School Press.

Cohen, W.M. and Levinthal, D.A. (1990). Absorptive capacity: A new perspective on learning and innovation. *Administrative Science Quarterly*, 35(1), 128–152.

Cook, S. and Brown, J. (1999). Bridging epistemologies: The generative dance between organizational knowledge and organizational knowing. *Organization Science*, 10(4), 381–400.

Csikszentmihalyi, M. and Rathunde, K. (1990). The psychology of wisdom: An evolutionary interpretation. In R.J. Sternberg (ed.), *Wisdom: Its Nature, Origins, and Development* (pp. 25–51). New York: Cambridge University Press.

Dalkir, K, (2005). *Knowledge Management in Theory and Practice.* Oxford: Elsevier.

Davenport, T.H. (1994). Saving IT's soul: Human-centered information management. *Harvard Business Review*, 72(2), 119–131.

Davenport, T.H. and Prusak, L. (1998). *Working Knowledge: How Organizations Manage What They Know*. Boston: Harvard Business School Press.

Dixon, R.A. and Baltes, P.B. (1986). Toward life span research on the functions and pragmatics of intelligence. In R.J. Sternberg and R.K. Wagner (eds), *Practical Intelligence* (pp. 203–235). New York: Cambridge University Press.

Drucker, P. (1999, October). Beyond the information revolution. *The Atlantic*. Retrieved from http://www.theatlantic.com/magazine/archive/1999/10/beyond-the-information-revolution/304658/1 (accessed September 7, 2015).

Duhigg, C. (2012). How companies learn your secrets. *New York Times*, February 16. Retrieved from http://www.nytimes.com/2012/02/19/magazine/shopping-habits.html?pagewanted=alland_r=0andpagewanted=print (accessed September 7, 2015).

Earl, M. (2001). Knowledge management strategies: Towards a taxonomy. *Journal of Management Information Systems*, 18(1), 215–233.

Einstein, A. (1954, March 24). To J. Dispentiere, Albert Einstein Archive 59–495. Retrieved from http://ffden-2.phys.uaf.edu/webproj/211_fall_2014/David_Reynolds/david_reynolds/page3.html (accessed September 22, 2015).

Fiol, C.M. and Lyles, M.A. (1985). Organizational learning. *Academy of Management Review*, 10(4), 803–813.

Gleick, J. (2011). *The Information: A History, a Theory, a Flood*. New York: Pantheon.

Gray, H. (1974). *Gray's Anatomy*. Philadelphia: Running Press.

Halberstam, D. (1992). *The Best and the Brightest*, 20th anniversary edn. New York: Ballantine Books.

Hall, S.S. (2010). *Wisdom: From Philosophy to Neuroscience*. New York: Alfred A. Knopf.

Hedberg, B. (1981). How organizations learn and unlearn. In P.C. Nystrom and W.H. Starbuck (eds), *Handbook of Organizational Design* (pp. 8–27). London: Oxford University Press.

Hislop, D. (2013). *Knowledge Management in Organization: A Critical Introduction*, 3rd edn. Oxford: Oxford University Press.

Huber, G.P. (1990). A theory of the effects of advanced information technologies on organizational design, intelligence, and decision making. *Academy of Management Review*, 15(1), 47–71.

——. (1991). Organizational learning: The contributing processes and the literatures. *Organization Science*, 2(1), 88–115. Special Issue: Organizational Learning: Papers in Honor of (and by) James G. March.

Kane, R. (2010). *Ethics and the Quest for Wisdom*. New York: Cambridge University Press.

Kitchener, K.S. and Brenner, H.G. (1990). Wisdom and reflective judgment: Knowing in the face of uncertainty. In R.J. Sternberg (ed.), *Wisdom: Its Nature, Origins, and Development* (pp. 212–229). New York: Cambridge University Press.

Liew, A. (2013). DIKIW: Data, information, knowledge, intelligence, wisdom and their interrelationships. *Business Management Dynamics*, 2(10), 49–62.

MacCormack, J. (2012). *9 Algorithms that Changed the Future: The Ingenious Ideas that Drive today's Computers*. Princeton: Princeton University Press.

Mata, F.J., Fuerst, W.L., and Barney, J.B. (1995). Information technology and sustained competitive advantage: A resource-based analysis. *MIS Quarterly*, 19(4), 487–505.

Nonaka, I. (1994). A dynamic theory of organizational knowledge creation. *Organizational Science*, 5(1), 14–37.

Nonaka, I. and Takeuchi, H. (1995). *The Knowledge Creating Company: How Japanese Companies Create the Dynamics of Innovation*. New York: Oxford University Press.

Nonaka, I. and von Krogh, G. (2009). Tacit knowledge and knowledge conversion: Controversy and advancement in organizational knowledge creation theory. *Organization Science*, 20(3), 635–652.

O'Dell, C. and Grayson, C.J. (1998). If only we knew what we know: Identification and transfer of internal best practices. *California Management Review*, 40(3): 154–174.

Oxford (2014a). Search term: "Wisdom." Retrieved from http://www.oxforddictionaries.com/us/definition/american_english/wisdom (accessed September 7, 2015).
——. (2014b). Search term: "Anatomy." Retrieved from http://www.oxforddictionaries.com/definition/english/anatomy (accessed September 7, 2015).
——. (2014c). Search term: "Algorithm." Retrieved from http://www.oxforddictionaries.com/definition/english/algorithm (accessed September 7, 2015).
Rich, F. (2008). The brightest are not always the best. *New York Times*, December 6.
Rittel, H. and Webber, M. (1973). Dilemmas in a general theory of planning. *Policy Sciences*, 4, 155–159.
——. (1984). Planning problems are wicked problems. In N. Cross (ed.), *Developments in Design Methodology* (pp. 135–144). New York: Wiley.
Robinson, D.N. (1990). Wisdom through the ages. In R.J. Sternberg (ed.), *Wisdom: Its Nature, Origins, and Development* (pp. 13–24). New York: Cambridge University Press.
Rowley, J. (2007). The wisdom hierarchy: Representations of the DIKW hierarchy. *Journal of Information Science*, 33(2), 163–180.
Rowley, J. and Hartley, R. (2006). *Organizing Knowledge: An Introduction to Managing Access to Information*. Burlington, VT: Ashgate Publishing.
Rowley, J. and Slack, F. (2009). Conceptions of wisdom. *Journal of Information Science*, 35(1), 110–119.
Senge, P.M. (1990). *The Fifth Discipline: The Art and Practice of the Learning Organization*. New York: Currency/Doubleday.
Serenko, A. and Bontis, N. (2004). Meta-review of knowledge management and intellectual capital literature: Citation impact and research productivity rankings. *Knowledge and Process Management*, 11(3), 185–198.
Spender, J.C. and Scherer, A. (2007). The philosophical foundations of knowledge management: Editors' introduction. *Organization*, 14(1), 5–28.
Stanford, D. (2013). Coke engineers its orange juice – With an algorithm. *Business Week*, January 31. Retrieved from http://www.bloomberg.com/bw/articles/2013–01–31/coke-engineers-its-orange-juice-with-an-algorithm (accessed September 7, 2015).
Sternberg, R.J. (2003). *Wisdom, Intelligence, and Creativity Synthesized*. New York: Cambridge University Press.
Swart, J. (2011). That's why it matters: How knowing creates values. *Management Learning*, 42(3), 319–332.
Tsukayama, H. (2012). YouTube uploads 72 hours of video a minute. *Washington Post*, May 21. Retrieved from http://articles.washingtonpost.com/2012–05–21/business/35457795_1_youtube-partners-youtube-users-chad-hurley (accessed September 7, 2015).
Vasenska, I. (2013). Organizational learning and employee empowering increasing tourist destination performance. In V. Dermol, N.T. Širca, and G. Đaković (eds), *Active Citizenship by Knowledge management and Innovation: Proceedings of the Management, Knowledge and Learning International Conference 2013* (pp. 615–624). Bangkok, Thailand: ToKnowPress.
Vastag, B. (2011, February 10). Exabytes: Documenting the 'Digital Age' and huge growth in computing capacity. *Washington Post*. Retrieved from http://www.washingtonpost.com/wp-dyn/content/article/2011/02/10/AR2011021004916.html (accessed September 7, 2015).
Wallace, D.P. (2007). Introduction. In D.P. Wallace (ed.), *Knowledge Management: Historical and Cross-disciplinary Themes* (pp. 1–10). Westport, CT: Libraries Unlimited.
Zins, C. (2007). Conceptual approaches for defining data, information, and knowledge. *Journal of the American Society for Information Science and Technology*, 58(4), 479–493.

Chapter 5

Benefits and perils of virtual modes of organizing

A call for practical wisdom

Stefan Schellhammer and Stefan Klein

Introduction

Information and communication technology (ICT) has been and continues to be heralded as a means to empower the individual employee. Computer-supported cooperative work, specifically, denotes modes of organizing in which groups enjoy greater freedom in the design of their workspace. The IT-enabled workplace promises more individual and collective leeway in deciding when, where, how, and with whom to work. The use of these technologies in organizations is often portrayed as a win–win situation. The organization gains flexibility, productivity, and a more motivated and creative workforce. The employees are liberated from workplace restrictions that made it difficult to find a work–life balance. For the Millennial Generation and more generally for employees in an increasing number of industries, these technologies have become second nature. They are not just tools or systems that are used only for specific ends; instead, they constitute the background against which we make sense of how things are done.

In contrast to the optimistic view of ICT-enabled modes of work, a growing number of skeptical voices have raised their concerns about downsides and detrimental effects of technology-induced workplace transformation. Several studies have shown that constant availability, multi-tasking, and an increased pace of work can put employees' wellbeing at risk. Organizations strive to counter these undesired effects. New rules and incentives are put into place to restrain unsustainable work practices, or employees are less formally asked to refrain from them. For instance, emails are no longer forwarded in the evening to curb after-hours communication. Other companies rely on communication etiquette or suggestions to curtail a culture of 24/7 responsiveness. Irrespective of the particular approach, all of these measures target the symptoms of unhealthy work practices.

While informal appeals, incentives, and rules as well as particular technical design features are commonly accepted means to "correct" unsustainable behavior and to foster employees' wellbeing, we dispute the effectiveness of such measures for three reasons. First, general rules are inconsistent with the liberating, autonomy-reinforcing logic and direction of workplace transformation, and are likely to be resisted or circumvented. Second, such rules are unlikely to do justice to the speed of the transformation. Third, general rules are inconsistent with decentralized modes of organizing and the specific work conditions of teams. In sum: "rules and regulations, however necessary, are pale substitutes for wisdom" (Schwartz, 2011, p. 6).

Instead, we argue that the empowerment of individuals and teams should not be limited to technical tools, but needs to include a reflection of what matters and how to find an appropriate response to the dilemmas of modern work. Along with the blurring of boundaries and the multitude of communication channels, employees face new demands from inside and outside their organization. Balancing these demands, deciding when to respond and when not to respond, requires a distinct competence of responsibly considering the circumstances, finding out what might be appropriate, and taking values and goals, in particular the idea of a good life, into account. We refer to this competence as practical wisdom.

The chapter is structured as follows. The next section outlines how technology and related modes of organizing have unfolded over recent decades, leading to a dissolution of our classic understanding of the workplace. Next, by reference to the literature and our own empirical study, we outline the benefits and perils of virtual modes of organizing – portraying the experience of technology use as ambivalent if not paradoxical. Based on our empirical data, we demonstrate that rules and regulations are not enough to mitigate the undesired consequences of the IT-enabled workplace. Then, we discuss why we believe that the modern condition demands a cultivation of practical wisdom. We elaborate on some of the challenges of exercising and cultivating practical wisdom in the distributed organization. We conclude our chapter by discussing implications for practitioners as well as possible directions of future research.

The dissolution of the "workplace"

Organization and technology cannot be separated, but are mutually constitutive. The way our organizations work and the manner in which we organize work are fundamentally dependent on the technological infrastructure. Likewise, what technology is, what it is good for, and what it means are inseparable from the organizational background against which we make sense of it. The way we work individually and organize work collectively is constantly changing. The notions of "Industrialization," the "Age of the of the smart machine," or the "Age of technology" convey the idea that technological innovations shape the transition toward new ways of organizing that were inconceivable before. They continue to change our understanding of the seemingly invariant concept called "the workplace."

In 1988 Zuboff realized that she had the historic chance to witness the transformation of work driven by the diffusion of "smart machines." Knowledge and computer-mediated work would supplant the predominant blue-collar worker. Gradually the industrial mode of work, the understanding of work and organization, would be subject to "social amnesia." Future generations would find it difficult to understand this bygone age. They would take the new mode of organization for granted.

Twenty years ago, virtual organizations were envisioned as new, technology-enabled modes of organizing which promised to increase labor productivity, flexibility, distribution, and mobilization of competencies (Byrne, 1993; Davidow and Malone, 1993). Today, we acknowledge that in many companies the ideals of the virtual organization (Picot et al., 2008) have become a reality, liberating employees and organizations from the constraints of time and place that characterized the organizational "battleships" (Drucker, 1990) of the past. ICT-enabled modes of work have become second nature for many employees. Computer-supported cooperative work and related technologies are no longer perceived as "intruders" or "guests" (Ciborra, 2002); rather, they have become infrastructure, that is, they are taken for granted (Edwards, 2003).

In parallel, the notion of "workplace" has changed profoundly. Work used to be confined to particular working hours, which made it easier to separate private and professional life. Likewise, the workplace defined a physical space, such as a desk in a department in a particular building. The workplace – and the workplace only – was equipped with all the tools required to perform the employees' tasks. Collaboration was mainly restricted to co-located employees in the near vicinity. The work day consisted of clearly defined tasks that could be handled in a more or less sequential order. Today's technological infrastructure affords a different idea of the workplace. For example, Cisco's Connected Workplace has been designed for a generation that "probably wouldn't be able to work in a space with just private offices and high-walled cubicles" (Cisco, 2012, p. 2). "Their work hours are not the standard eight to five either. Instead, work and personal activities are often intermingled across the span of day and night, serving both personal preference and the communications needs of a global company" (2012, p. 1).

The workspace that is no longer a work*place* seems to benefit both the company as well as the individual employee. The authority to design the workspace is transferred to the employees who know what suits organizational demands and personal preferences best.

While in many companies this new workplace has become a reality, some already proclaim the next transition – the age of hyperspecialization (Malone et al., 2011) – as the epitome of the "boundaryless" and "networked" organization. Again, the assumption is that employees can use their increased autonomy to ameliorate the balance between personal preferences and professional demands.

Paradoxes and tensions in the new workplace

Researchers and practitioners have highlighted the benefits of the ICT-enabled organization. In a literature review on telecommuting, Pinsonneault and Boisvert (1999) cite numerous studies linking these new work arrangements with increased productivity, higher organizational flexibility, and more satisfied employees. A study by Cisco (2009) found that ICT-enabled work arrangements (that is, telecommuting) not only increased employees' quality of life but their quality of work as well. The idea of transferring more control of when and where to work to the individual employee was and still is considered a powerful way to harmonize work and private life.

Yet, technological innovations in the workplace, whether assembly lines, telephones, or personal computers, have always been viewed critically in the public discourse. Initial enthusiasm about the promises of these new technology-enabled modes of organizing quickly met with skepticism about (undesired) consequences for individual employees and society at large. Equally, the considerable role of ICT in the transformation of work has spawned a skeptical stance toward the effects of ICT on wellbeing. A growing public awareness of technology-induced occupational stress (Arnetz and Wiholm, 1997; EU-OSHA, 2009) is fueled by a widespread yet diffuse sense of an ever-increasing acceleration of life. Some of the negative effects of technology use are addressed in the growing body of technostress literature (Ayyagari et al., 2011; Riedl, 2013). A definition by Brillhart (2004, p. 302) captures the challenges of today's workplace as "the mind's attempt to deal with change, malfunctions, multitasking issues and the overabundance of technology and data that keeps employees working harder and giving them less down time when away from work." Time pressure, multi-tasking, and other symptoms for rising demands (cf. Lohmann-Haislah, 2012) are closely associated with ICT-enabled work arrangements.

Workplace(s) in the IT service industry

In order to gain a better insight into how work is organized on the micro level, we conducted an explorative, in-depth study of 14 individuals working in the IT service industry: an industry that is generally perceived as a forerunner in the application of new technologies. This industry not only counsels other industries about technology use but also encourages its employees to engage in virtual modes of organizing that correspond to their strong customer orientation and project-oriented way of working. Therefore, our aim was to understand whether and how the participants in our study balance demands and perceived control.

In many aspects, the organization of work follows best practices and state-of-the-art knowledge in the three companies we studied. Work is organized predominantly in projects. Employees are assigned to multiple projects based on their expertise. While the project plan is agreed upon with the client, new project specifications, as well as new client requests, need to be accommodated by the project team. The individual employees have considerable freedom in deciding when and where to work as long as deliverables and deadlines are met. This style of work is made possible by complex communication and collaboration technology. These provide differentiated technology or media repertoires for the employees, who use them in an equally differentiated manner.

While the participants report an intensification of work (demands), they simultaneously underscore the benefits of technology for not only coping with the demands of their work but also providing latitude about working time and space (control):

> . . . because of the freedom to organize your working time, I can – on a Friday morning – go to the hairdresser, but then read on a Sunday evening the emails to prepare the following week. (Max)
>
> I can read my emails everywhere [on the smartphone] . . . that's making me more flexible [in daily life] and faster. If something really important happens, I can read them and call back. (Tess)
>
> You cannot read all of it anymore, you cannot absorb all of the information [emails]. And then you are expected to attend numerous meetings – one after another. (Pia)

Still, the findings suggest that technology has become a mixed blessing as the flexibility it facilitates is regularly used to work more and longer hours. Moreover, even when the employer is not too demanding, the clients typically are. The clients' demands reflect their increasing dependency on technology, which in turn increases the level of urgency. In effect, many of the participants have to "serve two masters":

> Well, often there is a very ambitious schedule – determined by the customer – that has to be met. (Max)
>
> I take those [calls of customers outside office hours]. The customers usually don't know that. (Lea)

> *. . . in the last big project . . . I had about 1,600–1,700 unread emails, and I can read email quite well.* (Nele)

Technology has enabled the subtle transformation of work practices. Most of the participants report being "always on," that is, available for calls and checking emails way beyond normal working hours. Many participants acknowledge the benefits in terms of latitude to organize their work and productivity gains in accomplishing their tasks. However, technology has at the same time changed their work practices; it has crept into their daily routines and has led to an intensification of work, extended work hours, increasing demands regarding availability, and response times from their clients.

This transformation has resulted in practices of not taking real breaks and using time that earlier was perceived as unproductive – such as driving to work or waiting at the airport – for work. Mobile devices embedded in collaborative work infrastructures enable our participants to work (almost) anywhere and anytime. Breaks are regularly skipped in order to be able to finish some work or they are used to check emails or meet clients or colleagues:

> *A train ride is a time in which you can focus on your work.* (Leo)
> *I use the waiting time at the airport to sort emails. For me that is simply gaining time.* (Max)
> *Borderline between break and break . . . 'cause you are under supervision nonetheless.* (Leo)
> *I don't take them [breaks] consciously, only maybe if you go with colleagues to a coffee break.* (Alex)

We asked our participants to document stressful events during the day and compared their diary entries to physiological measurements (heart rate variability) on that day. Our findings confirm the literature on discrepancies between self-reported and measured stress (Brant et al., 2010). The interviews suggest that the participants have learned to live and work in a high-demand environment in which pressure and stress are commonly perceived as normal and manageable. Only when they notice symptoms such as headaches, stomach aches, cardiovascular problems, or even burnout does the chronic stress become apparent. In the physiological data we found little evidence of breaks. According to the interviews, most participants would keep breaks short or combine them with talking to customers, for example, at lunch.

Paradoxical consequences of the IT-enabled workplace

In our own study, users report ambivalent – even paradoxical – experience and perception of technology, which resonates with the findings in the literature (Jarvenpaa and Lang, 2005). This observation is confirmed by a report on the work conditions in the EU: "The 'modern' patterns of work organisation, while creating job satisfaction among workers . . . can, at the same time, create strain . . . The final outcome seems to be very much dependent on the context into which practices are introduced" (Eurofound, 2011, p. 32). The demands placed upon employees increasingly lead to adverse effects, taxing not only individuals' wellbeing but also individual and organizational performance: for example, loss of productivity (Aral et al., 2012) and loss of innovativeness (Levy, 2007).

While ICT has changed work practices, it has also crept into our daily routines. The very ways we choose to work and collaborate bring forward the "dark side of technology." As the shifts that have taken hold of society have happened gradually, we mostly take them for granted, not calling to attention our own agency in their creation. Therefore, we would like to sensitize the reader to the choices we have and the choices we make in our daily activities. The way organizations work, the way organizing unfolds, and the role technology plays in this is not inherent; rather, it is the result of individuals, groups, managers and politicians, and eventually of societies. The notion of practical wisdom directs our focus to the choices we make and the ways we live our lives. It describes the ability to deliberate and to make good or prudent choices in the "particular and concrete question of what to do in a particular circumstance" (Schwartz, 2011, p. 4). Specifically, it concerns how we design our individual as well as our collective work. In the following we will discuss in which ways practical wisdom might help people to act wisely in modern work environments.

The need for a complement of rules and regulations

Many of the work patterns we identified in our data feature prominently as stressors in the public and academic discourse, calling attention to the "dark side of technology": overload, overuse, and addiction are just some symptoms of the negative effects brought on by IT usage (cf. Tarafdar et al., 2013, p. 270). Triggered by the public discourse and alarming studies about the rise of psychological illnesses, organizations feel the need to implement protective measures to ensure employees' wellbeing.

The following three examples serve as illustrations:

1 In 2011 Volkswagen Germany decided to turn the email push service off after working hours. The measure initially targeted about 1,100 employees, while managers were exempt (McMillan, 2011).
2 In 2013 the German Ministry of Labor and Social Affairs issued new rules of conduct (Öchsner, 2013). Employees may only be contacted after hours in situations that are "exceptional" or that cannot be delayed until normal office hours. In addition, no one is obliged to be accessible after normal office hours.
3 In 2014 the German car manufacturer BMW signed an employment agreement that allows employees to record "mobile working time" – time spent working away from the office – as part of their regular hours of work. Furthermore, BMW grants employees a right to define hours in which they are not reachable at all (Spiegel Online, 2014).

In each of these examples, general rules were put in place to prevent employees from engaging in unhealthy behavior and to restrict self-exploitation of employees. Such rules essentially target two aspects of the phenomenon:

1 Individuals tend to over-exert themselves in an effort to satisfy either intrinsic or extrinsic motives. By excelling in terms of productivity and responsiveness, the individual gains a reputation as a productive member of the workforce. General rules with which all employees have to abide are intended to level the playing field. Thereby, these rules are assumed to curb undesired behaviors.

2   Synchronous but also asynchronous communication (for example, sending an email) has effects on others. Sending an email in the evening may signal to the recipient an (implicit) expectation to work immediately. Eventually, this might have a cascading effect. Therefore, the individual's behavior needs to be guided in order to prevent his or her actions from causing undesired effects in others.

Both aspects demonstrate how tightly the individual and social spheres are interconnected. Based on our empirical findings, we believe that rules per se are unlikely to produce the desired effect as they do not address the norms that govern work practices.

While Volkswagen and its workers' council, which suggested the measure, aim to protect employees from stress, the immediate effect is to reduce the employees' level of control. This can easily backfire and increase stress; for example, managers have told us that they read their emails on Sundays in order to prepare for the working week and avoid an avalanche of unread emails on Monday morning. Employees chose deliberately to work on emails outside normal office hours. The problem here is not that employees misuse their liberties, but rather the amount of email and the expectation to react the next day. It is the invisibility of the workload that leads colleagues and clients to this expectation. General rules counteract the direction of the transformation. They do not address the demands, but rather reduce the level of control. Hence, the rules alone are likely to be ineffective.

The German Ministry of Labor and Social Affairs' approach is less strict. It recognizes that in some instances employees need to make exceptions to the rule. As a general rule, it cannot specify when exactly a communication after hours is exceptional. Whether or not communication is exceptional is up to the individual employee to decide. Similarly, whether or not someone is willing to be accessible after hours is a decision the individual employee has to make. The rule assumes a uniform definition of work and private life that applies to all parts of the organization. Yet, communication is rarely constrained to colleagues within one organization. Instead, our data show that clients in particular are not familiar with work arrangements and do not abide with these restrictions, even if they are aware of them. In many instances general rules are unable to accommodate the specific work conditions of individuals and teams; that is, they conflict with other norms like customer orientation or teamwork. In these situations the effectiveness of such a rule is unlikely.

At BMW, the ability to record "mobile working time" grants employees the liberty to decide for themselves when and where to work. It essentially represents an effort to separate work and private life without compromising on flexibility. Still, whether or not checking for emails or taking a phone call is considered worthwhile to record is for the individual to judge. Likewise, how strictly and rigorously employees implement their right of non-reachability is up to them to decide. It does not stop incoming emails and it is a weak protection against the expectation of being up-to-speed the next day. It is the individual employee who has to judge what behavior is appropriate in each instance.

Rules and incentives do not prevent people from making choices. On the contrary, individuals are burdened with making decisions regardless of whether there is a rule in place or not. Particular situations demand making the right choice: should I not react to the client's email even though it is already late? Would it not be wise to let a colleague know about new developments even though he or she is already gone? Is being accessible already part of mobile working time? Should I give precedence to meeting the deadline or the regulations?

A call for practical wisdom

The Aristotelian (1926) concept of phronesis – practical wisdom – embraces the particularities in each situation. The wise person is not only knowledgeable in how to act but also knows what is the right thing to do. It is the wisdom to know when a situation demands following the rule, when to bend it, and when to break it. While the ambivalence of conflicting demands and interests is bracketed out from general rules, which inevitably abstract from the specific, it is this very situation of conflict and ambivalence that people mostly find themselves in. Practical wisdom combines a capability of skillful coping with a sense of what matters. The idea of implementing sustainable work practices requires both: (1) a reflection on the normative orientation of work practices; and (2) the cultivation of true expertise of how to skillfully balance the needs for work and leisure.

In his phenomenology of skillful behavior, Dreyfus (2002, p. 368) describes the first stage as a novice who "is then given rules for determining actions on the basis of these features [of the task domain]." In contrast, the:

> expert not only sees what needs to be achieved: thanks to a vast repertoire of situational discriminations he sees how to achieve his goal. Thus, the ability to make more subtle and refined discriminations is what distinguishes the expert from the proficient performer . . . he or she knows how to perform the appropriate action without calculating and comparing alternatives. What must be done, simply is done.
>
> (Dreyfus, 2002, pp. 368–371)

A sense of being able to perceive situations holistically and to act in response to what is needed under the specific circumstances distinguishes the expert. Truly learning a skill also implies seeing the world differently (Dreyfus and Kelly, 2011).

Skillful coping requires a sense of direction, a goal or a purpose, an idea about the good life, wellbeing, or happiness (*eudaimonia*) in Aristotle's words. In a similar vein, Aristotle portrays practical wisdom (phronesis) as the "master virtue essential to solving problems of specificity, relevance, and conflict that inevitably arise whenever character strengths must be translated into action in concrete situations" (Schwartz and Sharpe, 2006, p. 377). McKeown (2014) has elaborated on the importance and indeed benefits of focusing on what is essential, what one really cares about, what provides meaning and is worth pursuing. This will yield happiness as the goal of pursuing excellence in what we do: "Happiness is the consequence of taking pride in being excellent at what we do" (Stefanazzi, 2012, p. 3).

Sternberg's (1998, 2001) balance theory of wisdom conceives wisdom "as the application of tacit knowledge as mediated by values toward the goal of achieving a common good (a) through a balance among multiple intrapersonal, interpersonal, and extrapersonal interests and (b) in order to achieve a balance among response to environmental contexts" (1998, p. 353). Such knowledge is acquired from experience and from the ability to reflect on alternative courses of action. Thus, the wise person knows what to do in situations that are characterized by conflicting demands and interests. Yet, acting wisely is not to be confused with maximizing someone's – or one's own – interests; rather, it is the ability to find the right balance between multiple, potentially conflicting interests toward achieving a common good.

Workplaces are characterized by manifold, often conflicting, interests:

1   ICT has widened the range of possible actions in terms of their technical feasibility. It is technically feasible to respond to emails at night, to attend virtual meetings on weekends from home, to directly respond to requests, and to be available while attending a school play.
2   Flexibility, availability, and responsiveness are generally assumed to be economically beneficial. Actions bearing these characteristics are believed to further one's own career and to further the interests of the organization.
3   Leisure or breaks are necessary in order for people to recover and to regain strength. They are a key part of wellbeing and resilience in times of pressure.

Practical wisdom calls for balancing what is technically feasible, economically beneficial, but also sustainable, in regard to the wellbeing of the individual as well as the group.

Following Sternberg's (2001) argument, wisdom does not stop with balancing multiple interests as a kind of mental exercise, but requires striking a balance between three possible courses of action: adapting oneself to the environment, shaping the environment, or selecting a new environment. The environment at stake here is how we work individually as well as collectively: "What constitutes appropriate balancing of interests, an appropriate response to the environment, and even the common good, all hinge on values" (Sternberg, 2001, p. 231). Sternberg (2001, p. 231) sees values as an "integral part of wise thinking" and emphasizes that the exercise of practical wisdom requires the proper aims of a particular practice.

Our participants held senior positions and had considerable experience in their job and with the company. During the interviews, we got to know them as mature personalities not only in their job, but in their private life as well. Our data support the impression that we were confronted with conscientious employees who liked their job and were willingly contributing to their company's success. In most instances our participants found that the "right thing to do" was to:

1   extend their work day to a degree that work and private life become indistinguishable; and
2   intensify their work day by using breaks "productively."

All of our participants work in multiple teams that are formed to accomplish projects. Members of a project team rely on each other's performance. The teams are largely driven by objectives, demanding that milestones are met, irrespective of unexpected additional workload or changing deadlines. Apart from a general sense of professionalism, team spirit, loyalty, and customer orientation show up quite prominently as guiding norms. It seems that these norms cultivated in the immediate social context would take precedence over rules introduced at the company level. Being a good IT consultant means being customer-oriented, not letting your team down, and ensuring that the project is a success. Yet this often implies sacrificing personal needs, including a healthy lifestyle.

We found employees who were well aware of the pressures of work, but found themselves struggling to translate this insight into actionable measures. The value of taking "time to think" (Levy, 2007), rest, and recover has not been acknowledged as an individual as well as a collective (Perlow and Porter, 2009) responsibility. Yet it would be prudent to do so as studies have shown the importance of taking breaks, time off, and proper sleep on the quality of work (Crary, 2013; König et al., 2013; Perlow and Porter, 2009). The increase in stress-related illnesses, as well as the presented empirical evidence, illustrates an imbalance toward economically beneficial and technically feasible behaviors.

While it is up to the individual to act prudently, translating this insight into practical measures in a tightly connected work environment proves to be a formidable challenge.

Challenges for cultivating practical wisdom in the distributed organization

In modern, distributed organizations, employees find themselves in multiple projects with changing roles, different milestones, and changing team members. Coordination and collaboration in teams and with clients is mediated to a large extent by ICT. As we will show, the cultivation of practical wisdom under these circumstances is far from trivial.

Schwartz (2011) distilled four key characteristics required to exercise practical wisdom: practical wisdom requires knowledge about the *proper aims* (1) of a practice as orientation and motivation. The ability to act appropriately in a particular situation hinges on the ability to *perceive* (2) and read the particularities of a situation. Empathy and the ability to *deliberate* (3) about appropriate courses of action inform the wise person's ability to *act* (4).

We will discuss each of Schwartz's characteristics, illustrating them with our empirical data. We will do so in reverse order.

Act: employees in general enjoy an increasing repertoire of means to design their own workspace. While our participants embrace many of these considerable liberties, they do not see themselves in a position to implement structuring elements (for example, a quiet hour). It seems that individuals' designs are often hampered due to perceived – not necessarily actual – constraints at the group level. Effectiveness and the ability to meet targets, rather than efficiency, are valued and assessed. Furthermore, individuals are very much aware of dependencies and the resulting cascading effect that their own performance might have on others. Being unavailable for colleagues might impede the project. In a networked setting, this problem has been exacerbated since an individual's work is highly connected with others.

Deliberate: sending emails late at night, working over weekends, and responding straightaway are generally held in high esteem, distinguishing the productive and diligent from the lazy worker. Whether or not the mode of working is efficient is neither a topic at the individual nor at the team level. Again, deliberation is challenging since multiple teams and contexts would need to be taken into account. In addition, it is difficult to estimate the impact of one's own behavior on others.

Perceive: most of our participants did not perceive themselves as being under pressure, although their physiological data suggested otherwise. The awareness of their own resources seems limited. On a collective level, the networked organization clouds the actual workload and strain on individuals. The situation of the individual becomes opaque for colleagues and clients, rendering it difficult for them to take the individual's level of stress into account.

Proper aims: many of our participants exhibited a high level of conscientiousness in their work. The necessity of leisure, of taking time off as a prerequisite for being productive, creative, and resourceful is not reflected.

Our data suggest that work practices and the underlying norms and values are rarely the subject of an ongoing organizational discourse.

Implications for practitioners

After developing a sense of familiarity, users of ICT assign a role or place to the technology in their context of work and social relations (Riemer and Johnston, 2013). Eventually, the technology becomes an integral but taken-for-granted part of the (shared) work practice. Thereby, technology vanishes into the background. Being an IT service consultant means being well versed in ICT. It becomes an inevitable part of how work is done and indeed the identity of the consultants.

Weick (2007) has studied fatal accidents involving firefighters who were overrun by fast-moving bushfires. Many of these firefighters could have survived if they had dropped their tools and run for their lives. "Drop your tools" has become a metaphor in Weick's work of practical wisdom: under specific and extreme circumstances, dropping something essential that is part of one's identity might be lifesaving. Weick's analysis suggests that "dropping our tools" may be a crucial part of remaining sensitive to the effects of technology on our lives, the way it is mediating our experience (for example, Carr, 2010; Lanier, 2010) and our engagement with others (for example, Turkle, 2010).

Perlow and Porter (2009) demonstrate how the work ethic of being available 24/7 can translate into a vicious, self-enforcing cycle of responsiveness. Breaking out of this cycle does not require employees to abandon technology, but to renegotiate the nature of work of which it is part. Their research documents the importance of communication partners (teams) as a source for excessive demands, but equally as a resource to mitigate them by designing new (team) work practices, which recognize individual needs for rest and time off. Articulating and negotiating these needs means to recognize them and to act on them. It makes them a shared concern and creates opportunities for mutual caretaking.

The impact of rules to take breaks or to turn off email after office hours is a mixed blessing. While they recognize the problem and employees' needs, they fail to do so in a manner that takes care of the specific circumstances. There is a risk of undermining the spirit of empowering and granting control to the employees. Rules may serve as a trigger to start a reflection about what it means to act wisely in a productive but also sustainable manner. They may encourage individuals and teams to reconsider breaks as a valuable resource rather than unproductive time. Breaks are a valuable resource not only because they allow employees to recover and reflect but also because the effort of organizing time off requires them to critically rethink existing work patterns (cf. Perlow and Porter, 2009). It spawns the question of how to work smarter rather than harder.

Conclusions

ICT has permeated modern societies in unprecedented ways and is continuing to transform all facets of our lives, in particular the ways in which we work. While societal transformations inevitably yield utopian and dystopian responses (Ogburn, 1964), there are strong warning signals that the increasing pace and pressure is not just a passing phenomenon. Although we acknowledge the need for societies to engage in a discourse about how the good life can (again) become the measure of our human enterprise (Sedlacek, 2011), our focus throughout this chapter has been on the individual level.

ICT has become an effective tool to enrich and empower the lives of individuals and groups. Individuals enjoy an increased autonomy and control over their work organization. Simultaneously, it requires assuming responsibility for meeting targets, being up-to-speed, or being available. Yet, our analysis suggests a void in the public discourse, which mainly follows an economic logic of efficiency gains. By contrasting and indeed extending the discourse by the notion of practical wisdom, we find a language to: a) describe a different set of competencies; b) to thematize the good life as a goal of our endeavors; c) to acknowledge the dilemmas and ambivalences of technology use; and d) to articulate concrete options for action.

Acquiring practical wisdom in an organization implies becoming sensitive to the multiple causes and the underlying dynamics of stress. Practical wisdom provides a profoundly humane perspective on how to cope with the mixed effects of technology on our work and life. It essentially forces us to reclaim our ability and responsibility to make choices about what our work environment should be like. Practical wisdom calls for balancing what is technically feasible, economically beneficial but also sustainable in regard to the wellbeing of the individual as well as the group.

Reflection and critical thinking

1   ICT permeates modern societies and transforms work and life. Driven by an economic logic, it is the engine that drives the acceleration in modern societies.
2   The impact of technology is not one-sided, but inherently ambivalent: it empowers and enslaves, enriches and constrains, and it has become an inevitable tool that should be dropped under certain circumstances.
3   Rules and regulations do not prevent people from making choices. On the contrary, particular situations demand making the right decision.
4   Practical wisdom addresses a competency that becomes even more important in the interconnected workplace.
5   Practical wisdom provides a distinctly humane perspective on how to skillfully cope with the opportunities and demands of ICT-driven work and life.
6   Too often, we do not reflect and take charge of what our shared work environment should look like. Practical wisdom emphasizes the ability and responsibility to consciously act in the interest of a common good.

References

Aral, S., Brynjolfsson, E., and Van Alstyne, M. (2012). Information, technology, and information worker productivity. *Information Systems Research*, 23(3), 849–867.

Aristotle (1926). *Nicomachean Ethics*, H. Rackam (trans.). Boston: Harvard University Press.

Arnetz, B. and Wiholm, C. (1997). Technological stress: Psychophysiological symptoms in modern offices. *Journal of Psychosomatic Research*, 43(1), 35–42.

Ayyagari, R., Gover, V., and Purvis, R. (2011). Technostress: Technological antecedents and implications. *MIS Quarterly*, 35(4), 831–858.

Brant, H., Wetherell, M.A., Lightman, S., Crown, A., and Vedhara, K. (2010). An exploration into physiological and self-report measures of stress in pre-registration doctors at the beginning and end of a clinical rotation. *Stress (Amsterdam)*, 13(2), 155–162.

Brillhart, P.E. (2004). Technostress in the workplace: Managing stress in the electronic workplace. *Journal of American Academy of Business*, 5(1/2), 302–7.

Byrne, J.A. (1993). The virtual corporation. *Business Week*, February 7, 98–103.

Carr, N. (2010). *The Shallows: What the Internet is Doing to Our Brains*. New York: W.W. Norton and Company.

Ciborra, C. (2002). *The Labyrinths of Information: Challenging the Wisdom of Systems*. Oxford, UK: Oxford University Press.

Cisco (2009). Cisco study finds telecommuting significantly increases employee productivity, work-life flexibility and job satisfaction (press release). Retrieved from http://newsroom.cisco.com/dlls/2009/prod_062609.html (accessed September 7, 2015).

——. (2012). Gen Y flexible collaborative workspace. *Cisco Trends in IT*. Retrieved from http://www.citywomen.co.uk/wp-content/uploads/2014/04/Trends_in_IT_Gen_Y_Flexible_Collaborative_Workspace-Cisco.pdf (accessed September 7, 2015).

Crary, J. (2013). *24/7: Late Capitalism and the Ends of Sleep*. New York: Verso Books.

Davidow, W. and Malone, M. (1993). *The Virtual Corporation: Structuring and Revitalizing the Corporation for the 21st Century*. New York: Harper Paperbacks.

Dreyfus, H.L. (2002). Intelligence without representation – Merleau-Ponty's critique of mental representation. *Phenomenology and the Cognitive Sciences*, 1(4), 367–383.

Dreyfus, H.L. and Kelly, S.D. (2011). *All Things Shining: Reading the Western Classics to Find Meaning in a Secular Age*. New York: Free Press.

Drucker, P. (1990). The emerging theory of manufacturing. *Harvard Business Review*, 68(May–June), 94–102.

Edwards, P.N. (2003). Infrastructure and modernity: Force, time, and social organization in the history of sociotechnical systems. In T.J. Misa, P. Brey, and A. Feenberg (eds), *Modernity and Technology* (pp. 185–225). Cambridge, MA: MIT Press.

EU-OSHA (2009). *OSH in Figures: Stress at Work – Facts and Figures*. Luxembourg.

Eurofound (2011). Recent developments in work organisation in the EU27 Member States and Norway. Office for Official Publications of the European Communities. Retrieved from http://www.eurofound.europa.eu/ewco/studies/tn1102013s/tn1102013s.htm (accessed September 7, 2015).

Jarvenpaa, S.L. and Lang, K.R. (2005). Managing the paradoxes of mobile technology. *Information Systems Management*, 22(4), 7–23.

König, C.J., Kleinmann, M., and Höhmann, W. (2013). A field test of the quiet hour as a time management technique. *Revue Européenne de Psychologie Appliquée/European Review of Applied Psychology*, 63(3), 137–145.

Lanier, J. (2010). *You are Not a Gadget: A Manifesto*. New York: Alfred A. Knopf.

Levy, D.M. (2007). No time to think: Reflections on information technology and contemplative scholarship. *Ethics and Information Technology*, 9(4), 237–249.

Lohmann-Haislah, A. (2012). *Stressreport Deutschland 2012*. Bundesanstalt für Arbeitsschutz und Arbeitsmedizin, Dortmund. Retrieved from http://www.baua.de/dok/3430796 (accessed September 7, 2015).

Malone, T.W., Laubacher, R.J., and Johns, T. (2011). The age of hyperspecialization. *Harvard Business Review*, 89(July–August), 56–65.

McKeown, G. (2014). *Essentialism: The Disciplined Pursuit of Less*. New York: Crown Business.

McMillan, R. (2011, December 23). Volkswagen blocks BlackBerry use when most people use BlackBerries. Retrieved from http://www.wired.com/2011/12/vwemail (accessed September 7, 2015).

Öchsner, T. (2013, August 29). Neue Richtlinie im Bundesarbeitsministerium. *Süddeutsche Zeitung*. Retrieved from http://www.sueddeutsche.de/karriere/neue-richtlinie-im-bundesarbeitsministerium-geringstmoeglicher-eingriff-in-die-freizeit-1.1758132# (accessed September 7, 2015).

Ogburn, W.F. (1964). *On Culture and Social Change*. Chicago: University of Chicago Press.

Perlow, L.A. and Porter, J.L. (2009). Making time off predictable and required. *Harvard Business Review*, 87(October), 102–109.

Picot, A., Reichwald, R., and Wigand, R. (2008). *Information, Organization and Management*. Berlin: Springer.

Pinsonneault, A. and Boisvert, M. (1999). The impacts of telecommuting on organizations and individuals: A review of the literature, No. 99–09 (pp. 1–27). Retrieved from http://expertise.hec.ca/gresi/wp-content/uploads/2013/02/cahier9909.pdf (accessed September 7, 2015).

Riedl, R. (2013). On the biology of technostress: Literature review and research agenda. *ACM SIGMIS Database*, 44(1), 18–55.

Riemer, K. and Johnston, R.B. (2013). Rethinking the place of the artefact in IS using Heidegger's analysis of equipment. *European Journal of Information Systems*, 22(February), 1–16.

Schwartz, B. (2011). Practical wisdom and organizations. *Research in Organizational Behavior*, 31, 3–23.

Schwartz, B. and Sharpe, K.E. (2006). Practical wisdom: Aristotle meets positive psychology. *Journal of Happiness Studies*, 7(3), 377–395.

Sedlacek, T. (2011). *Economics of Good and Evil: The Quest for Economic Meaning from Gilgamesh to Wall Street*. Oxford: Oxford University Press.

Spiegel Online (2014). E-Mails und Anrufe in der Freizeit: BMW will ein "Recht auf Unerreichbarkeit." Retrieved from http://www.spiegel.de/wirtschaft/unternehmen/arbeitszeit-bmw-will-e-mails-und-anrufe-in-der-freizeit-ausgleichen-a-953770.html (accessed September 7, 2015).

Stefanazzi, M. (2012). Aristotle on the virtue of phronesis – Practical wisdom. Inter-disciplinary. net conference: Sins, vices and virtues. Prague. Retrieved from http://www.inter-disciplinary.net/at-the-interface/wp-content/uploads/2012/03/MStefanazziWpaper.pdf (accessed September 7, 2015).

Sternberg, R.J. (1998). A balance theory of wisdom. *Review of General Psychology*, 2(4), 347–365.

——. (2001). Why schools should teach for wisdom: The balance theory of wisdom in educational settings. *Educational Psychologist*, 36(4), 227–245.

Tarafdar, M., Gupta, A., and Turel, O. (2013). The dark side of information technology use. *Information Systems Journal*, 23(3), 269–275.

Turkle, S. (2010). *Alone Together – Why We Expect More from Technology and Less from Each Other*. New York: Basic Books.

Weick, K.E. (2007). Drop your tools: On reconfiguring management education. *Journal of Management Education*, 31(1), 5–16.

Zuboff, S. (1988). *In the Age of the Smart Machine*. New York: Basic Books.

Chapter 6

Empathy by design
Enhancing diversity in online participation

Caterina Desiato and Cindy Scheopner

Introduction

The Internet and social media have been argued both to support the emergence of a more participatory and diverse society, and to reinforce concentration of power and polarization (Dahlberg, 2007; Sunstein, 2001). The debate about whether – and under which conditions – they are beneficial or problematic for the wellbeing of individuals and societies remains open. This chapter looks at possible desirable outcomes of design and uses centered on practical wisdom, particularly empathy. We will argue that although social media may facilitate connecting with others, their current design resists constructive argumentation among diverse perspectives. Taking diverse perspectives into account is crucial for democratic dialogue and decision making that benefit, or at least do not harm, the people involved. A better understanding of the role of empathy in bridging diversity can help social media users, designers, and online deliberation practitioners to overcome some obstacles to thoroughly democratic debate.

Empathy involves a combination of intellectual understanding and emotional involvement that has the potential to engage individuals from diverse perspectives far more effectively than mere tolerance or recognition. This formulation of the concept of empathy has deep philosophical roots and is supported by recent neurological developments (Winerman, 2005). Empathy is more than an attribute of practical wisdom or a personality characteristic of a wise person; it is a relationship capable of expression in communities. This sort of empathetic engagement is essential to the effective functioning of deliberative democracies. Without empathy, the voicing of diverse perspectives may remain a nominal exercise of pluralistic tolerance that fails to leverage constructive argumentation. This can lead to an inauthentic consensus or the avoidance of conflict. In contrast, fully diverse participation facilitates creative and innovative solutions (Nemeth and Wachtler, 1983). Intercultural and organizational communication studies show how consensus decision making in diverse groups can bring about high-quality and far-sighted results (Doyle and Straus, 1976).

It has been argued that information technologies (ITs) can be used to facilitate or scale up direct participation (Carpini et al., 2004) and that the main challenge for e-democracy is to create a "dialogic space" where people can actually make decisions together (Anderson, 2005). However, we identify several shortcomings to be addressed in order for ITs to actually connect people beyond clusters and for deliberation systems to facilitate the integration of different perspectives. This chapter examines how empathy supports constructive argumentation in diversity and how this process may be supported by design.

Evolving empathy

The word "empathy" entered the English language as a translation of the German term *Einfühlung*, used in the late eighteenth century to describe the aesthetic experience of "feeling into" nature or works of art (Stueber, 2006). Philosophers such as Theodor Lipps, Edmund Husserl, and Edith Stein adapted the concept of empathy to account for our interaction with other people. In addition to gaining a sense of their experiences, Stein suggested that we can also learn more about ourselves from how we are perceived by others (Stein, 1964). Contemporary philosopher Karsten Stueber uses empathy to explain how we know other minds. In addition to what he calls "basic empathy" (recognizing other creatures as minded like us), Stueber distinguishes "reenactive empathy." This is the process of "using our cognitive and deliberative capacities in order to reenact or imitate in our own mind the thought processes of the other person" (Stueber, 2006, p. 21). He argues that it is this process which allows us to conceive other people as acting rationally and with purpose.

These approaches emphasize *understanding* the other person from *that* person's point of view. This is distinguished from putting ourselves in their place, imagining what we would do or how we would feel in the same or similar circumstance. It is also distinct from having *sympathy* for another, characterized as feeling concern for another from the perspective of one who cares about them (Stueber, 2014). Empathy also requires more than mere *tolerance* of a viewpoint with which one does not agree. Putting up with an opinion or belief we consider to be mistaken does not necessitate fully appreciating the other's reason for having the belief and/or emotional commitment to it. These distinctions are very helpful; however, this conception of empathy focuses primarily upon mental processes. The empathetic relationship we propose includes emotion along with rationality.

Intellect and emotion

In *Nicomachean Ethics*, Aristotle distinguished practical wisdom from understanding, saying that practical wisdom issues commands while understanding only judges what is fair (Aristotle, 1984, VI, section 5). We propose that this combination of evaluation and action is aided by the type of empathetic process he described in the *Poetics*, a work Anthony Kenny calls "the first essay in the broader field of aesthetics" (Kenny, 2013, p. x). Indeed, the hoped-for reaction of the audience that Aristotle believed is essential to a good performance resonates with the *Einfühlung* of German aesthetics. Aristotle said the purpose of tragedy is to call forth pity (brought on by unmerited misfortune) or fear (the misfortune of someone who is like us). In the hands of an accomplished poet, "he who hears the tale told will thrill with horror and melt to pity at what takes place" (Aristotle, 2006, Book XIV). The artistic work itself produces and then transforms these emotions through catharsis, which is an understanding of the performance through the feelings it evokes in an engaged spectator: a "felt understanding in which both passion and intelligence are transposed into the aesthetic key" (Schaper, 1968, p. 142). In balance between intellectual understanding and emotional involvement, spectators are liberated from overwhelming emotions that impede understanding of unfamiliar situations, but are still involved and directly connected. In this way, participants recognize human possibilities even when they are very different from their own experiences. Liberation from overwhelming emotions and emotional connection are both crucial in this process. Emotions are not a hindrance, but rather an integral part of the *felt understanding* of otherness.

The stimulation of emotion and the creation of group connection that Aristotle describes in the *Poetics* differs from the way that empathy is described in much contemporary wisdom literature. Empathy is considered to be a part of wisdom; however, it is often included in a list of attributes of practical wisdom with no further explication. Monika Ardelt (2003, p. 277) proposes a definition of wisdom as "an integration of cognitive, reflective, and affective dimensions." This concept of wisdom allows space for the emotional connection provided through empathy. Perhaps the closest approximation is that of Ute Kunzmann and Paul Baltes, who use brief videos to stimulate empathy in observers. They demonstrate that individuals with high levels of wisdom-related knowledge react with stronger emotions to the life challenges depicted. They predict, however, that these empathetic individuals will "down-regulate" their emotional responses "to distance themselves and to bring their wisdom-related knowledge into the foreground" (Kunzmann and Baltes, 2005, p. 124). Rather, we propose that the emotional response is fully empathetic when engaged in a catharsis that releases the emotion during a shared event rather than dampening it.

The robust explication of empathy that we propose is a combination of both intellect and emotion that is capable of being experienced in a group (Steuber, 2006; Weber et al., 2011). This formulation of the concept of empathy draws upon Aristotelian roots and incorporates the spirit of *Einfühlung* to bring feeling/emotion into our experience of others. A similar approach is used in research on intercultural communication (Gudykunst, 2004) and psychology (Rogers, 1957), where cognitive and affective components must also include communication so that others are able to *perceive* that we are being empathetic. Theresa Wiseman (1996) also notes that understanding another's perspective and feelings implies a non-judgmental approach, which creates a safe space to voice diverse opinions. It is this concept of empathy that supports constructive argumentation in diversity and holds promise for more effective online deliberation.

Deliberative democracy, consensus, and diversity

The discussions that are part of political decision making in Western governments tend to follow an adversarial mode of communication (Anderson, 2005; Bohm, 1996). However, there are increasing numbers of documented cases of deliberative democracy where decision making emerges from dialogue and mutual learning (Fishkin, 1995; Habermas, 2006; Mansbridge, 1983).

Definitions of deliberation vary in different traditions and studies, and can be very narrow in terms of participants' discourse style or structural characteristics (Mutz, 2006; Sanders, 1997). However, most share two elements: 1) hearing different perspectives on a given topic; and 2) reaching "enough common ground to move ahead" (Melville et al., 2005, p. 47). "Ahead" means the next phase in the decision-making process, which could be consensus as well as another practice, such as debate and majority vote informed by the deliberative process (Towne and Herbsleb, 2012). In this context, deliberation has a broad scope: any political discussion that involves exposure to differing perspectives (Mutz, 2006).

Consensus is frequently considered the *telos*, the end toward which deliberation is directed. There is considerable evidence that authentic consensus processes support a broader information base, group cohesion, higher participant satisfaction, and better, far-sighted, decision quality (Doyle and Straus, 1976; Kellermanns et al., 2011). Diverse consensus decision-making protocols are practiced worldwide in a vast variety of groups and organizations: businesses, grassroots movements, the Iroquois League of the Six Nations (Shannon, 2008), autonomous communities like the Zapatista community in Chiapas or smaller ones like Christiania in Denmark, and collaborative public policy projects, particularly for environmental issues (Barber, 1984), to cite a few examples. Consensus can also be built without deliberation or direct interaction. For example, the Delphi and Nominal Group techniques are used for finding consensus and do not entail direct interaction among the participants, who are sent other participants' contrasting arguments by an external investigator.

We adopt a definition of consensus where interacting feelings, values, and personal interests are acknowledged. Brian Auvine and colleagues (1978, p. xii) define consensus as:

> A decision making process in which all parties involved explicitly agree to the final decision. Consensus decision making does not mean that all parties are completely satisfied with the final outcome, but that the decision is acceptable to all because no one *feels* that his or her vital *interests* or *values* are violated by it. (Emphases added)

Contrary to a common misunderstanding, neither deliberation nor consensus is about changing participants' minds; each is about creating a common ground among participants by understanding and empathizing with other viewpoints (Mendelberg, 2002; Mutz, 2006). Keith Melville and colleagues (2005) affirm that in most cases people do not change their views, but they change their perception of others and the issue at stake in a way that makes it possible to identify broadly acceptable solutions.

In deliberation, the presence of other like-minded people can lead to the reinforcement of one's own positions. However, even a single different voice can make a radical difference in redressing biases in a group (Sunstein, 2003) and finding more creative solutions (Nemeth and Wachtler, 1983). Therefore, giving space to a wide diversity of voices might be more important than having big numbers and statistically representative samples (Hendriks, 2005). Maintaining dialogue within heterogeneity has also been found to reduce "framing effects" (Druckman, 2004), that is, it reduces the influenceability of participants' thoughts by the way in which an argument is presented.

Diana Mutz (2006) tested the effects of "experiential diversity," based on surveys about respondents' experiences of talking with someone who had a different view from their own. She found that exposure to political disagreement highly correlated with awareness of rationales for oppositional perspectives and also correlated with awareness of rationales for one's own perspective. Exposure to different views also correlated with "tolerance," operationalized as willingness to grant civil liberties to opposing groups.

Everett Rogers and colleagues (2005) showed that innovations spread more easily in heterophilious (diverse) networks (Rogers, 1983). Innovative and creative thinking is necessary to accommodate everyone's views. In the fields of diffusion of innovation and group communication, there is a general agreement that diversity can backfire when there is not enough common ground among participants. At the same time, the process of deliberation has been shown to possibly create common ground and bridge diversities.

It is also important to note that the emphasis on diversity must not lead to demonizing like-minded groups. Outlier individuals in the political spectrum tend to connect more with like-minded people (Rainie and Smith, 2012; Sunstein, 2001). Rather than just an expression of polarization, this behavior can be understood as necessary to share meanings and keep alive dissenting voices (Dahlberg, 2007; Sunstein, 2003) that make possible rather than hinder the diversity of political landscapes.

Engaging and bridging diverse perspectives

Despite agreement on the importance of diversity for deliberation, there is little discussion about how to actually facilitate diverse participation. Here we focus on challenges that need to be met, whether it is to achieve an authentic consensus or to broaden the base of the debate in other types of decision making.

According to Jürgen Habermas (1991, p. 36), consensus is supposed to emerge after rational and disinterested consideration of different ideas, by "authority of the better argument." Political theorists have set many different conditions to define a situation as deliberative. However, setting "high" standards and overemphasizing rational argumentation can hinder diverse participation (Coleman and Moss, 2012; Lee, 2011; Mutz, 2006). This "rationality paradigm" embodies codes of class, gender, and status that filter out many voices (Coleman and Moss, 2012).

Further, the mere presence of diverse stakeholders does not guarantee the expression and consideration of diverse perspectives and the benefits previously discussed for deliberation. Dissenting voices can be silenced by various group dynamics and broader interwoven discriminations based on gender, race, class, dis/ability, and age. It is crucial to avoid a "manufactured consent" (Herman and Chomsky, 1988) that is an expression of power asymmetries rather than a genuine meeting point among the diverse needs, feelings, and thoughts of the deliberating members (Dahlberg, 2007; Goldberg, 2011). In order to maintain the diversity, it is also important to avoid *groupthink*, a group cognition phenomenon where individuals agree on the perceived will of the group, without considering actual alternatives (Janis, 1972). As we will see below, protocol design can minimize these social and group dynamics.

Another open issue with diversity is the apparent tension between active political participation and exposure to opposing views (Mutz, 2006). Mutz describes an either/or scenario between being a passionate partisan or an open-minded distant listener. However, deliberation does not necessarily require distancing from emotions. Emotions can be actually leveraged for empathic connection, which facilitates bridging diversity. We will further discuss the rationality paradigm and the participation vs. diversity "dilemma" in the next section.

Limits of current technological engagement

Online deliberation is an emerging interdisciplinary field (Coleman and Moss, 2012). Many have argued that Internet-based technologies represent new opportunities to support deliberation with new tools, not only at a distance, and scale up deliberative and participatory practices (Carpini et al., 2004). However, any mediational means brings about both affordances and constraints, which can respectively empower and limit users (Wertsch, 1998). In the final section, we suggest design principles that counter some limitations of computer-mediated communication that are of particular importance to diverse online participation.

An obvious shortcoming is the exclusion of all potential interlocutors who do not have access or literacies (for example, written language literacy and/or new media literacy). This limitation skews participation mainly across class and ethnicity groups, while gender biases are generally more subtle, at least in countries where Internet access is very widespread: even though there is an increasing number of awareness-raising campaigns and counteractions, there is a documented tendency in computer culture to under-represent or misrepresent women, as well as "feminine" language and aesthetics (Kirk, 2009).

Online deliberation experiments often differ in terms of goals, process design, discussion tools, and architecture, and whether or not discussions are facilitated. However, there are common limitations, some "inherited" from traditional deliberation theory.

Disconnected discussions

There is wide agreement that commonly used social media and forums, as they are currently designed, do not facilitate diverse and constructive deliberation (Elliman, et al., 2007; Lampe et al., 2011; Wright and Street, 2007). Indeed, the threaded discussion architecture that characterizes online forums, mailing lists, and Social Network Sites (SNSs) like Facebook or Twitter, seems to resist the creative synthesis of different ideas (Hewitt, 2003).

Many efforts have focused on designing specific tools. Computer-supported collaborative work studies mainly analyze the effects of design variables, such as visualization or argument mapping tools, during controlled experiments (Arnott and Pervan, 2005). Generally, these studies do not draw much from human and political sciences on deliberation and diversity. Little is known about users' experiences, as well as what types of interactions and technical affordances favor diverse constructive argumentation in real-world e-democracy applications (Lampe et al., 2011).

Some lessons can be learned from the field of computer-supported collaborative learning. Andrew Tolmie and James Boyle (2000) suggest that equal status (peer-to-peer interactions) together with reviewability may create an ideal condition for "conceptual growth" that bridges different arguments. However, designing for equal status and reviewability alone is not sufficient. They suggest that: "the critical factors are those which provide a context and rationale for online communication by helping users to establish a *shared purpose*" (Tolmie and Boyle, 2000, p. 119, emphasis added).

Design features can facilitate or constrain certain forms of group cognition rather than others (Suthers and Hundhausen, 2003; Suthers, 2008), for example, having mutually – exclusive voting options is constraining in that it hinders the expression of mixed preferences or new ideas. Current online deliberation system design focuses on visual or procedural means to cognitively facilitate argumentative construction within a discussion. However, helping users establish a shared purpose of mutual understanding, both cognitively and affectively, is just as important. A lack of empathy among participants may render the cognitive affordances of the system ineffective. Instead, when there is a shared purpose of mutual understanding, a group may successfully appropriate relatively simple tools (see, for instance, recent open-source developments Econsensus.org or Loomio.org).

The rationality paradigm

Online deliberation projects often focus on design variables that facilitate the emergence of the "better" argument in terms of logic. In this way the system carries an inherent risk of dismissing valid perspectives only because they are not argued well. Moreover, a systemic lack of both cognitive and emotional validation inhibits the expression of diverse perspectives, so that one does not speak one's mind, or not as clearly as one could, which in turn makes it easier to be dismissed.

The need for emotional skills in political deliberation has been explicitly acknowledged only recently. Traditionally, deliberative theory does not address the role of emotions explicitly, or they are rather considered a hindrance to the process (Mendelberg, 2002; Morrell, 2010; Thompson and Hoggett, 2001). However, empathic connection has been encouraged and facilitated by deliberation practitioners (Mansbridge, 1983; Mendelberg, 2002) as a crucial element of deliberative forums and consensus conferences. Melville and colleagues (2005) underline how participants in face-to-face National Issues Forums are encouraged to tell stories to present their perspectives and therefore facilitate empathic connection and common ground even when participants' perspectives seem strongly conflicting. However, in Timothy Recuber's (2013) study, a "superficial empathy" toward shared online narratives is often followed by invalidations of the other's perspective. In part, discussion might have remained disconnected because participants from different perspectives were writing from different websites and did not share a common discussion space. Nonetheless, this study shows that recognizing and valuing the other's perspective does not automatically derive from sharing narratives. A deep empathy shift faces numerous challenges, beginning from the still-widespread belief that emotions do not have a place in deliberation, and the lack of recognition and training of emotional skills.

When deliberation scholars do acknowledge the role of empathy, they seem to focus only on the cognitive aspect and dismiss the emotive (Mendelberg, 2002; Morrell, 2010). Cognitive empathy is supposed to help find "the better argument" which would impose itself as self-evident, and this is assumed to require formal conditions. However, we have seen that the over-emphasis on rationality and formality often embody unrecognized codes of class, gender, and status that discourage or discredit the participation of women and minorities (Coleman and Moss, 2012; Hickerson and Gastil, 2008; Lee, 2011), excluding precious carriers of a "double epistemology" (Brooks, 2007). In other words, people from non-dominant social groups are usually familiar with both the worldview of the dominant population and their own. Mutz (2006) found that lower-income populations are significantly more likely to be exposed to opposing political views.

Along with undermining a deeply diverse participation, the rationality paradigm assumes that policy problems can be solved by logic. This assumption has often been questioned in moral philosophy. For instance, Charles Taylor (1989) explains that most controversial political issues cannot be resolved through a rational plan because ultimately they are moral controversies, not logical ones, and the first cannot be reduced to the second. Opinions on complex policy issues may never be informed enough; instead, they can be based on shared values that form a source of morality and identity for the individual. This does not mean that one's positions can never change, but understanding and bridging different moral plans might not be possible with logic alone; it might need the help of cognitive and affective empathy. Empathy, when taken into consideration, is regarded as both an outcome and an enabler of deliberation. Indeed, deliberative interaction, creates an opportunity for empathic expression, and empathy, in turn, allows for the creation of common ground for further deliberation and decision making (Mendelberg, 2002; Morrell, 2010).

Participation vs. diversity "dilemma"

We have seen that deliberation systems can support diversity by de-emphasizing formality and rationality. However, increasing diversity may not automatically increase authentic participation. Participants who experience diversity in everyday political conversations appear to be more likely to withdraw from discussion (Mutz, 2006; Thompson and Hoggett, 2001). Mutz (2006) shows that there is a widespread tendency, in several surveyed Western countries, to avoid confrontation with diversity whenever one can afford it. However, she also observes that the passionate partisan versus distant open-minded observer dilemma might be contingent upon a predominantly adversarial culture that does not educate people to value differences or to deal with the strong emotions that may arise when confronting different views (Mutz, 2006).

Emotional skills must be developed in order to facilitate participation in a diverse environment (Mendelberg, 2002; Thompson and Hoggett, 2001). Lee Rainie and Aaron Smith (2012, p. 2) found that: "A fifth of social networking site users have avoided making political comments on the sites for fear of offending others." Some 37 percent of social network sites (SNSs) users who exchange material about politics on the sites have gotten strong negative reactions when they posted political material, while 63 percent said they have never experienced such reactions. Interestingly, Republicans, Democrats, liberals, and conservatives among SNS users have all experienced the same level of emotional challenge. On any other questions about SNS use and behavior, Rainie and Smith found variance across participants' political positions. This shows that a major portion of the political arena might have something to learn from the concepts of catharsis and felt understanding introduced at the beginning of this work. The liberation of negative emotions when facing the unfamiliar can be part of an empathic relationship rather than an inhibiting process. William Gudykunst (2004), who focuses on situations where people do not know each other personally, affirms that empathy (also comprising cognitive, affective, and communication components) is the skill that most consistently emerges in discussions about effectively communicating with strangers.

Implications for general audiences

Whether one uses commonly available social media or specifically designed deliberation systems, it is possible to engage with people who have diverse perspectives in reciprocally enriching ways. We have seen that users may refrain from expressing a different perspective in an online post for fear of causing offence or a backlash. The awareness that empathy helps bridge diversity can be empowering. Users who strive to understand others' perspectives and to hear their feelings can expect to reach a certain depth of constructive dialogue with diversity. Practicing empathic communication can also improve users' experiences with diversity, for example, talking in the first person without judging the others, or expressing one's feelings without holding the others responsible for them.

As mentioned above, we do not suggest avoiding affinity groups. The tendency to interact more with like-minded people or with users who share similar backgrounds is not negative per se; on the contrary, it is vital to maintaining a rich diversity of perspectives (Dahlberg, 2007; Sunstein, 2003). Nonetheless, it is important to engage constructively with people from different standpoints, not necessarily to change each other's views, but to become more aware of one's own position and to develop a deep consideration – a felt understanding of the broader implications in terms of other people's feelings – of personal and collective decisions.

Implications for designers and deliberation practitioners

Ideally, in order to design deliberation systems that support empathy and diversity, the design process itself should be characterized by collaboration and empathic connection with maximally diverse stakeholders at all design stages. Even as early as the requirements and users' needs analysis stage, it is very important to involve putative or potential users with diverse perspectives on online deliberation and diverse backgrounds and social groups, putative or potential users and non-users who might be affected in different ways by the system, and other online deliberation "expert" designers or thinkers. The design team should consider inviting non-users who do not have Internet access or literacies to participate in the design process in order to understand possible ways to enrich the online deliberation with their perspectives. This approach can draw largely from participatory design (Ehn, 1992) and empathic design (Crossley, 2003), but would be slightly less user-centered. However, this may seem counterintuitive: in order to support empathy to bridge diversity, the process will need to engage participants with views that challenge widespread beliefs among users. As Shaowen Bardzell notes: "It would seem that serving *existing* needs – the traditional approach to Human Computer Interaction (HCI) – is conservative and perpetuates the status quo. Conversely, an activist stance is problematic because it seems to privilege the social values of the designer" (2010, p. 1304, emphasis added). Inviting participants with views that may challenge existing needs as well as designers' perspectives can be a way to cope with this ethical dilemma. Once the stage is set for an empathic collaboration team of diverse stakeholders, the suggestions below become completely secondary to the actual work of the team.

While it is important to invite and facilitate the participation of members from different social groups both at the design and usage level, it is just as important not to label participants or ask them to necessarily self-label themselves in those terms. In this way, participants from any social group may feel less constrained by ingroup and outgroup expectations, and may feel able to voice more and more diverse ideas and feelings. These social definitions do not need to be banned; they may emerge if relevant and if the participants feel it is appropriate.

The design of users' profiles can have an impact on the way social identities play out. An example of facilitating empathy and diversity in online discussion is to consider social constructions of gender. Men and women have been shown to perform similarly in tasks requiring empathy skills; however, men's empathy drops as soon as the gender variable is made apparent, even by simply checking a gender box in a pre-test form (Fine, 2010). Although women are not necessarily more empathic than men, their communication is often affected by existing stereotypes and expectations as well, in ways that may disadvantage them in deliberative contexts, particularly considering the widespread rationality paradigm and the belief that women are empathic and emotional. Similarly, for any stereotype-based expectation of poor performance, when the association of an individual with the stereotyped group is highlighted, the individual's performance drops. Therefore, a design that allows participation without labeling users or forcing them to self-define in terms of stereotyped identities (for example, having to check gender, ethnicity, and so on) helps to avoid stereotype threats and framing.

Association with social groups can still emerge when users find it appropriate. Creative alternatives can be found together with users, since social categories are likely to emerge eventually anyway (Walther et al., 2001). Discrimination does happen online; however, pseudonymity can afford some equality of status and at the same time prevent possible de-individualizing effects also attributed to reduced social cues (Tolmie and Boyle, 2000).

Although we suggest avoiding traditional structures that might be divisive or facilitate stereotypical dynamics, this is not to say that deliberation should be unstructured. On the contrary, the design is crucial as deliberation outcomes seem highly context-dependent (Carpini et al., 2004) and there are examples in the literature where suboptimal deliberative conditions have led to divisive or biased results (Goven, 2003; Carpini et al., 2004). What is argued here is that structure and facilitation could focus less on formality and more on affective empathy. If the design excludes *a priori* the very emotional and human expressions that facilitate connection in diversity, we might be designing quite an elitist program, reinforcing existing biases of the already-dominant views. Graphic design should be comfortable and welcoming, avoiding extremely "cold" colors and sharp lines that often reflect the predominant "masculinity" of both computer culture and cognition-centered deliberation. For instance, representing the deliberating group as a circle might be more conducive to a safe non-judgmental space to speak one's mind.

It is important to have a transparent and simple process (Doyle and Straus, 1976), with agreed-upon rules or guidelines that all participants can master. Those who do not have the relevant access or literacies should be able to refer to mediators. Guidelines should incorporate basic empathic communication tips and should be easily accessible at all steps of the process, even if participants went through an initial briefing or online tutorial. Some tips may be given a privileged visibility in the interface: for instance, general guidelines could be accessible from a drop-down top-level menu, but there might be a "Triggered?" button in a more central position to access tips to "drain" the emotional overload and express one's feelings in a way that elicits empathy.

Having a simple set of roles can help as well (Doyle and Straus, 1976). Whenever participants are involved in more than one session, empathic connection and participants' empowerment can be supported by rotating roles. Although facilitation risks leading or even censoring the discussion, emotionally skilled facilitation can make a great difference in avoiding inauthentic consensus and groupthink. A brief training or tip sheet on empathic communication is sufficient. Facilitators should rotate and possibly be part of the discussion as well, so that leading or censoring tendencies may become more apparent as they are not assumed to have a "neutral" position. As an example, general assemblies of the Occupy Wall Street movement have been using a simple set of rotating member roles – a facilitator, a stack taker (who keeps track of who wants to talk), and a recorder – who are also part of the discussion. Facilitators use flow charts or other agreed-upon guidelines to streamline and ensure the authenticity of the consensus process, and any other participant is empowered to interrupt the discussion when he or she sees a flaw in the process as well.

Software agents might cover some empathy and diverse participation-enhancing roles. A recent effort in computer-supported consensus decision making implemented artificial agents to seek participation and consensus (Tenorio-Fornés and Hassan, 2014). Rather than seeking participation and consensus directly – with the risk of pressing toward inauthentic agreement – such agents could suggest empathic communication guidelines, welcome and brief newcomers, pose follow-up questions that facilitate the consideration of diverse perspectives, point to ways to invite someone with a fresh look on the issue at stake, and similar ways to facilitate users to find a deep consensus within diversity.

Of special concern is the present lack of detailed research aimed at understanding whether diverse and minority positions are actually given consideration in deliberative contexts (Hickerson and Gastil, 2008; Lee, 2011). Andrea Hickerson and John Gastil (2008) found that women and men who participated in a deliberative poll reported similar levels of satisfaction (which was not the case in earlier studies), but they suggest that women might have been unaware of discriminating conditions which are often invisible because of their "normality" and that a discourse analysis might find different results. When testing or piloting an online deliberation system, we recommend including critical analysis of deliberations as part of the system evaluation. Such analysis can inform future developments of the system and prevent current shortcomings in facilitating diversity.

Conclusion

The possibilities for empathetic engagement in online deliberation are many, but they will remain unsupported unless foundational assumptions are examined. Creative solutions can arise once the assumptions now considered to be neutral (such as privileging rationality at the expense of emotional engagement) are challenged. Deliberative democracy and online design may incorporate lessons from disciplines such as intercultural communication to facilitate the creation of connections and allow participants to discover common ground. Facilitating emotional and cognitive empathy supports a regeneration of the democratic process and a more viable settlement between reason and emotion in contemporary societies at large (Richards, 2004). The newest technologies are best informed by taking into consideration more ancient articulations of practical wisdom. We have suggested some implications for design and possible helpful features, but context-specific affordances for empathy and diversity in online deliberation systems emerge when the design process itself is an exercise of practical wisdom.

References

Anderson, L. (2005). E-government to e-democracy: Communicative mechanisms of govern-ance. *Journal of E-Government*, 2(1), 5–23.

Ardelt, M. (2003). Empirical assessment of a three-dimensional wisdom scale. *Research on Aging*, 25(3), 275–324.

Aristotle (1984). *Nicomachean Ethics*, W.D. Ross (trans.). Retrieved from http://ebooks.ade-laide.edu.au/a/aristotle/nicomachean/contents.html (accessed September 8, 2015).

——. (2006). *Poetics*, S.H. Butcher (trans.). Retrieved from http://www.gutenberg.org/files/1974/1974-h/1974-h.htm (accessed September 8, 2015).

Arnott, D. and Pervan, G. (2005). A critical analysis of decision support systems research. *Journal of Information Technology*, 20(2), 67–87.

Auvine, B., Densmore, B., Extrom, M., Poole, S., and Shanklin, M. (1978). *A Manual for Group Facilitators*. Madison, WI: Center for Conflict Resolution.

Barber, B.R. (1984). *Strong Democracy: Participatory Politics for a New Age*. Berkeley, CA: University of California Press.

Bardzell, S. (2010). Feminist HCI: Taking stock and outlining an agenda for design. In *Proceedings of the SIGCHI Conference on Human Factors in Computing Systems* (pp. 1301–1310). New York: Association for Computing Machinery.

Bohm, D. (1996). *On Dialogue*. New York: Routledge.

Brooks, A. (2007). Feminist standpoint epistemology. In S.N. Hesse-Biber and P.L. Leavy (eds), *Feminist Research Practice* (pp. 53–82). Thousand Oaks, CA: Sage.

Carpini, M.X.D., Cook, F.L., and Jacobs, L.R. (2004). Public deliberation, discursive participa-tion, and citizen engagement: A review of the empirical literature. *Annual Review of Political Science*, 7, 315–344.

Coleman, S. and Moss, G. (2012). Under construction: The field of online deliberation research. *Journal of Information Technology and Politics*, 9(1), 1–15.

Crossley, L. (2003). Building emotions in design. *Design Journal*, 6(3), 35–45.

Dahlberg, L. (2007). Rethinking the fragmentation of the cyberpublic: From consensus to con-testation. *New Media and Society*, 9(5), 829–849.

Doyle, M. and Straus, D. (1976). *How to Make Meetings Work*. New York: Jove Books.

Druckman, J. (2004). Political preference formation: Competition, deliberation, and the (ir)relevance of framing effects. *American Political Science Review*, 98, 671–686.

Ehn, P. (1992). Scandinavian design: On participation and skill. In P.S. Adler and T.A. Wino-grad (eds), *Usability: Turning Technologies into Tools* (pp. 96–132). New York: Oxford Uni-versity Press.

Elliman, T., Macintosh, A., and Irani, Z. (2007). A model building tool to support group delib-eration (eDelib): A research note. *International Journal of Cases on Electronic Commerce*, 3(3), 33–44.

Fine, C. (2010). *Delusions of Gender: How Our Minds, Society, and Neurosexism Create Dif-ference*. New York: W.W. Norton and Company.

Fishkin, J. (1995). *The Voice of the People*. New Haven: Yale University Press.

Goldberg, G. (2011). Rethinking the public/virtual sphere: The problem with participation. *New Media and Society*, 13(5), 739–754.

Goven, J. (2003). Deploying the consensus conference in New Zealand: Democracy and de-problematization. *Public Understanding of Science*, 12(4), 423–440.

Gudykunst, W.B. (2004) *Bridging Differences: Effective Intergroup Communication*, 4th edn. Thousand Oaks, CA: Sage.

Habermas, J. (1991). *The Structural Transformation of the Public Sphere: An Inquiry into a Category of Bourgeois Society*. Cambridge, MA: MIT Press.

——. (2006). Political communication in media society: Does democracy still enjoy an epistemic dimension? The impact of normative theory on empirical research. *Communication Theory*, 16(4), 411–426.

Hendriks, C. (2005). Consensus conferences and planning cells: Lay citizen deliberations. In J. Gastil and P. Levine (eds), *The Deliberative Democracy Handbook: Strategies for Effective Civic Engagement in the 21th Century* (pp. 80–110). San Francisco: Jossey-Bass.

Herman, E.S. and Chomsky, N. (1988). *Manufacturing Consent: The Political Economy of the Mass Media*. New York: Pantheon Books.

Hewitt, J. (2003). How habitual online practices affect the development of asynchronous discussion threads. *Journal of Educational Computing Research*, 28(1), 31–45.

Hickerson, A. and Gastil, J. (2008). Assessing the difference critique of deliberation: Gender, emotion, and the jury experience. *Communication Theory*, 18(2), 281–303.

Janis, I.L. (1972). *Victims of Groupthink: A Psychological Study of Foreign-Policy Decisions and Fiascoes*. Boston: Houghton Mifflin.

Kellermanns, F.W., Walter, J., Floyd, S.W., Lechner, C., and Shaw, J.C. (2011). To agree or not to agree? A meta-analytical review of strategic consensus and organizational performance. *Journal of Business Research*, 64(2), 126–133.

Kenny, A. (2013) Introduction. In *Aristotle: Poetics* (pp. vii–xxxviii). Oxford: Oxford University Press.

Kirk, M. (2009). *Gender and Information Technology: Moving beyond Access to Co-create Global Partnership*. Hershey, PA: Information Science Reference.

Kunzmann, U. and Baltes, P.B. (2005). The psychology of wisdom: Theoretical and empirical challenges. In R.J. Sternberg and J.A. Jordan (eds), *A Handbook of Wisdom: Psychological Perspectives* (pp. 110–135). New York: Cambridge University Press.

Lampe, C., LaRose, R., Steinfield, C., and DeMaagd, K. (2011). Inherent barriers to the use of social media for public policy informatics. *The Innovation Journal: The Public Sector Innovation Journal*, 16(1), Art. 6.

Lee, C.W. (2011). Five assumptions academics make about public deliberation, and why they deserve rethinking. *Journal of Public Deliberation*, 7(1), Art. 7.

Mansbridge, J. (1983). *Beyond Adversary Democracy*. Chicago: University of Chicago Press.

Mansbridge, J., Hartz-Karp, J., Amengual, M., and Gastil, J. (2006). Norms of deliberation: An inductive study. *Journal of Public Deliberation*, 2(1), Art. 7. Retrieved from http://services. bepress.com/jpd/vol2/iss1/art7 (accessed September 8, 2015).

Melville, K., Willingham, T.L., and Dedrick, J.R. (2005). National Issues Forums: A network of communities promoting public deliberation. In J. Gastil and P. Levine (eds), *The Deliberative Democracy Handbook* (pp. 37–58). San Francisco: Jossey-Bass.

Mendelberg, T. (2002). The deliberative citizen: theory and evidence. In M.X. Delli Carpini, L. Huddy, and R. Shapiro (eds), *Research in Micropolitics: Political Decision Making, Deliberation and Participation* (pp. 151–193). Bingley, UK: Emerald.

Morrell, M.E. (2010). *Empathy and Democracy: Feeling, Thinking, and Deliberation*. University Park, PA: Penn State University Press.

Mutz, D.C. (2006). *Hearing the Other Side: Deliberative versus Participatory Democracy*. New York: Cambridge University Press.

Nemeth, C.J. and Wachtler, J. (1983). Creative problem solving as a result of majority vs. minority influence. *European Journal of Social Psychology*, 13(1), 45–55.

Rainie, L. and Smith, A. (2012). Social networking sites and politics. Pew Internet and American Life Project. Retrieved from: http://www.pewinternet.org/2012/03/12/main-findings-10 (accessed September 8, 2015).

Recuber, T. (2013). Occupy empathy? Online politics and micro-narratives of suffering. *New Media and Society*, October 6. DOI:10.1177/1461444813506971.

Richards, B. (2004). The emotional deficit in political communication. *Political Communication*, 21(3), 339–352.

Rogers, C. (1957). The necessary and sufficient conditions of therapeutic change. *Journal of Consulting Psychology*, 21, 95–103.

Rogers, E.M. (1983). *Diffusion of Innovations*. New York: Free Press.

Rogers, E.M., Medina, U.E., Rivera, M.A., and Wiley, C.J. (2005). Complex adaptive systems and the diffusion of innovations. *The Innovation Journal: The Public Sector Innovation Journal*, 10(3), 579–584.

Sanders, L.M. (1997). Against deliberation. *Political Theory*, 25(3), 347–376.

Schaper, E. (1968). Aristotle's catharsis and aesthetic pleasure. *Philosophical Quarterly*, 18(71), 131–143.

Shannon, T. (2008) *Iroquois Diplomacy on the Early American Frontier*. New York: Penguin.

Stein, E. (1964) *Zum Problem der Einfühlung* [*On the Problem of Empathy*], W. Stein (trans.). The Hague: Martinus Nijhoff. (Original work published 1917.)

Stueber, K.R. (2006). *Rediscovering Empathy*. Cambridge, MA: MIT Press.

——. (2014). Empathy. In E.N. Zalta (ed.), *The Stanford Encyclopedia of Philosophy*, Spring edn. Retrieved from: http://plato.stanford.edu/archives/spr2014/entries/empathy (accessed September 8, 2015).

Sunstein, C.R. (2001). *Republic.com*. Princeton: Princeton University Press.

——. (2003). *Why Societies Need Dissent*. Cambridge, MA: Harvard University Press.

Suthers, D.D. (2008). Empirical studies of the value of conceptually explicit notations in collaborative learning. In A. Okada, S. Buckingham Shum, and T. Sherborne (eds), *Knowledge Cartography* (pp. 1–23). Cambridge, MA: MIT Press.

Suthers, D.D. and Hundhausen, C. (2003). An experimental study of the effects of representational guidance on collaborative learning. *Journal of the Learning Sciences*, 12(2), 183–219.

Taylor, C. (1989). *Sources of the Self: The Making of the Modern Identity*. Cambridge, MA: Harvard University Press.

Tenorio-Forñes, A. and Hassan, S. (2014). Towards an agent-supported online assembly: Prototyping a collaborative decision-making tool. In *Proceedings of COLLA 2014: The Fourth International Conference on Advanced Collaborative Networks, Systems and Applications* (pp. 72–77). Red Hook, NY: Curran Associates.

Thompson, S. and Hoggett, P. (2001). The emotional dynamics of deliberative democracy. *Policy and Politics*, 29(3), 351–364.

Tolmie, A. and Boyle, J. (2000) Factors influencing the success of computer mediated communication (CMC) environments in university teaching: A review and case study. *Computers and Education*, 34(2), 119–140.

Towne, W.B. and Herbsleb, J.D. (2012). Design considerations for online deliberation systems. *Journal of Information Technology and Politics*, 9(1), 97–115.

Walther, J.B., Slovacek, C., and Tidwell, L. (2001). Is a picture worth a thousand words? Photographic images in long-term and short-term computer-mediated communication. *Communication Research*, 28(1), 105–134.

Weber, B., Marsal, E., and Dobashi, T. (2011) *The Politics of Empathy: New Interdisciplinary Perspectives on an Ancient Phenomenon*. Berlin, Germany: LIT.

Wertsch, J. (1998). *Mind as Action*. New York: Oxford University Press.

Winerman, L. (2005). The mind's mirror. *American Psychological Association Monitor*, 36(9), 48. Retrieved from http://www.apa.org/monitor/oct05/mirror.aspx (accessed September 8, 2015).

Wiseman, T. (1996). A concept analysis of empathy. *Journal of Advanced Nursing*, 23(6), 1162–1167.

Wright, S. and Street, J. (2007). Democracy, deliberation and design: The case of online discussion forums. *New Media and Society*, 9(5), 849–869.

Chapter 7

Wisdom in praxis

How engineers use practical wisdom in their decision making

Bernard McKenna, Roberto Biloslavo,
and Anita Trnavcevic

Introduction

Although it has been crucial to the development of our contemporary economy, the way that engineers go about their work has never been systematically analyzed. Whether it be the ongoing provision and maintenance of urban water, sewage, and transport infrastructure or the inventions emerging from nanotechnology or physiological mechatronics, engineers' work has a strong impact on our standard of living and strongly influences the potential for creating and maintaining civil society. Recently, Kathryn Montgomery's *How Doctors Think* (2006) asked a simple question that had not been particularly considered before. Montgomery's central finding was that physicians "start from the demands of the patient's condition and not from the demand of generalizable knowledge" (2006, p. 31). She asserts that physicians deploy phronesis "to fit their knowledge and experience to the circumstances of each patient" (2006, p. 32). Notwithstanding that it may not be an obvious association between the work of engineers and that of physicians, the etymology of the word "engineer," from the Latin roots *ingeniare* ("to contrive, devise") and *ingenium* ("cleverness"), may add some plausibility. The modern definition of an engineer is a professional practitioner who has displayed high levels of aptitude in applying scientific knowledge, mathematics, and ingenuity to develop solutions for technical, societal, and commercial problems. Fundamental to this role is a relationship of trust that society has with engineers and their works. That society needs to be able to trust that such professions will put their knowledge to good use not just for the patient or client but also for society – that they will act wisely – provides a point of similarity between the two professions.

This chapter starts with that assumption: that wise engineers adopt a phronetic approach to their work. To understand the notion of the phronetic engineer, we first outline a set of characteristics derived from a theory of wisdom. Then we consider the nature of the cognitive complexity involved in engineering decision making to see that it is intricately involved with intuition and the capacity for metacognition. Finally, we propose that wise engineering judgment must be virtuous to be truly wise. The chapter concludes by understanding that the wise professional archetype is characterized by possessing a balance of virtues.

The stereotypical understanding of an engineer is that they simply apply established knowledge to technical problems to derive a solution in a manner typically explained by Eilon: "the decision-maker has several alternatives and . . . his [sic] choice involves a comparison between these alternatives and an evaluation of their outcomes" (1969,

p. 172). In only the most routine of engineering cases is this the case; furthermore, when considering the wise rather than stereotypical engineer, it is vital, as Aristotle did, to separate *techne* and phronesis. *Techne* is a craft-based capacity of "knowing how to" use resources to produce something useful or aesthetic. While useful as a calculative technology, *techne* is not concerned with contributing to the eudamonic life of society. Wise judgment, according to Aristotle, needs a transcendent element. This transcendent capacity is largely contained in the concept *sophia*, a difficult and – although he calls it "the most precise of the sciences" – still unclear notion outlined in *Nicomachean Ethics* (1984, VI: 1145a 7–12; X: 7–9). It is that which is concerned with features that remain "always the same" (1984, VI: 1141a 24–5). The application of *sophia* thus allows us to go beyond the physical confines of *techne*, "to transcend the world of transient finitude" (Long, 2002, p. 39). Admittedly, *sophia* has been rather theoretically neglected in contemporary understandings of wisdom, and its transcendent dimension may well sit at odds with the practical world of engineering. But it should not sit at odds with wise engineering. Whereas phronesis is more easily understood as rational and virtuous processes for society living well, *sophia* is transcendent and precedes phronesis. Put simply, *sophia* can be understood as an understanding of the oneness or interconnectedness of all things as well as intuitive knowing (Trowbridge, 2011). Both of these aspects can be seen as transcendent. A sense of interconnectedness implies the foundation of wisdom: that the purpose of life is to flourish. Similarly, intuitive knowing is based on an "unbiased mindfulness" (Rosch, 2007, p. 14) in which people can to varying degrees move beyond their "imprisoning consciousness" to make connections that are unavailable in the logical and knowledge-laden processes of normal work life.

Phronesis, drawing on the transcendent, is wise action, or "the ability to find some action in particular circumstances which the agent can see as the virtuous thing to do" (Hughes, 2001, p. 105). Phronesis provides a degree of value rationality to balance the instrumental rationality of *techne* (Flyvbjerg, 2004), which resonates with Weber's concern that the industrial age had supplanted "wertrational" (or value-oriented) with "zweckational" (or technocratic) thinking.

A theory of wisdom

Wisdom manifests in six ways (Biloslavo and McKenna, 2013; Rooney et al., 2010). First, wise people are knowledgeable and are able to draw sound conclusions by evaluating the salience and ontological foundations of propositions and practices. Second, wise people are able to use non-rational factors such as intuition, past experience, and subjective feelings when they make decisions and judgments. Third, wise people are able to articulate their thoughts and judgments in aesthetic and creative ways. A fourth characteristic of wise people is that they are humane and virtuous, acting in a way that contributes to eudaimonic society not just in the present but also for the longer term. Supplementing this as a fifth characteristic is moral conation, which is the capacity "to take moral action in the face of adversity and persevere through challenges" (Hannah et al., 2011, p. 664). Finally wise people are practical.

This wisdom framework is used to consider how engineers go about their work to determine the ways in which engineering thinking can produce wise action. We begin by looking more closely at the cognitive processes involved in decision making.

Cognitive processes in engineering decision making

A useful starting point for understanding the nature of engineering decision making is Cognitive Continuum Theory built on the work of Kenneth R. Hammond (1996, 2000; Hammond et al. 1987). Hammond proposed that cognitive tasks have different properties depending on the context and also that cognition occurs along a continuum from intuition to analysis depending on the task at hand. An analytical task is one where the process of deciding or solving can be explained (Hammond, 1996), and is commonly described as "deductive, rigorous, constrained, convergent, formal and critical" (Allinson and Hayes, 1996, p. 122). In the Cognitive Style Index, it is understood as implying "processing information in an ordered, linear sequence" (Allinson and Hayes, 2012, p. 2). Intuition, on the other hand, is a cognitive process that produces a solution or decision without using a conscious, logically articulable process (Hammond, 1996). A further element is that responses "are reached with little apparent effort, and typically without conscious awareness . . . [and] involve little or no conscious deliberation," as proposed by Hogarth (2001, p. 14). This distinction has been categorized by Stanovich and West (2000) as System 1 and System 2 cognitive functioning. System 1 refers to our intuitive system, which is typically fast, automatic, effortless, implicit, and emotional. System 2 refers to reasoning that is slower, conscious, effortful, explicit, and logical.

The task properties of any work activity are determined by the task complexity, the level of ambiguity of its content, and the manner in which the task presents itself, such as the potential for decomposition into subtasks (Cader et al., 2005). Judgment tasks that are "ill-structured" are more likely to induce intuitive cognition, while "well-structured" tasks are more likely to use "analytical" processes. Thus, cognition might oscillate between intuition and more rational modes. Engineers have frequently been the subjects of Hammond's empirical work. He has found that "the closer the engineers were on the cognitive mode predicted by the task structure, the better was their overall judgement performance" (Cader et al., 2005, p. 401).

A further level of difficulty is added to complexity when we consider the actual processes that underlie apparent rational decision making, particularly when issues of risk and finance are concerned. A fundamental weakness of the rational model was exposed by Herbert Simon (1955, 1992), who, with his colleagues (Cyert and March, 1963), developed a model that anticipates that intuitive decision making occurs in unstable conditions. Unstable conditions are characterized by time constraints, the need for large amounts of data, or the unreliability of the available data (Khatri and Ng, 2000). For these reasons, decision makers have only so-called "limited rationality" available. Empirical evidence supports the proposition that instability and uncertainty tend to incite intuitive judgment. Top managers in computer companies when making decisions were shown to use "gut feeling" significantly more in relation to judgment and experience than similar people in banks and utility companies.

Under these circumstances, instead of maximizing the value of decision making (i.e., a difference between expected benefits and costs), the decision-making process is limited to a search for information and alternative solutions to the point where a potential solution satisfies the decision maker. This means that engineers might stop searching for the best solution when they reach a solution that is good enough. In technical terms, this represents a point beyond which incremental benefits no longer match the costs to achieve them. Clearly, the selection of the components of this cost–benefit analysis involves not just relevant knowledge but also the scope of the analysis and the moral principles to be applied. To sum up, Simon's model of decision making identifies intuition, attitudes, values, and experiences as crucial to the decision-making process.

A crucial aspect of a decision-making process is the perception of the decision-making environment. Perceptions are formed by sensory stimuli. Senses enable people to receive and value data and information from their environment. However, George Miller's (1994) work shows that people are limited in terms of processing information and developing perceptions. Most of us have the cognitive capability to simultaneously process five to nine chunks or pieces of information. In other words, human short-term memory is limited to a finite amount of information that can be stored for computation. If this limitation is exceeded, then selected perceptions (for example, we "hear" only what we are interested in at certain points of time and space) or even simplifications of the decision-making environment occur.

One area where this problem has been particularly researched is environmental and built environment management, as scientific principles are considered in conjunction with aesthetic issues. Research by Stamps (2004), for example, indicates that at a certain point, "the marginal effect of quantity of elements and quantity of different kinds of elements is asymptotic to subjective impressions of responses such as complexity or diversity" (2004, p. 14). It is reasonable to conclude then that "the information load is simply too great with respect to human capabilities." Seminal research in this area by Rachel and Stephen Kaplan and associates concludes that environmental preferences are determined by four informational variables: coherence (immediate understanding), complexity (immediate exploration), legibility (inferred understanding), and mystery (inferred exploration). One study by Kaplan et al. (1989) was designed to determine the relative ability of certain variables to predict quality preference. The variables included aesthetic factors such as physical attributes (for example, land form such as slope and diversity and land cover) and empirical "scientific" information. A significant finding was that "mystery," which is inferred exploration with the promise of new but related information, was the "flagship informational variable" (1989, p. 527) rather than "complexity"-based information, which is characterized by richness, intricacy, and multiple elements. In other words, it is the more speculative orientation that predicted decision making rather than greater amounts of more complex information.

In complex situations, the final decision emerges from negotiations and compromises. In these circumstances, the matter can be taken out of the hands of an individual engineer by the organization or the engineer is cornered into an inappropriate decision. Such was the case when Morton Thiokol overrode the advice of its engineer, Allan McDonald, not to launch the space shuttle Challenger because he could not assure them that the O-ring would operate at the temperature prevailing at the launch (McDonald and Hansen, 2009). Modern projects are usually far too complex for a single engineer to make decisions; they require teams of engineers, each specializing in a portion of the project. Today, an engineering project is essentially a complex communication and negotiation process involving engineers, site workers, project managers, and clients. The people involved in the process are responsible for deciding what to do, when to do it, what information is needed, and what tools need to be used (Sommerville and Kotonya, 1998). While communication can be difficult, project decisions must be made that will affect other collaborators. This is even more significant if we acknowledge that engineering is a field where data are often presented with little context. Because such data are difficult to understand at first glance, a lot of experience is needed to make a judgment which is, in turn, subjectively conditioned.

In such situations, we fill in the gaps in our perceptions (for example, stereotyping, categorization, heuristic judgments, and prejudices, the "rule of thumb" judgments) in order to have better control over the situation. This is what Herbert Simon in his "bounded rationality theory" calls "small world" (1945, as cited in Beach and Connolly, 2005). However, relying on "small world" can lead to wrong judgment. In fact, deploying subjective judgment of probability of development of a specific event can lead us to conclusions that are very different from real or objective probability. The genre and narrative conventions of engineering judgment are presented as algorithmic, which is an application of rules that are derived from quantitative empirical research. However, it is known that heuristics are frequently employed based on exemplars derived from experience. Nonetheless, a narrative fiction of algorithmic judgment is maintained.

Intuition

Intuition is not the same as insight, which "arises suddenly, especially in cases of longer, deliberate and unsuccessful thinking about a problem – and often after a period of incubation and rumination when thinking activities have been stopped" (Harteis et al., 2008, p. 69). Insight "literally means seeing the solution to the problem," and can usually explain the solution's elements and their logical inter-relationships; thus it is "conscious and explicable" (Sadler-Smith and Shefy, 2004, p. 81). Thus, a person with intuition has "the capacity to explore possible meaningful relationships between apparently unrelated events and phenomena pertinent to that situation" (Intezari and Pauleen, 2013, p. 161).

Much of our understanding about heuristic decision making comes from the work of Amos Tversky and Daniel Kahneman (Kahneman and Tversky, 1979, 2000; Tversky and Kahneman, 1974). Indeed, Daniel Kahneman's 2002 Nobel Memorial Prize in Economic Sciences undercut the claims to rationality in traditional economic theory by showing how people make judgments and decisions under uncertain conditions using rules of thumb rather than rational analysis, often based on past events and loss aversion as well as reacting to the framing of the question. Research into the decision making of financiers (Kakabadse et al., 2008; MacKenzie, 2009; Zaloom, 2004) shows that such responses are not confined to "lay" decision makers. This is not to say that engineering decision making is capricious. Of course, design, maintenance, and repair of technology are in many ways soundly based on applied empiricism and experience. Rather, the focus is on judgment, the essence of wisdom, particularly in projects where the issues frequently call not so much for technical expertise as judgment. Judgment beyond mere expertise might be called upon in any number of engineering situations. For example, fracking, where coal and gas seams are hydraulically fractured by high-pressure pumping of water, sand, and chemicals into wells, has become enormously popular in the USA and Australia as a means of extracting natural gas, which is then pumped to facilities where it is converted into liquefied natural gas (LNG). LNG has been touted as a dramatic, if medium-term, remedy to oil shortages and to reduce greenhouse gas emissions. Furthermore, in Australia it has produced a valuable new export commodity for an energy-hungry China in particular. Of considerable concern, however, is that using this method to extract gas also removes huge amounts of groundwater and can collapse aquifers. In the state of Queensland, a government report suggests that 100,000 ML of water will be removed from the Surat Basin alone (Water, 2012). Elsewhere in Australia, profound concerns have been raised by many farmers, whose land rights are overridden by mining leases, that arable land which is relatively limited in the continent will be permanently lost for short-term and unequally distributed gain. Clearly the technology of fracking has proved itself at one level to be enormously efficient in yielding gas. However, the breadth of judgment that engineering companies use in developing LNG mining is extremely limited given the commercial demands to win and fulfill mining engineering contracts.

While the left-right brain hemispheres is a popular classificatory system for separating intuitive and analytical judgment, this is far too simplistic because intuitive judgment (and creativity, for that matter) is not performed in one hemisphere. Furthermore, such an internalist approach fails to take into account the context in which such performances occur (Harteis et al., 2008). A more useful framework for understanding how intuition works, particularly from an engineering perspective, would include the knowledge base underlying intuition and would consider issues of time, whether decisions aim to be optimal or *satisficing*, the degree of risk aversion, and framing.

The knowledge underlying intuitive judgment and decision making can range from the "fast and frugal characteristics" displayed by, for example, chicken sexers, who take less than two seconds to make a decision and do so with 98 percent accuracy (Harteis et al., 2008), to those with a rich knowledge basis of which they may be unaware and which may have transformed over time as a result of double-loop learning (Argyris and Schön, 1978). Another factor that affects decision making is the timeframe for deciding. The busier that people are, the more they have on their minds, and the more time constraints they face, the more likely they will be to rely on System 1 thinking. Thus, the frantic pace of life, which is likely to lead us to rely on System 1 thinking much of the time, can lead to costly errors. A third element affecting the nature of decision making is whether the desired outcome is an optimal or a satisficing one. Such desired outcomes may be the result of the decision maker's personality (for example, the desire to protect against failure) or because time constraints do not allow for an optimal decision-making process. According to Schwartz et al. (2011), not only is the attempt to make decisions to maximize utility fraught with difficulties, such as the information gap and information processing, but it may also be less preferable for other reasons. A person who adopts a robust satisficing decision strategy "maximizes the robustness to uncertainty" (2011, p. 213) to satisfice the outcome by asking two questions: what will be a "good enough" outcome and will it do so under the widest range of possible future states of the world? It is worthy of note that satisficers tend to be more satisfied with their decisions and happier overall (Iyengar et al., 2006).

A particular concern is judgment in conditions of risk where the engineers' orientation to risky decisions is crucial. Tversky and Kahneman (1981) found that people differently value outcomes that represent gains for them or their client compared to those that represent losses, even if both are equal in absolute terms. Because losses psychologically hurt more than the good feeling provided by gains, people tend to be loss averse. Furthermore, in general, people overweight small probabilities (for example, 0.01 vs. 0) and underweight medium to high probabilities (for example, 0.4 vs. 0.5). Based on their results, Kahneman and Tversky's prospect theory (1979) asserts that people are risk averse with high probability of gains and low probability of losses, and are risk seeking with low probability of gains and high probability of losses. Besides considering an individual's propensity to give different values to gains and losses and to small and high probabilities, prospect theory shows that reference points used by people to assess gain and losses are not fixed, but change over time and are conditioned by aspirations, expectations, opportunity costs, and social comparison (Heath et al., 1999). The consequences of such decisions can be catastrophic, which means that the true meaning of probability and value that are assigned to each alternative should be considered. For example, an engineer who is naturally inclined to risk taking or is very confident in his or her own abilities could well define a reference point very low. Consider, for example, determining appropriate risk in relation to safety when seeking maximum possible speed in car racing. While there is probably little doubt about the technological excellence of the design, the human factor that makes a judgment about appropriate risk could potentially be very dangerous.

Another area of concern in decision making raised by Tversky and Kahneman is that of framing, which occurs in the stage where the outcome or consequence options for making decisions are framed: the "decision frame" (1981, p. 454). The various ways in which the contingencies and outcomes are framed are known to influence judgments. Contingency framing includes both the certainty effect and the pseudo-certainty effect. The certainty effect posits that "a reduction of the probability of an outcome by a constant factor has more impact when the outcome was initially certain than when it was merely probable" (1981, p. 455). The pseudo-certainty effect occurs when the description of a problem alters according to the sequence of presentation or by the manner of introducing causal contingencies. The framing of outcomes centers on the understanding that "outcomes are commonly perceived as positive or negative in relation to a reference outcome that is judged neutral" (1981, p. 456). Manipulation of the reference point, whether conscious or unconscious, can determine whether the judge will evaluate an outcome as a gain or as a loss.

Discourse perspective

These notions of framing, which concern the internal processes of people making decisions, do not consider the broader framework that creates the way that options are framed. We would argue that the framing of problems is a discursive act that is overtly or implicitly political. From a discourse perspective, the engineer's task could be understood as operating at a meso-discursive, or organizational, level. A discourse analytic approach assumes that specific communicative interactions are, to some extent, constituted by a broader contextual framework, the macro-perspective. Because the language of any discursive site evolves interdependently with concrete situations rather than in either an "abstract linguistic system" or "the individual psyche of speakers," every utterance is "only a moment in the continuous process of verbal communication" (Volosinov, 1994, p. 59). Hence, the utterance has a synchronic dimension, being of its own contextual moment, and a diachronic dimension, being part of ongoing social change (Morris, 1994). Thus, the micro levels of discourse, the "capillary" level of the subject (Foucault, 1980, pp. 96–101), have a range of discourses made available to it by meso or organizational levels of discourse, and macro levels (Alvesson and Kärreman, 2000; Conrad, 2004; House et al., 1995). Consistent with this three-level discursive relationship is the understanding that language is "imbricated" in social relations (Fairclough, 1995, p. 73). In other words, our discursive practices are inextricably involved in day-to-day activities and social relationships.

Thus, when an engineer, singly or more usually as part of a team, makes a decision, the problem has to a large extent been "framed" within the macro-discursive framework within which the organization (meso-level) operates and, consistent with that, within the meso-discursive framework within the organization itself. The macro-discursive framework is framed by a dominant sociopolitical ethic that is currently dominated by neo-liberal principles of individualism, globalization, market principles, and small government (Tickell and Clark, 2001; Tickell and Peck, 2003) and a belief in inevitable progress (Bauman, 1992). At the meso-discursive level, organizational members adopt a "particular ethic of personhood – a view of what persons are and what they should be allowed to be" (Du Gay, 2003, p. 675). These produce "norms and techniques of conduct," which, if contravened, imperil their organizational survival (Du Gay, 2000, p. 78; 2003). At the macro-discursive level, frames "are embedded in historical and material contexts" (Fiss and Hirsch, 2005, p. 30). Sense making occurs as an "ongoing retrospective development of plausible images that rationalize what people are doing" (Weick et al., 2005, p. 409). Organizational actors organize their sense of what is to be done within these macro- and meso-discursive levels. Technological, political, economic, ethical, and professional discourses intersect at the moment that engineers utter a statement.

Through sense making, identity "unfolds," say Weick et al. (2005) in social contexts with other actors. Sense making is a process to establish meaning in organizational life. It involves the language of written and spoken texts as well as enacted roles. Crucial to this meaning is the schematic formulation of "salient categories" of organizational knowledge and subject positions. These subject positions are frequently formalized in organizations according to skills, knowledge, and experience. To locate oneself comfortably within an organization, our personal identity in a psychological sense must be consistent with the role identity of the organization. Stable personal and occupational identities need to display three features: authenticity, which manifests itself as "integrity of self and behavior within and across situations"; coherence, "the extent to which a story makes sense on its own terms across different episodes"; and legitimacy, where personal self-narratives embed within a larger canonical cultural discourse (Ibarra and Barbulescu, 2010, pp. 140–142). The subjective expression of this identity – for example, one's clothing, workspace, hours worked, relationship with others, agency, and authority – is enacted every day. Supporting this conception of the way in which organizational identity is enacted is Buse et al.'s (2013) study of women engineers who stayed in or left the profession. Women who remained in engineering expressed high levels of self-efficacy, identified themselves strongly as an engineering professional, and enacted social roles that involved reciprocal engagement with others, including clients and co-workers, collaboration, and advice.

Superimposing on the role of engineer is a professional identity. Although the topic has not been extensively researched, one study shows that professionals communicate a higher degree of perceived competence and exhibit varying patterns of identification with their profession and their organization (Pratt et al., 2006). Professional identity extends beyond the organization to an institutional level such that an individual's self-definition as a member of a profession is enacted as a professional role (Chreim et al., 2007). Those who identify themselves as a professional align with strongly institutionalized beliefs and values that define their professionalism to the extent that it prescribes and proscribes various behaviors. Engineers could be seen as possessing four identities; personal, organizational, technical, and professional. The most appropriate disposition that is essential for professional integrity is an authentic sense of self across the four identities in a variety of situations. However, at particular times, one identity is more salient (Gunz and Gunz, 2008; Stryker and Burke, 2000).

In ethical situations, it is vital that a professional commitment to values-based principles underlies an engineer's judgment and behavior. However, engineers face serious dilemmas when their personal and professional ethics do not comply with organizational imperatives. In a brave and honest revelation of his role in the Ford Pinto debacle, Dennis Gioia (1992) reveals how his sense of personal identity as a deeply ethical person was contradicted by his role in the Ford Motor Company in 1972 and 1973 as the Field Recall Coordinator. The Pinto model had been fast-tracked as Ford responded to the Japanese companies' increasing market share during the petrol crisis by producing small cars. Although prototype testing had shown that the fuel tank ruptured with relatively light impact, the imperative to get the car onto the market overruled the ethical option of redesigning. In fact, the solution to the problem was relatively simple as the tank was punctured by protruding bolts from the axle that could have been re-positioned. Essentially, engineers were guided by a "common sense" rule of thumb within Ford promoted by Lee Iacocca, the "charismatic" Ford CEO, that "safety doesn't sell." As Field Recall Coordinator, Gioia was extremely busy dealing with various issues arising from different Ford models. Although he noticed emerging data indicating the Pinto fuel tank was a problem with fatal consequences, Gioia did not take decisive action. In fact, he owned a Pinto which he later sold to his sister.

Gioia's reflective analysis 20 years later is significant in terms of the theoretical framework developed so far in this chapter of micro-level sense making within a meso-discourse (Ford as a company) that in turn operates within the epistemic and sociopolitical (or ideological) framework of a particular time and place. Gioia posits that "my own schematized (scripted) knowledge influenced me to perceive recall issues in terms of the prevailing decision environment . . . [where] the scripts did not include ethical dimensions" (1992, p. 385). Furthermore, he proposes that in a complex organizational world, schematizing or scripting occurs because it "saves a significant amount of mental work" (1992, p. 386).

Organizational routines

Gioia's story leads inevitably to understanding that almost all engineers work within an organization and that these organizations develop routines for good reasons. However, routines can produce unintended consequences and tend to occlude intuition. Thus, it could be said that routine is of a lower cognitive order than analysis, which incorporates some conscious choice of analytical tool. Thus, the "template" report is not uncommon in engineering firms that regularly deal with particular sorts of issues such as determining the technical compliance of machinery with standards or evaluating the geological characteristics of core samples. At a higher cognitive level, however, engineers draw on a range of possible analytical tools to solve a problem. So, for example, large grinding mills (SAG mills), which crush and abrade mineral ores to "feed" size, provide problems for engineers who need to resolve the tension between increasing the milling speed for quicker output and the potential damage to the mill itself in the longer term. Over time, however, engineers who deal frequently with this may develop routines of analysis. Routine decision making is fast because an individual is not excessively thinking about it, and consequently their efficiency increases. The disadvantage of such a mode of decision making is that the routine may limit an engineer's capacity to notice that the situation has changed and that consequently his or her decision under the new conditions is inappropriate. The nature and role of routines in organizations was comprehensively established by Feldman and Pentland (2003). Significantly, they shifted the framing of routines away from structural models to emphasize the importance of agency and thus subjectivity and power. The wise engineer understands the role of routine in organizations, but is also aware of the dangers of mindless routinization.

On the positive side, routines enhance coordination and control, they economize cognitive resources, reduce uncertainty and instability, and provide a store of knowledge (Becker, 2004). However, routines can induce mindless conformity, lack of adaptivity, reduced creativity and motivation, and can produce "competency traps" that lure organizations into using the success of prior applications again in future similar, but different, situations (March, 1991). The wise engineer's agentive capacity, which "involves the ability to remember the past, imagine the future, and respond to present circumstances" (Feldman and Pentland, 2003, p. 95), also calls on the wise engineer to adapt to changing contexts and, from time to time, reflexively question the underlying assumptions of routine practices and "common sense" (McKenna and Rooney, 2008). Setting aside for one moment the complex macro-environment in which an organization operates at the meso-level, the engineer can be seen as having a degree of agency within the more inflexible organizational structure, which comprises the processes, practices, and relationships of the organization. It is not only an ethical evasion for an engineer to claim that structure eliminates individual agency, but also it does not correctly represent how organizations work. Although the organizational structure is reproduced by the repetition of its members' activities, a process of structuration also occurs, as agentive acts continually reformulate the structure. This process of structuration (Giddens, 1984) is based on understanding the difference between institutional rules and resources that are reproduced as well as social systems that are reproduced practices. It is at the level of practice that institutional structure is modified. This distinction between institutional rules and social practices has been theorized as the difference between the ostensive and performative aspects of organizational routines (Feldman and Pentland, 2003). The ostensive aspect refers to standard operating procedures and taken-for-granted norms that play a role in producing tacit knowledge. The performative aspect refers to "the specific actions taken by specific people at specific times when they are engaged in an organizational routine" (2003, p. 95).

This distinction implies agency, the capacity to "choose to do otherwise" (Giddens, 1984, p. 4). Positing an agentive subject assumes a reflexive, acting subject with a sense of identity shaped to varying degrees by a combination of socially available roles and unconscious motivations as well as sets of values. Understanding the organizational subject from both a sociological and psychological perspective is difficult but necessary. Giddens has done this in a formidable, if slightly imperfect, way according to Groarke (2002). From a macro-structural perspective, Giddens locates the modern subject in a transformational framework of globalization ("action at distance") and detraditionalization ("the excavation of traditional contexts of action": Groarke, 2002, p. 562). Given the decontextualized arena of social action, the subject relies on trust to provide ways to believe in the world in certain ways and to defend their sense of the world. People develop a sense of security, says Giddens in *The Consequences of Modernity* (1990), according to the confidence they have in the "continuity of their self-identity and in the constancy of the surrounding social and material environments of action" (as cited in Groarke, 2002, p. 562). The stable organizational subject is thus one who "trusts" the routine of everyday practices that shape perception in certain ways and help to form their self-identity. It is in this way that routine and reflexive, agentive practices construct and reconstruct the professional role identity particularly in complex environments (Chreim et al., 2007) typical of the engineer's environment.

The wise engineer

The Ancient Hellenic concept of *eudaimonia* was adopted by Aristotle as the *telos* of human life. Whereas the Ancient Hellenes assumed that the *telos* of life was happiness, only some adopted a view that such happiness needed to be rooted in virtuous practice. However, Aristotle drew a line from the human *telos* through virtuous practice to the wellbeing of *eudaimonia*: by choosing to exercise one or more of the virtues, "right action" will ensue (MacIntyre, 1985). This teleological perspective thus eschews the consequentialism of much contemporary decision making, but it is not deontological in the Kantian sense. Of all the virtues, phronesis is the greatest, though it is not possible without the presence of other virtues (MacIntyre, 1985). The personal expression of virtue clearly produces social outcomes. Notwithstanding that the primacy of "social justice" is contested among neo-Aristotelians (Hope, 2013), we adopt Nussbaum's (2006) position that eudaimonic outcomes must be founded on the assumption of human dignity, a precondition of which is economic, political, and social justice. Thus, *eudaimonia* is understood as the "human flourishing" or the "well-being" of society (Nussbaum, 1994, p. 15).

Just as Aristotle rejected the notion that a *eudaimon* (a person enacting the virtues) does not do so for the sake of temporary personal happiness (pathos), so too does contemporary psychology distinguish between *eudaimonia* and hedonia. The life-span psychologist Carolyn Ryff developed her notion of psychological wellbeing (PWB), describing a person's self-realization (Ryff, 1989), directly from Aristotle's works (Ryff and Singer, 2008). The six dimensions of PWB devised by Ryff include self-acceptance, positive relations with others, personal growth, purpose in life, environmental mastery, and autonomy. Although her studies have found that purpose in life and personal growth decline with age, there is evidence that a higher initial PWB, notwithstanding later decline, benefits people's health behaviors, including their neurobiological processes, and "appears to be tied to more adaptive patterns of brain circuitry" (Ryff and Singer, 2008, pp. 31–32).

However, though enhanced personal wellbeing is a good incentive for virtuous wise behavior, the more important reason in the case of engineering practice is that it will promote socially eudaimonic outcomes. Much of this chapter has focused on the features of cognitive behavior in engineering work to understand that judgment involving complex or extensive data necessarily invokes varying degrees of intuition. Yet the genres of engineering practice often compel engineers to maintain a fiction of analytical and algorithmic deduction. In engineering reports, for example, engineers convert real-world entities, events, and processes into scientific concepts in their analysis and findings before reconstruing it back into real-world phenomena (McKenna, 1997). This suggests that the public display of intuitive judgment may appear at odds with the subject role of engineer as understood by others, which, as a result, leads to a dissonance with the professional identity. This use of intuitive judgment based on experience can create difficulties for engineers and even expose them to legal action.

Even where intuitive judgment seems to be overridden by manuals, engineers' decision making still requires making judgments about conflicting objectives, the reliability of information, and salient factors to consider. One such case occurred during the Brisbane (Australia) floods in December 2010 and January 2011 in a series of rain events that killed 35 people statewide and caused $AUD 2.4 billion in damage. Years before, in response to the catastrophic 1974 Brisbane floods, the state government constructed the Wivenhoe Dam, the state's biggest, in order to reduce the peak flood height by one meter. As a result of months of wet weather followed by a cyclone, the Brisbane River and the Bremer River coursing through the adjacent city of Ipswich peaked on the morning of January 13, 2011, flooding more than 28,000 homes. In an ensuing judicial inquiry, three engineers who operated the dam at the height of the flood faced potential criminal charges, as their actions were referred to the Crime and Misconduct Commission (CMC) to determine whether their post-flood reports and testimony were accurate. Sensibly, the CMC dismissed the matter, but not before the engineers had been publicly vilified by one journalist in one of the nation's leading papers and had experienced considerable stress. The judge heading the inquiry stated that the flooding in Ipswich and Brisbane could have been reduced if the dam level had been reduced to 75 percent of its drinking water capacity before the December rains. However, just three years prior, the dam contained just 17 percent of its capacity because of a prolonged El Niño drought. Although La Niña conditions returned, the near-catastrophe brought about by the drought was still very fresh in people's minds.

The engineers' decision whether to release water depended heavily on information provided by the highly regarded Bureau of Meteorology, a federal agency. Of course, other variables such as the dryness of the earth in the 13,570 km^2 catchment area as a result of the drought would affect the degree of water run-off, which is relatively difficult to determine. The whole catchment area, which had preceding heavy spring rain, underwent a post-cyclonic deluge for four days from January 7, 2011, producing very high water levels in Wivenhoe Dam and other nearby dams. The operations manual for the dam's engineers (as quoted in van den Honert and McAneney, 2011, p. 1157) provides a set of objectives in descending order:

1   ensuring the structural safety of the dams;
2   providing optimum protection of urbanized areas from inundation;
3   minimizing disruption to rural life in the valleys of the Brisbane and Stanley Rivers;

4   retaining the storage at Full Supply Level (for water supply purposes) at the con-
     clusion of the Flood Event;
5   minimizing impacts to riparian flora and fauna during the drain-down phase of
     the flood.

Thus, as van den Honert and McAneney (2011) point out, three of the objectives (2, 3,
and 5) may contain an inherent contradiction of another (4). The manual also provides
four strategies to operate the dam during a flood. These strategies – W1, W2, W3, and
W4 – are set out in an algorithmic path that takes account of the Wivenhoe Dam level
(if it exceeds 68.5 meters, it requires W1). But if above that level, then it requires consideration of the flow at two points, one downstream and one upstream (W2 and W3),
and a different strategy should the dam exceed 74 meters (W4). Thus, compliance
with the manual required choices about release rates and whether to accept weather
forecasts, stream flow information, and drain-down times (Queensland Floods Commission of Inquiry, 2012). In fact, the Bureau of Meteorology's rain forecasts on
January 7 and 8 were out by considerable amounts, 266 mm compared with a forecast
117 mm (van den Honert and McAneney, 2011). Of further concern for the engineers
was that necessary releases of water that flood properties downstream are identified
as a "dam release flood" by the Insurance Council of Australia's hydrologists, which
brings enormous liability implications for the government.

   Thus, to be wise, engineers must not only be knowledgeable but must also evaluate
the salience and reliability of information available to them. At a further level, engineers need from time to time to question the ontological foundations of propositions
and practices. For example, natural weather events are classified in terms of their likelihood: thus, a particular rain event might be described as a "100 year event." However,
global warming is already affecting weather patterns, as NASA and the International
Panel on Climate Change (2013) clearly state. To put this into Aristotelian terms,
the *technē* is based on an episteme, or underlying knowledge base (Aristotle, 1960).
However, Aristotle differentiates infallible episteme from fallible *doxa* and *logismos*
(Barker, 2005). An appropriate contemporary notion of *doxa* is Bourdieu's definition:
"spontaneous belief or opinion [that] . . . would seem unquestionable and natural"
(Bourdieu and Eagleton, 1992, p. 112) or "things people accept without knowing"
(p. 114). Furthermore, people have the capacity for nous, an intuitive capacity that
should act to check actions based purely on the processes of *technē*. Nous, says Aristotle, "is concerned with the ultimate particular . . . [It is] of definitions, for which
there is no reasoning" (Aristotle, 1984, Bk 6, 1142b: 9, 25–28). It can also be defined
as "the insightfulness that makes up for the imprecision of rationality" (Dunne, 1997,
p. 15). Applied to organizations, this capacity for nous forms what Kriger and Malan
call the "invisible . . . soft data" comprising among other things thoughts, feelings,
and volitions (1993, p. 393).

   However, contemporary conditions are not propitious for wise practice, with Küpers
and Pauleen asserting that practices in organizations and institutions are situated
today on a "hostile ground for growing phrónêsis . . . because of technocratic regimes,
excessive managerialism, systems of surveillance and accountability discourses, in
which professionals have numerous and frequently conflicting ruling bodies to which
they are answerable" (2013, p. 5). Given this environment, it is vital to wise practice
that the ethical professional display conation, which in philosophy and psychology

has been understood as a vital element of a trilogy of traits that also include the cognitive and emotional. Conative traits refer to motivation, interests, or more generally "will" (Ericsson et al., 2006, p. 155): it is a proactive volition (Huitt and Cain, 2005). Moral conation is the capacity "to take moral action in the face of adversity and persevere through challenges" (Hannah et al., 2011, p. 664). Moral conation is impossible unless it is incorporated into a suite of proper inclinations and habits that are based on self-awareness and emotional and social intelligence (cf. Eikeland, 2008). This wise disposition comes about through a process of reflexive practice founded on critique and openness to experience, which is the foundation to effective experiential learning (Kolb, 1984). A professional who exercises moral conation would display sufficient courage to do the right thing for the right reasons, regardless of pre-existing rules, laws, norms, or duties (Schwartz and Sharpe, 2006). This requires more than mere compliance with regulations and codified business ethics (McKenna and Rooney, 2012; Rooney et al., 2013) because these often produce an unintended consequence of moral de-skilling.

A further important component of a wise engineering disposition is the emotional component of affect, particularly emotional regulation. It is now well established that emotion and other aspects of affect are fundamental to, not separate from, cognitive processes. However, rather than the hot and cold duality theories of emotion–cognition-based behaviors (for example, Bernheim and Rangel, 2004; Deutsch and Strack, 2006), we assume that attentional and emotional control is carried out by "synergistic" parallel processing streams in the brain (Fichtenholtz and LaBar, 2012; Pessoa, 2008). We also argue that emotional regulation is important because the amygdala initiates reactions to emotionally significant stimuli to various parts of the brain. Evidence shows that emotional reactions can impair effective cognitive functioning, particularly attentional focusing. Anxiety, for example, can affect cognitive functioning. This is particularly so in instances of negative external appraisal where events are "appraised as unchangeable and the self is appraised as helpless and lacking in control" (Matthews and Wells, 2000, p. 80) or a person's negative metacognitive outlook (for example, a pessimistic rather than optimistic frame). We also know from neuroeconomics research of the ostrich effect (shielding oneself from psychologically discomforting information) and that immediate emotions shape our choices (Hodgkinson and Healey, 2011; Loewenstein et al., 2008).

Thus, regulating emotions is important for effective judgment based on clear cognition (Damasio, 2000). Furthermore, the disposition that successfully regulates emotions displays other positive features. Aristotle's wider notion of catharsis, which includes emotional empathy, proposes that people have the capacity to develop insight, to create new meanings and to (re-)organize existing meanings, understandings, and knowledge about all aspects of reality, including such things as human fallibility through what might be called emotional learning. Catharsis fundamentally inspires and emotionally stimulates the imagination to see alternative and better ways of working. According to Berczeller's psychological analysis of Aristotle's catharsis, the "essence of every emotional process is adaption" so that the "unlike attributes of the outside world and our inner subjective life . . . can get along" (1967, p. 269). Regulating negative emotions can be achieved by behavioral regulation, although this is less desirable as it might reduce expressive action, but not dampen unpleasant experience. It also worsens memory and increases sympathetic nervous system activation.

A preferable form is cognitive regulation, which "neutralizes negative experience without impairing memory and might decrease physiological arousal" (Ochsner and Gross, 2005, p. 243). A person's regulatory response is largely determined by normal and pathological variations in wellbeing and social behavior. Emotional intelligence, which comprises emotional regulation and emotional empathy, is positively related to transformational leadership (Barling et al., 2000; Mandell and Pherwani, 2003), and there is evidence that it is also positively related to wisdom (Bergsma and Ardelt, 2012; Kunzmann and Baltes, 2003; Zacher et al., 2013).

Professional balance

At the core of wise practice is balance and integration as one seeks eudaimonic outcomes by mastering the basic dialectics inherent in life: between good and bad, positivity and negativity, dependency and independence, certainty and doubt, control and lack of control, finiteness and eternity, strength and weakness, and selfishness and altruism (Staudinger and Glück, 2011). Another leading wisdom researcher, Robert Sternberg (2001, p. 230) proposes a Balance Theory of Wisdom in which people apply:

> tacit as well as explicit knowledge as mediated by values toward the achievement of a common good through a balance among (a) intrapersonal, (b) interpersonal, and (c) extrapersonal interests, over the (a) short and (b) long terms, to achieve a balance among (a) adaptation to existing environments, (b) shaping of existing environments, and (c) selection of new environments.

Significantly, ancient wisdom traditions and contemporary psychology tend to agree on what constitutes not just wisdom but also the life well lived. A lifestyle that incorporates self-awareness and self-discipline, openness to experience (Helson and Srivastva, 2001, 2002; Mickler and Staudinger, 2008), and empathy has been evident in wisdom writings over the centuries (Cooper, 2012; Curnow, 2010; Küpers, 2013). Thus, philosophy, psychology, and neurobiology are telling us similar stories and developing techniques such as the S-ART model comprising self-awareness, self-regulation, and self-transcendence to develop prosocial behaviors (Vago and Silbersweig, 2012). The role of mentors in providing feedback and an external Archimedean reference point is important in developing the wise professional practitioner (Ericsson, 1996). The concern with these developments, however, is that they become fads and quick fixes rather than being founded on the understanding that phronesis is not an instrumentalist process (Dunne, 1997; Küpers and Pauleen, 2013).

Excessive focus on the psychological aspect of wisdom can occlude the importance of the sociology of practice. Born into our world, we make sense of our experience through a life-world, which is "the anonymous creation of meaning that forms the ground of all experience" (Dunne, 1997, p. 109) and which forms our historically located consciousness (Gadamer, 1979). This experience in life and the conscious and subconscious memories of it are critical in producing intuitive insight and prescience (Edelman and Tononi, 2000; Vygotsky, 1986; Wade, 1996). Within an organization, "the intelligibility of any proposition is derived from its placement within the system" of meaning (Gergen, 2001, p. 21). The social order that we impose on that system of meaning is not just cognitive, but also has relational and ethical dimensions within an overarching framework of values, attitudes, and ideologies that manifest as organizational behaviors (Uhl-Bien, 2006).

How engineers think, then, has a significant influence on the type of society that we are continuously creating. From a cognitive perspective, recognizing and acknowledging that in many cases judgments are made at the intuitive end rather than the analytic end of the cognitive continuum, particularly in complex and dynamic situations, should liberate engineers to articulate this when dealing with peers and clients. Such recognition has implications for creative problem solving and speculating about futures. From an organizational perspective, it was seen that routine can play a positive role, but that critique of the ontological assumptions inherent in those routines wards off such negative outcomes as competency traps and diminished motivation. Superordinating this understanding of the cognitive and organizational processes of engineering is the proposition that the most appropriate *telos* of all human activity is *eudaimonia*, or social flourishing. To achieve this, a wise professional engineer deploys intellectual and moral virtues to better society rather than serve the narrow interests of the client or the employer. In doing this, the wise engineer can also feel reasonably assured that his or her own psychological and social wellbeing will be enhanced. Given that the notion of the wise engineer has not been researched or written about, this chapter hopefully provides an impetus to a new conversation.

Conclusions

As a profession, engineering involves a relationship of trust with society at large which extends beyond their client relationship. Rather than understanding engineering as applying scientific knowledge to technical problems, the professional engineer could be reconsidered as a wise person whose core virtue is the unselfish pursuit of *eudaimonia*, or human flourishing. Because engineers make significant decisions in a political, economic, social, and cultural context, their judgments go beyond mere expertise to incorporate complex contextual factors as well as ethical and societal considerations. Thus, they strongly influence the eudaimonic potential of society.

In practice, the wise person combines *technē* and phronesis. Separating the two is the rather vague notion of *sophia*, which involves a transcendent dimension of understanding the interconnectedness of all things as well as intuitive knowing.

Cognitive capacity would include cognitive complexity, but also intuition and metacognition. The type of task and context, and the complexity of information can determine the extent to which engineers use the three cognitive elements (complex cognition, intuition, and metacognition). Furthermore, because of bounded rationality, heuristics, which are fallible, can be drawn on in decision making. A wise engineer, then, displays a metacognitive capacity that understands the ontological foundations of knowledge, the limitations of routinized applications, the subjective factors of decision making (for example, risk aversion), the framing of questions, and the potential fallibility of intuition.

Considered from a discourse perspective, an engineer can be located as operating at the meso-level of an organization and the micro-level of interpersonal relations and communication. However, a wise engineer understands the broader macro-discursive component that frames knowledge and practice within an ideological and epistemological framework. This framework is not unitary, but involves dialectic forces. A wise practitioner is able to balance and integrate these dialectical forces (for example, good and bad, certainty and doubt, selfishness and altruism) to produce eudaimonic outcomes.

By identifying wisdom as crucial in his or her professional work, the professional identity of a wise engineer would superordinate their personal, organizational, and technical identity. However, the extent which an engineer can act as a wise professional is related to his or her agentive capacity. To use that agency often involves conation or the will and courage to choose the right course of action.

Reflection and critical thinking

1   To what extent do engineers extend their professional relationship of trust with the client to the trust that society places in their work? If engineers were to create an equivalent to doctors' Hippocratic Oath, what would it say?
2   Dennis Gioia admitted his culpable role in the Ford Pinto disaster by adopting the CEO's culture and by inattention. What can we learn about professional responsibility from this story?
3   To what extent do manuals and codification take away the engineers' capacity for wise judgment when deviation from these manuals and codes can expose them to civil and criminal action? Can this be considered a moral de-skilling?
4   As the Wivenhoe Dam example shows, when engineers applied reasonable assumptions to a manual's directions, it still led to a serious flooding problem. Does this support Küpers and Pauleen's assertion that organizational and institutional practices of surveillance and accountability processes can actually present conflicting "imperatives"?
5   To what extent can an engineer draw on intuition, experience, and subjective feelings in performing his or her professional role?
6   Mentoring is a vital element of passing on important cultural practices and tacit and intuitive knowledge, while providing the inexperienced practitioner with the space to make mistakes. How would a wise engineer provide proper mentoring?

References

Allinson, C.W. and Hayes, J. (1996). The cognitive style index: A measure of intuition-analysis for organizational research. *Journal of Management Studies*, 33(1), 119–135.
——. (2012). *The Cognitive Style Index: Technical Manual and User Guide*. London: Pearson.
Alvesson, M. and Kärreman, D. (2000). Varieties of discourse: On the study of organizations through discourse analysis. *Human Relations*, 53(9), 1125–1149.
Argyris, C. and Schön, D. (1978). *Organizational Learning*. Reading, MA: Addison-Wesley.
Aristotle (1960). *Posterior Analytics*. Cambridge, MA: Harvard University Press.
——. (1984). *Nicomachean Ethics*, H.G. Apostle (trans.). Grinnell, IO: The Peripatetic Press.
Barker, E.M. (2005). Aristotle's reform of Paideia. Retrieved from http://www.bu.edu/wcp/Papers/Anci/AnciBark.htm (accessed September 9, 2015).
Barling, J., Slater, F., and Kelloway, E.K. (2000). Transformational leadership and emotional intelligence: An exploratory study. *Leadership and Organization Development Journal*, 21(3), 157–161.
Bauman, Z. (1992). *Intimations of Postmodernity*. London: Routledge.

Beach, L.R. and Connolly, T. (2005). *The Psychology of Decision Making: People in Organizations*, 2nd edn. Thousand Oaks, CA: Sage.

Becker, M.C. (2004). Organizational routines: A review of the literature. *Industrial and Corporate Change*, 13(4), 643–677.

Berczeller, E. (1967). The "aesthetic feeling" and Aristotle's catharsis theory. *Journal of Psychology*, 65(2), 261–271.

Bergsma, A. and Ardelt, M. (2012). Self-reported wisdom and happiness: An empirical investigation. *Journal of Happiness Studies*, 13(3), 481–499.

Bernheim, B.D. and Rangel, A. (2004). Addiction and cue-triggered decision processes. *American Economic Review*, 94(5), 1558–1590.

Biloslavo, R. and McKenna, B. (2013). Evaluating the process of wisdom in wise political leaders using a developmental wisdom model. In W. Küpers and D.A. Pauleen (eds), *Handbook of Practical Wisdom: Leadership, Organization and Integral Business Practice* (pp. 111–132). Farnham: Gower.

Bourdieu, P. and Eagleton, T. (1992). Doxa and common life: In conversation. *New Left Review*, 191, 111–121.

Buse, K., Bilimoria, D., and Perelli, S. (2013). Why they stay: Women persisting in US engineering careers. *Career Development International*, 18(2), 139–154.

Cader, R., Campbell, S., and Watson, D. (2005). Cognitive Continuum Theory in nursing decision-making. *Journal of Advanced Nursing*, 49(4), 397–405.

Chreim, S., Williams, B.E., and Hinings, C.R. (2007). Interlevel influences on the reconstruction of professional role identity. *Academy of Management Journal*, 50(6), 1515–1539.

Conrad, C. (2004). Organizational discourse analysis: Avoiding the determinism-voluntarism trap. *Organization*, 11(3), 427–439.

Cooper, J.M. (2012). *Pursuits of Wisdom: Six Ways of Life in Ancient Philosophy from Socrates to Plotinus*. Princeton: Princeton University Press.

Curnow, T. (2010). *Wisdom in the Ancient World*. London: Duckworth.

Cyert, R.M. and March, J.G. (1963). *A Behavioral Theory of the Firm*. Englewood Cliffs, NJ: Prentice Hall.

Damasio, A. (2000). *The Feeling of What Happens: Body, Emotion and the Making of Consciousness*. London: Vintage Books.

Deutsch, R. and Strack, F. (2006). Duality models in social psychology: From dual processes to interacting systems. *Psychological Inquiry*, 17(3), 166–172.

Du Gay, P. (2000). Entrepreneurial governance and public management: The anti-bureaucrats. In J. Clarke, S. Gerwirtz, and E. McLaughlin (eds), *New Managerialism, New Welfare?* (pp. 62–81). London: Sage.

——. (2003). The tyranny of the epochal: Change, epochalism and organizational reform. *Organization*, 10(4), 663–684.

Dunne, J. (1997). *Back to the Rough Ground: Practical Judgement and the Lure of Technique*. Notre Dame, IN: University of Notre Dame Press.

Edelman, G.M. and Tononi, G. (2000). *A Universe of Consciousness: How Matter Becomes Imagination*. New York: Basic Books.

Eikeland, O. (2008). *The Ways of Aristotle: Aristotelian Phronesis, Aristotelian Philosophy of Dialogue, and Action Research*. Bern: Peter Lang.

Eilon, S. (1969). What is a decision? *Management Science*, 16(4), 172–189.

Ericsson, K.A. (1996). *The Road to Excellence: The Acquisition of Expert Performance in the Arts and Sciences, Sport and Games*. Mahwah, NJ: Erlbaum.

Ericsson, K.A., Charness, N., Hoffman, R.R., and Feltovich, P.J. (2006). *The Cambridge Handbook of Expertise and Expert Performance*. Cambridge: Cambridge University Press.

Fairclough, N. (1995). *Critical Discourse Analysis: The Critical Study of Language*. Harlow: Longman.

Feldman, M.S. and Pentland, B.T. (2003). Reconceptualizing organizational routines as a source of flexibility and change. *Administrative Science Quarterly*, 48(1), 94–118.

Fichtenholtz, H.M. and LaBar, K.S. (2012). Emotional influences on visuospatial attention. In G.R. Mangun (ed.), *The Neuroscience of Attention: Attentional Control and Selection* (pp. 250–266). Oxford Scholarship Online [e-book]: DOI:10.1093/acprof:oso/9780195334364.001.0001

Fiss, O.C. and HIrsch, P.M. (2005). The discourse of globalization: Framing and sensemaking of an emerging concept. *American Sociological Review*, 70(1), 29–52.

Flyvbjerg, B. (2004). Phronetic planning research: Theoretical and methodological reflections. *Planning Theory and Practice*, 5(3), 283–306.

Foucault, M. (1980). *Power/Knowledge: Selected Interviews and Other Writings, 1972–1977*, C. Gordon (ed.), C. Gordon, L. Marshall, J. Mepham, and K. Soper (trans.). Brighton: Harvester Press.

Gadamer, H.-G. (1979). *Truth and Method*, 2nd edn. London: Sheed and Ward.

Gergen, K.J. (2001). *Social Construction in Context*. Thousand Oaks, CA: Sage.

Giddens, A. (1984). *The Constitution of Society: Outline of a Theory of Structuration*. Cambridge: Polity Press.

——. (1990). *The Consequences of Modernity*. Cambridge: Polity Press.

Gioia, D.A. (1992). Pinto fires and personal ethics: A script analysis of missed opportunities. *Journal of Business Ethics*, 11(5–6), 379–389.

Groarke, S. (2002). Psychoanalysis and structuration theory: The social logic of identity. *Sociology*, 36(3), 559–576.

Gunz, S. and Gunz, H. (2008). Ethical decision making and the employed lawyer. *Journal of Business Ethics*, 81(4), 927–944.

Hammond, K.R. (1996). *Human Judgement and Social Policy: Irreducible Uncertainty, Inevitable Error*. New York: Oxford University Press.

——. (2000). *Judgment under Stress*. New York: Oxford University Press.

Hammond, K.R., Hamm, R.M., Grassia, J., and Pearson, T. (1987). Direct comparison of the efficacy of intuitive and analytical cognition in expert judgment. *IEEE Transactions on Systems, Management, and Cybernetics*, 17(5), 753–770.

Hannah, S.T., Avolio, B.J., and May, D.R. (2011). Moral maturation and moral conation: A capacity approach to explaining moral thought and action. *Academy of Management Review*, 36(4), 663–685.

Harteis, C., Koch, T., and Morgenthaler, B. (2008). How intuition contributes to high performance: An educational perspective. *US-China Education Review*, 5(1), 68–80.

Heath, C., Larrick, R.P., and Wu, G. (1999). Goals as reference points. *Cognitive Psychology*, 38(1), 79–109.

Helson, R. and Srivastva, S. (2001). Three paths of adult development: Conservers, seekers and achievers. *Journal of Personality and Social Psychology*, 80(6), 995–1010.

——. (2002). Creative and wise people: Similarities, differences, and how they develop. *Personality and Social Psychology Bulletin*, 28(10), 1430–1440.

Hodgkinson, G.P. and Healey, M.P. (2011). Psychological foundations of dynamic capabilities: Reflexion and reflection in strategic management. *Strategic Management Journal*, 32(12), 1500–1516.

Hogarth, R.M. (2001). *Educating Intuition*. Chicago: University of Chicago Press.

Hope, S. (2013). Neo-Aristotelian social justice: An unanswered question. *Res Publica*, 19(2), 157–172.

House, R.J., Rousseau, D.M., and Thomas-Hunt, M. (1995). The meso-paradigm: A framework for the integration of micro and macro organizational behavior. *Research in Organizational Behavior*, 17(1), 1–114.

Hughes, G.J. (2001). *Aristotle on Ethics*. London: Routledge.

Huitt, W. and Cain, S. (2005). An overview of the conative domain. *Educational Psychology Interactive*. Retrieved from http://www.edpsycinteractive.org/brilstar/chapters/conative.pdf (accessed September 9, 2015).

Ibarra, H. and Barbulescu, R. (2010). Identity as narrative: Prevalence, effectiveness, and consequences of narrative identity work in macro work role transitions. *Academy of Management Review*, 35(1), 135–154.

Intezari, A. and Pauleen, D.J. (2013). Students of wisdom: An integral meta-competencies theory of practical wisdom. In W.M. Küpers and D.J. Pauleen (eds), *Handbook of Practical Wisdom: Leadership, Organization and Integral Business Practice* (pp. 155–174). Farnham: Gower.

International Panel on Climate Change (2013). *Climate Change 2013; The Physical Science Basis*. New York: Cambridge University Press. Retrieved from http://www.ipcc.ch/report/ar5/wg1 (accessed September 9, 2015).

Iyengar, S.S., Wells, R.E., and Schwartz, B. (2006). Doing better but feeling worse: Looking for the "best" job undermines satisfaction. *Psychological Science*, 17(2), 143–150.

Kahneman, D., and Tversky, A. (1979). Prospect theory: An analysis of decision under risk. *Econometrica*, 47(2), 263–291.

Kahneman, D. and Tversky, A. (2000). *Choices, Values and Frames*. New York: Cambridge University Press and Russell Sage Foundation.

Kakabadse, A., Lake, A., and Kakabadse, N. (2008). *The Elephant Hunters: Chronicles of the Moneymen*. Basingstoke: Palgrave Macmillan.

Kaplan, R., Kaplan, S., and Brown, T. (1989). Environmental preference: A comparison of four domains of predictors. *Environment and Behavior*, 21(5), 509–530.

Khatri, N. and Ng, H.A. (2000). The role of intuition in strategic decision making. *Human Relations*, 53(1), 57–86.

Kolb, D.A. (1984). *Experiential Learning: Experience as the Source of Learning and Development*. Englewood Cliffs, NJ: Prentice Hall.

Kriger, M.P. and Malan, L.-C. (1993). Shifting paradigms: The valuing of personal knowledge, wisdom, and other invisible processes in organizations. *Journal of Management Inquiry*, 2(4), 391–398.

Kunzmann, U. and Baltes, P.B. (2003). Wisdom-related knowledge: Affective, motivational, and interpersonal correlates. *Personality and Social Psychology Bulletin*, 29(9), 1104–1119.

Küpers, W. (2013). The art of practical wisdom: Phenomenology of an embodied, wise "interpractice" in organization and leadership. In W. Küpers and D. Pauleen (eds), *A Handbook of Practical Wisdom: Leadership, Organization and Integral Business Practice* (pp. 19–45). Farnham: Gower.

Küpers, W. and Pauleen, D.J. (2013). Introducing a handbook of practical wisdom for our times. In W. Küpers and D.J. Pauleen (eds), *A Handbook of Practical Wisdom: Leadership, Organization and Integral Business Practice* (pp. 1–18). Farnham: Gower.

Loewenstein, G., Rick, S., and Cohen, J.D. (2008). Neuroeconomics. *Annual Review of Psychology*, 59, 647–672.

Long, C.P. (2002). The ontological reappropriation of phronesis. *Continental Philosophy Review*, 35(1), 35–60.

MacIntyre, A. (1985). *After Virtue: A Study in Moral Theory*, 2nd edn. London: Duckworth.

MacKenzie, D. (2009). *Material Markets: How Economic Agents are Constructed*. Oxford: Oxford University Press.

Mandell, B., and Pherwani, S. (2003). Relationship between emotional intelligence and transformational leadership style: A gender comparison. *Journal of Business and Psychology*, 17(3), 387–404.

March, J.G. (1991). Exploration and exploitation in organizational learning. *Organization Science*, 2(1), 71–87.

Matthews, G. and Wells, A. (2000). Attention, automaticity, and affective disorder. *Behavior Modification*, 24(1), 69–93.

McDonald, A.J. and Hansen, J. (2009). *Truth, Lies, and O-rings: Inside the Space Shuttle Challenger Disaster*. Gainesville, FL: University Press of Florida.

McKenna, B. (1997). How engineers write: An empirical study of engineering report writing. *Applied Linguistics*, 18(2), 189–211.

McKenna, B. and Rooney, D. (2008). Wise leadership and the capacity for ontological acuity. *Management Communication Quarterly*, 21(4), 537–546.

——. (2012). Making sense of Irrealis in the GFC. *Culture and Organization*, 18(2), 123–137.

Mickler, C., and Staudinger, U.M. (2008). Personal wisdom: Validation and age-related differences of a performance measure. *Psychology and Aging*, 23(4), 787–799.

Miller, G.A. (1994). The magical number seven, plus or minus two: Some limits on our capacity for processing information. *Psychological Review*, 101(2), 343–352.

Montgomery, K. (2006). *How Doctors Think: Clinical Judgment and the Practice of Medicine*. Oxford: Oxford University Press.

Morris, P. (1994). *The Bakhtin Reader: Selected Writings of Bakhtin, Medvedev, Voloshinov*. London: Edward Arnold.

Nussbaum, M. (1994). *The Therapy of Desire: Theory and Practice in Hellenistic Ethics*. Princeton: Princeton University Press.

——. (2006). *Frontiers of Justice*. Cambridge, MA: Belknap Press.

Ochsner, K.N. and Gross, J.J. (2005). The cognitive control of emotion. *Trends in Cognitive Sciences*, 9(5), 242–249.

Pessoa, L. (2008). On the relationship between emotion and cognition. *Nature Reviews Neuroscience*, 9(2), 148–158.

Pratt, M.G., Rockmann, K.W., and Kaufmann, J.B. (2006). Constructing professional identity: The role of work and identity learning cycles in the customization of identity among medical residents. *Academy of Management Journal*, 49(2), 235–262.

Queensland Floods Commission of Inquiry (2012). *Queensland Floods Commission of Inquiry: Final Report*. Retrieved from www.floodcommission.qld.gov.au (accessed September 9, 2015).

Rooney, D., Mandeville, T., and Kastelle, T. (2013). Abstract knowledge and reified financial innovation: Building wisdom and ethics into financial innovation networks. *Journal of Business Ethics*, 118(3), 447–459.

Rooney, D., McKenna, B., and Liesch, P. (2010). *Wisdom and Management in the Knowledge Economy*. New York: Routledge.

Rosch, E. (2007). What Buddhist meditation has to tell psychology about the mind. *AntiMatters*, 1(1), 11–21.

Ryff, C.D. (1989). Happiness is everything, or is it? Explorations on the meaning of psychological well-being. *Journal of Personality and Social Psychology*, 57(6), 1069–1081.

Ryff, C.D. and Singer, B.H. (2008). Know thyself and become what you are: A eudaimonic approach to psychological well-being. *Journal of Happiness Studies*, 9(1), 13–39.

Sadler-Smith, E. and Shefy, E. (2004). The intuitive executive: Understanding and applying "gut feel" in decision-making. *Academy of Management Executive*, 18(4), 76–91.

Schwartz, B., Ben-Haim, Y., and Dacso, C. (2011). What makes a good decision? Robust satisficing as a normative standard of rational decision making. *Journal for the Theory of Social Behaviour*, 41(2), 209–227.

Schwartz, B., and Sharpe, K.E. (2006). Practical wisdom: Aristotle meets positive psychology. *Journal of Happiness Studies*, 7(3), 377–395.

Simon, H.A. (1945). *Administrative Behavior: A Study of Decision-Making Processes in Administrative Organization*. New York: Free Press.

——. (1955). A behavioural model of rational choice. *Quarterly Journal of Economics*, 69(1), 99–118.

——. (1992). What is an explanation of behavior? *Psychological Science*, 3(3), 150–161.

Sommerville, I. and Kotonya, G. (1998). *Requirements Engineering: Processes and Techniques.* New York: John Wiley & Sons.

Stamps III, A.E. (2004). Mystery, complexity, legibility and coherence: A meta-analysis. *Journal of Environmental Psychology*, 24(1), 1–16.

Stanovich, K.E. and West, R.F. (2000). Individual differences in reasoning: Implications for the rationality debate? *Behavioral and Brain Sciences*, 23(5), 645–726.

Staudinger, U.M. and Glück, J. (2011). Psychological wisdom research: Commonalities and differences in a growing field. *Annual Review of Psychology*, 62, 215–241.

Sternberg, R.J. (2001). Why schools should teach for wisdom: The Balance Theory of Wisdom in educational settings. *Educational Psychologist, 36(4)*, 227–245.

Stryker, S. and Burke, P.J. (2000). The past, present, and future of an identity theory. *Social Psychology Quarterly*, 63(4), 284–297.

Tickell, A. and Clark, G.L. (2001). *New Architectures or Liberal Logics? Interpreting Global Financial Reform.* Future Governance Working Paper 3. Hull: University of Hull.

Tickell, A. and Peck, J. (2003). Making global rules: Globalisation or neoliberalisation. In J. Peck and H. Yeung (eds), *Remaking the Global Economy* (pp. 163–182). London: Sage.

Trowbridge, R.H. (2011). Waiting for sophia: 30 years of conceptualizing wisdom in empirical psychology. *Research in Human Development*, 8(2), 149–164.

Tversky, A. and Kahneman, D. (1974). Judgment under uncertainty: Heuristics and biases. *Science*, 185(4157), 1124–1131.

——. (1981). The framing of decisions and the psychology of choice. *Science*, 211(4481), 453–458.

Uhl-Bien, M. (2006). Relational leadership theory: Exploring the social processes of leadership and organizing. *Leadership Quarterly*, 17(6), 654–676.

Vago, D.R. and Silbersweig, D.A. (2012). Self-awareness, self-regulation, and self-transcendence (S-ART)—A framework for understanding the neurobiology of mindfulness. *Frontiers in Human Neuroscience*, 6, 296. Retrieved from http://www.ncbi.nlm.nih.gov/pmc/articles/PMC3480633 (accessed September 9, 2015).

Van den Honert, R.C., and McAneney, J. (2011). The 2011 Brisbane floods: Causes, impacts and implications. *Water*, 3(4), 1149–1173.

Volosinov, V.N. (1994). Marxism and the philosophy of language, L. Matejka and I.R. Titunik (trans.). In P. Morris (ed.), *The Bakhtin Reader: Selected Writings of Bakhtin, Medvedev, Voloshinov* (pp. 50–61). London: Edward Arnold.

Vygotsky, L. (1986). *Thought and Language*, T.A. Kozulin (trans.). Cambridge, MA: MIT Press.

Wade, J. (ed.). (1996). *Changes of Mind: A Holonomic Theory of the Evolution of Consciousness.* New York: State University of New York Press.

Water (2012). Coal seam gas mining and groundwater: A review of the controversies around and potential impacts of CSG in Australia. *Water: Official Journal of the Australian Water and Wastewater Association*, 39(7), 46–48.

Weick, K.E., Sutcliffe, K.M., and Obstfeld, D. (2005). Organizing and the process of sensemaking. *Organization Science*, 16(4), 409–424.

Zacher, H., McKenna, B., and Rooney, D. (2013). Effects of self-reported wisdom on happiness: Not much more than emotional intelligence? *Journal of Happiness Studies*, 14(6), 1697–1716.

Zaloom, C. (2004). The productive life of risk. *Cultural Anthropology*, 19(3), 365–391.

Chapter 8

Atomic/nuclear weapons and energy technologies

The need for wisdom[1]

Mara Miller

Introduction

In facing the challenges posed by atomic and nuclear weapons (ANWs) and nuclear energy technologies (NETs; collectively ANWETs),[2] society has so far confined its efforts to generating and applying scientific and technological data, information, and knowledge (DIK).[3] But ANWETs present some of the most important and urgent issues facing us; it is therefore important to incorporate wisdom in every stage of both consideration and action. Yet they are also among the most difficult to face (by "face," I mean to consider or decide to think about in preparation for action; the reasons for the difficulty are analyzed below). Even the difficulties are complex, because:

1 atomic and nuclear technologies differ in terms of their capabilities and in underlying processes;
2 weapons require different understanding and handling than energy technologies;
3 governments, the military, and power companies present different problems – and solutions – from those in the hands of rogue states or terrorists;
4 weapons require thinking about disasters we caused in the past, nuclear energy preventing possible disasters in the future, and historical events which present different cognitive, moral, and emotional challenges than hypothetical or even predictable events in the future; and
5 historical events present different cognitive, moral, and emotional challenges than do hypothetical or even predictable events in the future.

But what can we mean by wisdom?

Defining wisdom

Wisdom is best understood not as a personal characteristic – an attribute of the lucky aged – but as the culmination of a progression of data, information, knowledge, and understanding. By "understanding," I refer to knowledge that is complex, a typical condition in many fields where effective functioning depends upon knowledge of one or more subfields, often becoming "intuitive." An orchestra conductor needs knowledge of composers' repertoires, musical styles, capabilities of different instruments, and of individual musicians, perhaps of audiences and boards of directors. And we might say of such a conductor that her knowledge has deepened over time, that she has gained understanding as her experience and information accumulate. Before approaching wisdom, then, we need to extend our DIK "pyramid," inserting "understanding" between knowledge and wisdom. We also should recognize it as a characteristic not only of individuals, but also of populations, workforces, and institutions.

But wisdom moves beyond understanding. Regarding atomic and nuclear weapons and energy, there are (at least) 10 crucial dimensions of wisdom:

1 The ability to go beyond immediate interests and needs, to take the long view.
2 The ability to go beyond one's own and/or one's group's interests and subjective point(s) of view, intellectually and practically; to understand other points of view, even (taking it further) to empathize, even when (taking it yet further) one may not be able to agree with or accommodate them.
3 The ability to combine knowledge from varied contexts in useful ways, enabling us to make connections and recognize similarities – and differences – that apply to a problem.
4 The ability to hold off on action until the time is appropriate, a sensitivity to what the ancient Greeks called *kairos*, a concept spread throughout the monotheistic West (especially Judaism and Christianity) through Ecclesiastes 3:1: "To everything there is a season" (and most recently through the song "Turn, Turn, Turn").
5 Self-knowledge, the ability to recognize one's own strengths and weaknesses, virtues and flaws, and even morally neutral qualities of character, so as to take them into consideration and relate them to the problem at hand.
6 Recognizing the way in which one's own psychological "baggage" – one's personal history and the lessons we have learned – affects one's thinking, emotions, and reactions.
7 Taking responsibility for one's own actions (past and future).
8 The ability to recognize where the general rules of the knowledge base do not apply due to local or specific variation (in many cases, such knowledge can eventually be subsumed into objective knowledge).
9 Discerning, and sometimes setting, boundaries when something is not relevant or appropriate.
10 Knowing when to refrain from acting. Wisdom has an inherent action dimension and an inaction dimension, the capacity to refrain from acting when that is what is called for, the *wu wei* of Daoism). We commonly understand wisdom not simply as a cognitive state or set of attributes, but as an ability to act or refrain from acting in certain ways – to behave in accordance with these "larger" views, to forego immediate gratification in lieu of long-term benefits and benefits to others or the wider community.

These capabilities are typically predicated on a basis of maturity and mental health. The first four of these characteristics amount to ways of seeing the "bigger picture." Number four, *kairos*, comprises an ability to weave together the first three – different kinds of knowledge, what is applicable to different entities and over different lengths of time, and to compensate for them in the interests of accuracy, truth, and fairness. Numbers five, six, and seven carry heavy implications for action or inaction.

These are cognitive and emotional skills and values that can be taught. Indeed numbers one, two, three, and five are typically inculcated through the social sciences and humanities, especially psychology, history, literature, sociology, and philosophy. They also comprise fundamentals of the world's "major" religions, those that philosopher Karl Jaspers (1883–1969) called axial-age religions, that developed between 500 BCE and 200 CE in Persia, India, China, and the Middle East (Judaism, Christianity, Zoroastrianism, Confucianism, Daoism, Buddhism, Hinduism, and so on) that moved beyond local and clan "nature" deities to aspire to universally applicable principles (as opposed to requesting benefits and propitiating gods) and that offered not only solutions to individuals' and community practical needs (health, triumph in battle, fertility) but that also asked questions about the larger meaning of life and the good life for individuals and communities. These "wisdom skills" are also learned through various forms of psychotherapy, "12-Step Programs," support groups, and so on.

Similarities between ANWETs and other technologies

ANWETs are intricately intertwined with other technologies in numerous ways. They rely on information and communications technologies (ICTs) for their production, deployment, surveillance, and delivery systems; many technologies depend on them for power. Technologies share many characteristics:

1   they are complex not only physically and technologically, but also in their social (and other) ramifications, often in seemingly unrelated areas;
2   their effects may be very long-lasting, even permanent;
3   they may also alter human behavior and/or entire environments, even permanently;
4   the changes they bring about are often invisible, with political, ethical, and practical implications that go unnoticed;
5   they may be commercialized for post-industrial consumer culture; and
6   while they increase control in some ways, especially for some stakeholders, they force loss of control over some areas of our lives and communities, sometimes unpredictably.

Differences between ANWETs and other technologies

These similarities, however, only point to equally important differences between ANWETs and other technologies, especially information technologies (ITs):

1   ANWETs lack the thrill factor – space exploration's excitement, relief and gratitude at new medical technologies, and the convenience and sheer fun of flying, driving, and underwater technologies.
2   Most ITs and other technologies are designed to improve life; ANWs destroy it.
3   Thus, ANWs terrify – threatening our control and peace of mind in ways that require not only science but also art for their amelioration.
4   There is a "repugnance factor" (see Miller, in preparation); effects of radiation on bodies are painful to contemplate, nauseating to see even in photographs – and for good reason: repulsion is a physiological reaction protecting us from physical harm.

5   ANWETs present special concerns in terms of both safety and security, since both can easily result in sudden disasters, intentionally and accidentally, severe, widespread, or global, typically long-lasting, and make the physical environment difficult (or impossible) to remediate. And disasters themselves are highly complex events and processes that are "difficult to think" (Oliver-Smith, 2002, p. 23) (see below).
6   Nuclear disasters may also make environments permanently uninhabitable.
7   Their special deadliness in the hands of terrorists means they require oversight on many levels – oversight that itself demands not only knowledge but also wisdom.
8   Moreover, ANWETs strike at the heart of essential core beliefs: that technology is beneficial and controllable; that we have control over our environment and therefore can store materials in a safe, predictable, and unchanging environment over a long period; that we can recover from disaster; and that we are good people who do not hurt children or bomb civilians.
9   Atomic and nuclear effects create a strong version of the reaction I call "tertiary trauma," the trauma caused by exposure to traumatizing events "through the mediation of witnesses' accounts, texts, photographs, and so on" (from Miller, 2012, especially pp. 159–160).

As a result, few technological developments have been more terrifying, more challenging ethically and emotionally, or more demanding of wisdom than nuclear technologies. Moreover, as nuclear power plants proliferate globally and nuclear weapons are developed by more (and sometimes less stable) states and by independent agents, the need to address these challenges becomes more urgent (Union of Concerned Scientists, n.d.), resulting in an increased need for wisdom at every stage and level of consideration and implementation.

Yet for a combination of reasons, both objective and subjective, we seem reluctant to cultivate wisdom with regard to nuclear issues. In addition to a general avoidance of thinking about the bombings of Hiroshima and Nagasaki, there is an unwise resistance even to *considering* positions opposed to one's own, a rush to judgment that precludes wise decision making and prevents new ways to develop and apply wisdom. Far from serving as a model for understanding other technological innovations, our seven decades of experience with ANWETs seems to have resulted in a black hole in which data and information dominate our "understanding," with even knowledge all too rare – and wisdom largely missing.

This chapter explores the need for and use and cultivation of wisdom regarding ANWETs. Wisdom cannot simply be loaded on top of pre-existing priorities/entities/activities or at the apex of our data/information/knowledge/understanding pyramid (see note 3; Bohn, 1994); it must inform those three as they are collected, created, or discovered – although specific recommendations for incorporating it at these levels remains beyond the scope of this chapter.

Disaster

Like other industrial technologies, ANWETs demand consideration not only in and of themselves, but also in terms of their potential misuse, accidents, and disasters. Yet disasters continue to be "difficult to think" on their own, especially as part of ongoing activities such as energy production that are presumably peaceful and beneficial, and now routine. As recent researchers have observed, our ways of thinking about disasters remain unsatisfactory; consequently, our ways of dealing with them are also unsatisfactory. As disaster research has progressed over the past several decades, disasters are coming to be recognized as more complex than was thought. Kenneth Hewitt (1997, p. 26, quoted by Oliver-Smith, 2002, p. 3) recognizes three categories of disaster agents: "natural hazards (atmospheric, hydrological, geological, and biological), technological hazards (dangerous materials, destructive processes, mechanical, and productive), and social hazards (war, terrorism, civil conflict, and the use of hazardous materials, processes, and technologies)"; "Triple Disasters" (the earthquake, tsunami, and damage to the Fukushima nuclear power plant that resulted in the irradiation of the surrounding environment) of March 11, 2011 show how easily they can cascade or trigger one another, to tragic nuclear effect.

Anthropologist Anthony Oliver-Smith recommends recognizing disasters, first, not as discrete events with clear beginnings and endings, but as *processes*, results of long-contrived patterns of interaction between society, precipitating forces, and the environment that create patterns of vulnerability over time. He further characterizes disasters as "multidimensional": "all-encompassing occurrences, sweeping across every aspect of human life, impacting environmental, social, economic, political, and biological conditions" (Oliver-Smith, 2002, p. 24).

Christopher L. Dyer (2002, p. 165) points out that technological disasters often "have cumulative effects known as 'secondary disasters' (Erickson 1976), which include cultural, social and economic impacts that persist long after the event and that negatively alter or destroy affected communities (Dyer 1993)."[4] Dyer (2002, p. 164) recommends paying more attention to the ways in which secondary disasters can result in what he terms the "punctuated entropy paradigm:" a "*permanent* decline in the adaptive flexibility of a human cultural system to the environment brought on by the cumulative impact of periodic disaster events [that] explains the nonrecovery of human systems after a disaster . . . [since] the opportunity for recovery is compromised by repeated disruptions to the human system."

Like other disasters, nuclear disasters are processual, multi-dimensional, and can lead to secondary disasters with punctuated entropy.

Moreover, disasters related to ANWETs typically carry a special need to react urgently. In ways that contrast with our overall need to strategize for long-term safety and security, with atomic or nuclear events requiring an urgent response, it becomes important in two distinct timeframes – the immediate response and the need to be proactive regarding prevention – since to the extent that we deny the problems that crop up, postpone dealing with them, or procrastinate in confronting these issues in general, we increase the likelihood of incurring an emergency in the future. Such planning is already part of the normal military, corporate, and governmental handling of nuclear issues. But when it occurs within the dominant social paradigm's framework of understanding in terms of adversarial relations, zero-sum game theory, and economic and systems theory that ignores human emotions and insight, there are limits to what it can accomplish.

Difficulties of facing the issues

ANWETs are difficult to face for three kinds of reasons – objective, subjective, and blended – that is, the ways they interact. Understanding these reasons helps us understand the need for wisdom – and what kinds of wisdom we need.

Objective difficulties

ANWETs present unique challenges, making wisdom especially crucial for a variety of reasons, including: 1) objective factors such as the unique degree and type(s) of danger they pose; 2) their spatial, geographical, and temporal scales (mentioned above); 3) the multiplicity of their effects; 4) the invisibility of radiation; and 5) the consequent need to rely on expert and technical evidence. In addition, 6) the newness of ANWETs means we have not had the centuries – indeed, millennia – that most cultures have had for developing social and technical coping mechanisms addressing natural disasters indigenous to their locales.[5] Moreover, 7) some symptoms, (such as people seeming fine, then suddenly succumbing to fatal disease) are unfamiliar (in ways that interact with subjective factors; see below). Since 8) ANWETs are scientifically complex, they require elaborate cooperation among companies, agencies and governments for their development, safe use, and oversight. This scientific complexity leads to further problems: 9) decisions continue to be made by technocrats, meaning first 9a) that they are often beyond oversight ("transparency" is limited) and, second, 9b) that these individuals are often employed by companies or local or regional governments with vested interests in the NW/NETs and limited interest in exploring both "worst-case scenarios" and even, in many cases, actual outcomes.[6] Their danger and complexity 10) demand *regulation* for safe use – regulation at all levels, which itself requires oversight – and by disinterested parties.[7]

Moreover, undesirable ANWETs events 11) easily result from and/or interact with other kinds of disasters.

Given all this, it is perhaps not surprising that needs for safety and security, scientific complexity, and the public's *reactions to* information dissemination by the "nuclear establishment" both shape the dissemination of DIK about ANWETs and too frequently limit it to "experts" – who are selected by industrial/commercial and governmental/military powers. These powers and their experts must indeed have DIK access. But 12) in a democracy, the public also needs access (Arkin, 2014). Where should we draw the line between needs for safety and security, and the elimination of security by dispersing DIK too broadly? How should we draw that line during periods of disaster – when people's (including first responders' and nuclear authorities') cognitive abilities are impaired by fatigue, injury, stress, and hunger? And 12a) commercial and industrial agents' need for privacy is also legitimate, given their need to make a profit; however, in both commercial and governmental cases, the need to protect their reputations and limit legal and financial liability often trump the public's right to know. 12b) The desire to avoid criticism and public humiliation has, in many cases, led to censorship of DIK. (See below.) 13) In addition to censorship (both admitted and secret), there are documented cases of governments and companies covering up the truth and/or issuing deceptive data and information – practices which also inculcate widespread public mistrust.

Subjective difficulties

Subjective factors also make ANWETs difficult to face. The fact that atomic and nuclear disasters remain real possibilities in our future leads not only to anxiety and evasion/denial, but also to questioning why we tolerate these risks. While this could be a wise questioning, it more frequently leads instead to cognitive dissonance – the holding of conflicting attitudes, beliefs, or behaviors that results in discomfort, and to the consequent desire for dissonance reduction, by changing one of the attitudes, beliefs, or behaviors to reduce the discomfort and restore balance and harmony.[8]

One means to dissonance reduction regarding potential dangers is the adoption of a "no-risk" thesis, as analyzed by anthropologist Robert Paine (2002, p. 68): "The no-risk thesis is one of cognitive repression of risk." It is the societal equivalent of the individual's psychological phenomenon of "denial," comprising:

> the preclusion of doubt and the effective elimination of ambiguity . . . the shutting out of perceptions of the world, and of what is or is not possible, that others may hold. It also involves shutting out the perceptions other people have of those who embrace no-risk; the notion of insulation is thus crucial. A person or group, then, that proceeds and persists with its enterprise despite its associated danger and does so without risk calculations, ideally embraces the no-risk thesis.
>
> (Paine, 2002, p. 69)

This is the very antithesis of wisdom. Yet people do embrace the "no-risk" hypothesis with regard to ANWETs. One of the studies Paine analyzes is of radiation protection experts, studied by Sharon Stephens in the same volume. He points out:

> The radiation protection experts flounder for a politically acceptable way of letting an anxious and suspicious public know that there are risks attached to nuclear energy and nuclear accidents, and that their knowledge is none too reliable. Yet the message the experts send to the public is essentially: Stop thinking about risks, everything is under control.
>
> (Paine, 2002, p. 72)

People often embrace danger; the worst danger comes from pretending that the real dangers do not exist.

There are three further points to note. First, insofar as we accommodate ourselves to the adoption of the no-risk hypothesis (for some aspect of our lives), it generates value where otherwise none would exist. The result is a logic of extreme behavior in extreme circumstances.

Second, this sense of value predicated on the no-risk hypothesis, with its extreme human behavior, may create or promote extreme circumstances, sometimes intentionally, in a self-reinforcing cycle. Third, behavior that looks "extreme" to an outsider observer is likely to be understood as "adaptive" in the minds of the committed (Paine, 2002, p. 69). Paine (2002, p. 71) finds that "ritualized behavior tends to take the place of rational calculation, and in neither case is risk calculated."

Combinations of objective and subjective factors

Interactions between subjective and objective factors may create new difficulties, such as feedback loops, and subjective orientations (or attitudes, and so on) so widely shared within a social or scientific community as to mimic "objectivity." A number of complexities augment the difficulties of cognitive processing at times of disaster.

Miscellaneous factors

In addition to deficiencies in our models of disaster, few populations are (mentally or organizationally) prepared, and physically outfitted, to deal with industrial disasters in general and radiation accidents and disasters in particular (a subjective liability). This places warning, containment of effects, rescue, recovery, and rebuilding in the hands of experts to an unusual degree – a simple matter of fact, widely shared among many societies that are otherwise different. These experts need both scientific language and professional cognitive and emotional frameworks to help them cope – but both the language and the distancing frameworks place them even further from the public whom they are obligated to help at time of enormous stress.

Anthropologist S. Ravi Rajan describes a pattern he calls "missing expertise," objectively demonstrable but varying according to local culture and disaster, in which "the production of the potential for [a new, typically technological] risk is not matched by a concomitant creation of expertise and institutions with the wherewithal to help mitigate a crisis, should one ensue." In such cases, while some problems have been foreseen and prepared for, others are completely ignored and there is no one to address them when they do arise. Often this relates to special difficulties involving local knowledge (from sociological and political to topographical and biological); the knowledge in accordance with which the new systems have been instituted is "objective" and scientific, thus failing to take into account local deviation from the norms of the society that generated that "objective" knowledge.

This relates to the concept of "categorical politics," which refers to "the civil society, and in particular, activist organizations . . . forms of political intervention that are driven solely by framing social problems via some overarching structural analysis, and that either ignore or dismiss phenomena that are not visible through their theoretical lens." His concern is that "the combination of missing expertise in the state and the preponderance of categorical politics within civil society often produces a pattern of vulnerability that results in perpetrating chronic disasters" (Rajan, 2002, pp. 237–238). Other blended objective/subjective factors include experts' and first responders' legitimate needs to distance themselves psychologically/emotionally, and others' (victims', witnesses') equally valid needs (to survive personally, to prioritize finding family) that may conflict with those of experts and first responders. Subjective factors also include those that have been objectively (quantitatively, scientifically) verified: certain now well-documented idiosyncrasies in human cognitive processing (such as risk-assessment under various conditions) and crowd behavior in disasters – which Irving Janis (1962) has shown is by no means principally driven by panic – and so on.

Complexities multiplying the problems: feedback loops

Workers at NET companies may also find themselves in the double role of victims in an accident – meaning their abilities to act and think normally may be affected, and their personal and family interests may be opposed to their work responsibilities.

Feedback loops complicate cognitive processing and dissemination of DIK, making wisdom more imperative. At times of actual or threatened disasters, conflicts arise over everyone's, including the experts', need for expertise, the experts' need to protect themselves from tertiary trauma and to distance themselves psychologically, and their consequent retreat into hyper-rational abstract language and arcane jargon, the demands placed upon experts to lie – out of legitimate fears of inflaming public fear and/or the fear of public humiliation or retaliation – and the public's increasing mistrust of experts. These mutually reinforce one another, leading to feedback loops between the perceived needs to contain information (whether legitimate or not is irrelevant to this point) and people's awareness that they have been misled or lied to, and their resulting mistrust.

A second feedback loop results from censorship. Censorship is not only an objective "fact" about a culture (during a certain period) – it is one that deeply shapes that culture, including people's willingness to take on risk (of punishment, incarceration, death at the hands of authorities, and the risks posed by the censored information itself). And it not only occurs at the current time, but affects the future dissemination of DIK, which has not flowed freely throughout the system during the censorship period. Beyond that, censorship over time leads to customs of "self-censorship," so that people may continue habits of not sharing information and knowledge even after legal censorship ends.

Combinations of objective and subjective factors: temporality

We have already seen how the needs for urgent response to disasters and urgent planning for possible future disasters and other incidents may conflict with the overall long-range orientation crucial to nuclear planning of all kinds. Temporality, philosophers' term for our understanding and experience of time, is an important factor in understanding how we fall short in dealing with ANWETs. There are at least three aspects to this: the (objectively verifiable) temporalities inherent in radiation and related events; the multiple objective and subjective temporalities of unfolding disasters themselves; and the temporality of past/future or historical versus hypothetical events. Since wisdom typically incorporates nuanced and sophisticated awareness of time, it will prove helpful in addressing these difficulties.

Temporalities of disasters in general

Disasters in general unfold according to peculiar and varying temporalities:

1   Many people find their inner sense of time distorted in emergency situations, speeding up and slowing down unpredictably.
2   Disasters prompt immediate response – which is often, however, "hurry up and wait" for conditions to change so that the aid can reach victims.
3   First responders, whose own instinctive urge is to rush, are trained to approach methodically and carefully – to "take their time" even against the urging of desperate bystanders or victims.
4   Beyond this, anthropologist Oliver-Smith urges us to reframe disasters as processes that are the outcomes of behaviors and patterns of events long in the making, rather than as the instantaneous inescapable cataclysms we normally view them as.
5   Other disaster analysts point out that the few days we commonly think of as "the disaster" open a new stage in a society's life that may change over months, years, or decades – or, as Dyer and Rajan remark, may be permanent.

The anomalous temporality of radiation

Like the symptoms of radiation poisoning that had never before been witnessed, the temporality of atomic/nuclear events and radiation's effects are anomalous by the standards of normal (pre-atomic) physics. Objectively, there is the (in some cases unfathomably) long life of radioactivity, which varies with the isotope (whose invisibility makes it impossible to identify, confirm, and quantify without special equipment, adding to the uncertainty), and which can therefore have long-lasting effects. Although some human cultures have conceptualized lengths of time that are in themselves inconceivable – Hindu and Buddhist *kalpas*, modern astronomers' light years – we rarely try to use them in everyday planning. Our plans for storage of nuclear waste suffer from this shortsightedness and might be remedied by adopting the Seneca-Iroquois principle of planning for the next seven generations.[9]

There are also the peculiarities of the temporal unfolding of radiation symptoms. Rather than the typical curve of effects diminishing over time, some radiation effects strengthen or appear suddenly after months, even years. Such variables wreak havoc with customary systems of time and temporality, making wisdom all the more crucial. The threat of nuclear accidents and of the use of nuclear weapons, with their potential to destroy whole environments and even the earth, cast a pall on several generations' understanding of their future.

The past: the use of the atomic bombs on Hiroshima and Nagasaki

The US is the only agent to have used atomic weapons. (Any justification for doing so and the reasons it should *not* have done so are outside this chapter's purview.) International law already proscribed the bombing of civilians.[10] International condemnation of the 1937 bombing of Guernica by Nazi pilots at Franco's request had been severe; indeed, unannounced bombing of civilians by both the Allies and the Axis powers soon became routine during World War Two.

This moral opprobrium means that our experience with our past use of atomic weapons weighs us down and makes it psychologically (and socially, emotionally) difficult to confront the ANWETs issues. In addition to terror regarding possible repetition, many of us, including US citizens, feel guilty and/or ashamed, or at least conflicted about them, regardless of whether we were even alive at the time.

It is this subjective response – our inner conflict and/or inner certainty – that concerns us here. Even the certainty with which many have assured me that the US "had" to drop the bombs is presented with such vehemence that one cannot help but recognize it as a defensive posture. These feelings of moral repugnance, of revulsion both at violating international customs and legal agreements and at violating them in such an abhorrent way (exacerbated by the second bombing, which may not have "been necessary," even if the first was), make it all the more difficult to confront any of the related issues – and to cultivate wisdom. But they are also why the job cannot be done right unless we cultivate wisdom.

A sense of collective guilt, shame, and/or embarrassment makes it very difficult to contemplate these actions. Yet even this collective guilt is especially difficult to think about because very few people had any decisive role in their manufacture or delivery, much less in the decision making. (The situation is quite unlike those in Nazi Germany and in the US with regard to indigenous populations.) While most living US citizens may be said to have benefited in at least some way by the dropping of the atomic bombs, in what sense are they responsible for decisions and actions taken by our government without their knowledge (and perhaps before their birth)?

This brings us to the issues of collective versus individual memory and collective versus individual guilt – areas coming under increasing scholarly scrutiny, but which are also the subject of some (although not enough!) examination within existing wisdom traditions.

These are not the only such decisions that people have been rethinking over the past half-century, of course; the atomic bombings take their place among genocides and anti-ethnic actions of many kinds. Yet the top-secret nature of the atomic events and their restriction to so few individuals absolves most of us from a sense of responsibility – a seeming complacence we should re-examine, especially since, given that we have profited from them, we may bear responsibility for ongoing situations in particular, and since our non-responsibility, to which we have understandably become accustomed, does *not* carry over to situations today.

The future

The US continues to be the only major power not to renounce "first use" of nuclear weapons. It consequently bears responsibility for continuing implicit threats against the rest of the world – as well as for continuing production. In addition, the transportation of radioactive materials and the safe, long-term storage of nuclear arsenals and nuclear waste cannot be guaranteed; leakage is also a problem. (In some cases, as at Rocky Flats, Colorado, nuclear waste is buried atop seismic faults, susceptible to earthquake.) The Union of Concerned Scientists recently released a report saying that safety and security measures and training at US nuclear facilities are not meeting avowed standards. As I write, senior federal nuclear expert Michael Peck, formerly Diablo Canyon's lead on-site inspector, has issued a 42-page confidential report charging that "the Nuclear Regulatory Commission is not applying the safety rules it set out for the plant's operation" (Blood, 2014).

Ethics and moral issues

The use of ANWs and both permitting or facilitating accidents or terrorism with NETs are morally repugnant; this can result in shame, embarrassment, and guilt – all of which can make it more difficult to face the issues. Professors frequently cite guilt and shame as reasons that they and others do not teach about them. Reparations and apologies are two means by which countries recently have begun to redress the wrongs they have perpetrated against populations; however, these remain only partial – though necessary and valuable – solutions, unless we address other issues as well.

These other issues include serious debate over:

1 how and why such events occur;
2 what can be done to prevent them in the future;

3   why we are so vulnerable to them in the first place; and
4   what we can do to make ourselves stronger.

Most religions include these aspects of moral development for individual persons, but they are rarely developed for populations as a whole – although certainly the emphasis of many religions on living within a like-minded community of believers, be they Amish, Buddhist, Christian, or Muslim, moves in this direction and acknowledges our vulnerabilities and the difficulties of maintaining ethics challenged by the standards of another community. What we need, however, is further exploration of how communities of different kinds and sizes and with differing types of organization can develop wisdom outside of the ties of shared religion – and how they can share their values without insisting on permanent affiliation or identification with the group, on shared belief, on generating hatred, or creating an "other" whom our in-group despises. The peace studies and wisdom movements focus on construction of positive action.

We also must take seriously Jonathan Shay's (2002, 2010) three-part concept of moral injury, which pertains when the agreement over what is morally correct has been betrayed by someone considered a legitimate authority in a high-stakes situation.[11] Exploration of moral injury has focused especially on effects of witnessing and on therapy; it should be expanded to encompass perpetrators and exploration of the moral and ethical dimensions per se.

The need for wisdom

As we have seen, nuclear/atomic technologies present special challenges. But what is wisdom in and for this context? How does wisdom enter into our relations with atomic bombings and nuclear energy? More importantly, whether it has in the past or not, should it in the future? And, if so, how? How do we even identify wisdom? Where can we see it so as to be able to study it? What does wisdom even mean in this connection? What further developments in wisdom should we be trying to encourage – and by/ among whom? How can wisdom be cultivated and enhanced within a given individual and within communities – including business and research communities? What examples do we have of such developments of wisdom and how might they apply in this case?

Do ANWETs require more – or different kinds of – wisdom? And, if so, how and why? This chapter relies on findings from industrial disasters such as Bhopal. How can we ensure that we learn everything we need to across types of technology and/or disaster? An early conference on changing medical ethics at Yale University illustrated the pitfalls of relying on medical experts in extreme care and end-of-life issues and how important it is to include all stakeholders.

Should we be trying to change our models? Traditionally the Western model understands wisdom as something: a) that was a property of individuals, not societies or communities; and b) that would develop almost naturally with aging – if it developed at all. In Asia, by contrast, wisdom has been cultivated more deliberately as part of the various religious traditions. And historically we turn to leaders to institutionalize social change. However, the anti-nuclear power movement in southwestern Massachusetts succeeded largely because it avoided leadership and centralization, allowing a hydra-headed approach.

Equally importantly, what, if anything, might we learn about how to handle other forms of technology by developing our capacity for wisdom in relation to ANW/NET? Is this set of developments really so anomalous, so *sui generis*, that there is nothing to apply to other fields of technology?

Wisdom and the dominant social paradigm

But many modern systems of thought and education, which are widespread in what is referred to as the current Dominant Social Paradigm (DSP) (Catton and El Dunlap, 1980), actively *counter* our propensity to realize these capabilities, damaging our abilities to develop these skills and values, and preventing us from communicating about them easily. They do this by (among other things – this list is not exhaustive) teaching us to understand social problems in terms of "zero-sum games"[12] and individual-versus-society adversarial relations (the latter the spine of most modern Euro-American social and political philosophy and legal thought); by promulgating dichotomous thinking ("subjective versus objective," qualitative versus quantitative, material versus spiritual, cognitive versus emotional, scientific versus artistic, nature versus nurture), which often promotes clarity, but at the expense of truth, accuracy, nuance – and wisdom; by ignoring the subtleties of non-linguistic communication that contribute to empathy with others; by under-valuing empathy and subjective modes of understanding and processing – and, for that matter, deriding well-established paradigms of knowledge and skill that do not fit the DSP, thereby lowering the prestige of skills and values, and even social roles and institutions that do not fit the DSP. While these modern skills and values have proven invaluable – indeed, how could we have manufactured nuclear bombs without them? – we must go beyond them now if we are to survive and thrive in the post-modern – post-atomic – era. Fortunately, there is a growing movement, including many scientists and even government agencies, that has begun this process.

Western, Eastern and other wisdom traditions, theologies, and spiritual approaches contribute to our development of wisdom, and thus can have a positive impact on our relationship with and use of technologies. From an Aristotelian perspective, of course, simply knowing what the right course of action is goes a long way in enabling us to do it, but in addition, a number of Eastern and other strategies can help enormously, particularly in countering our panicky resistance to facing the issues.

Developing and cultivating wisdom for dealing with both ANWETs and disasters

What does wisdom consist of in this context? Minimally, it would require that we follow Socrates' and Shakespeare's injunction to "Know thyself," including the limits of our power (scientific, political, and other). We must acknowledge our acts in the past and our "sins of omission" as well – the safeguards we are not taking, the truths we did not tell. We must begin thinking in the long term – and bring into the discussion over just which long-term costs are permissible more of those who will share in paying those costs. (Admittedly there will always be some – children, the unborn – who might bear the burden of nuclear accidents without having any say.) We must practice thinking hypothetically – including the question "what if we don't know everything?"

Understanding why it is necessary to confront our use of atomic weapons in the past and of nuclear power

In light of the tertiary trauma, the revulsion, the self-reproach, the unpleasantness, difficulties and risks, what can possibly justify imposing this knowledge on ourselves, much less others?

The gist so far has been that the difficulties posed by atomic and nuclear weapons and energy technologies require us to approach them with wisdom. But there is another perspective as well. What would considering them wisely contribute to our own development as individuals and societies? There are (at least) 17 reasons ANWETs are important for all of us to think about, to come to terms with – to develop wisdom regarding.

This task leads immediately to the need for wisdom, given the obvious inadequacy of the standard categories (of data, information, and knowledge) that are used to address the situation. Although they are invaluable – indeed, essential – in relation to atomic and nuclear weapons and energy, they are limited relative to our needs. These distinctions among DIK are especially important as our teaching about the atomic bombings can easily get bogged down completely at the level of data or information.

Conclusions, implications for practitioners and general audiences

This chapter analyzes our need for wisdom in dealing with atomic and nuclear technologies primarily in terms of the dangers and challenges these technologies present us with – whether we are willing to recognize them or not. But in the end, there is another perspective on our need for wisdom in this regard, namely, what we have to gain from cultivating the wisdom to confront these issues and their risks and our deeds not only in practical terms, but also as individuals, as a nation, and community members of various kinds. It is not just a matter of increasing our safety and security – of trying to increase the odds of continuing in our world as a relatively safe and pleasant place to live rather than an apocalyptic nightmare, important as that is – but also of developing ourselves. It is a matter of developing individual and collective wisdom so as to deal with – even resolve – issues of atomic and nuclear safety and security, disasters already caused and possible in the future, moral and physical and other damage done and preventable, so that we preserve and develop ourselves, our societies, and our environments, and become better and stronger. This can only be done if we develop and use wisdom regarding our atomic and nuclear weapons and energy technologies.

Compared to information technologies, ANWETs permit far less active involvement and manipulation, yet they have the power to transform the lives of all of us, often without our foreknowledge. There is no one who is unaffected, no one who is free to opt out. We must all take responsibility rather than leaving the decision making in the hands of nuclear experts.

In particular, we must all explore ways in which our communities and organizations can develop wisdom so as to generate more solutions on different levels and of different kinds. The peace studies and wisdom movements are leaders in positive action. Wisdom cannot simply be loaded on top of pre-existing priorities/entities/activities or at the apex of our data/information/knowledge/understanding pyramid; it must inform our thinking and our actions as consistently possible.

Reflection and critical thinking

1   Atomic and nuclear weapons and energy technologies present issues that are both important and urgent; we should therefore incorporate wisdom in every stage of both consideration and action.
2   Wisdom, a combination of skills and values that should culminate in the progression of data, information, knowledge, and understanding, should be developed not only in individuals, but also in populations, workforces, and institutions.
3   ANWETs require thinking about disasters; because these are so horrific and are intrinsically "difficult to think," this is especially difficult and especially necessary – and wisdom is needed.
4   Past atomic disasters we have caused raise issues of moral injury, guilt, shame, horror, and self-disgust, making it difficult to contemplate our actions. Wisdom is needed if we are to integrate this part of our past and take responsibility for our actions.
5   Wisdom regarding ANWETs is not just a matter of increasing safety and security, but of developing ourselves individually and collectively.

I stated above that our seven decades of experience resulted in a black hole in which data and information dominate our "understanding," to the extent that even knowledge is all too rare – while wisdom about how to handle these and similar issues is largely missing. Far from serving as a model for understanding other technological innovations or guiding us in self-knowledge and in preservation of our species, our cultures, and our environment, they have been abscesses causing continuing pain and damage to us as individuals, as nations, and as communities of various kinds. Wisdom as we move forward can change that.

Notes

1   I would like to thank the organizers and audiences at the Hiroshima Peace Studies Institute's Conference on Teaching about the Atomic Bombings (2003), the University of Hawaii at Manoa's Numata Conference in Buddhist Studies (2014) and Center for Japanese Studies, Drexel University, and the Canterbury Historical Society (Christchurch, NZ), for opportunities to present my ideas about the atomic bombings and for their feedback and perspectives, and Professor Paul Bracken and the other members of the Yale School of Management for the opportunity to participate in their faculty seminar on nuclear weapons.
2   In spite of the differences between atomic and nuclear technologies, this chapter examines primarily issues that ANWETs have in common. Although atomic and nuclear technologies differ, for brevity's sake I have shortened the acronym with the understanding that both energy and current weaponry are nuclear, not atomic.
3   I refer here to Roger Bohn's classic distinctions between data, information, and knowledge: "Data are what come directly from sensors, reporting on the measured level of some variable. Information is data that have been organized or given structure – that is, placed in context – and thus endowed with meaning . . . Knowledge goes further; it allows the making of predictions, causal associations, or predictive decisions about what to do" (Bohn, 1994, p. 61).

4 References are to Erickson, K. (1986). *Everything in its Path: Destruction of Community in the Buffalo Creek Flood*. New York: Simon & Schuster; Dyer, C.L. (1993). Tradition loss as secondary disaster: The long-term cultural impacts of the Exxon Valdez oil spill. *Sociology Spectrum*, 13(1), 105–126.
5 Dyer (2002, p. 164) points out that: "For noncumulative events such as . . . earthquakes, or floods, societies possess adaptive flexibility, also described as 'equilibration' . . . Equilibration – adjustment to changed environmental conditions in the face of new sociotechnological exigencies – is well documented in the ethnographic literature."
6 This phenomenon is well-studied in disaster-containment and-management literature, as well as by anthropologists, for example Hoffman and Oliver-Smith (2002).
7 Sharon Stephens (2002, p. 94) states that: "Every country with a nuclear industry has at least one nuclear regulatory agency. The United States has at least sixteen federal agencies and twenty congressional committees, and each of the fifty states has its own regulators." According to Catherine Caufield (1989, p. 167): "Together, these groups make up what its supporters call the radiation protection community and its critics refer to as the nuclear establishment."
8 Leon Festinger's (1957) cognitive dissonance theory suggests we have an inner drive to hold all our attitudes and beliefs in harmony and avoid disharmony (or dissonance). See also Festinger (1959, 1964); and Festinger and Carlsmith (1959).
9 According to Seneca/Haudenosaunee chief, legal scholar, Civil War hero, and Cabinet-level commissioner Ely Parker (1844–1865): "The Seventh Generation philosophy is integral to Haudenosaunee life," (PBS, n.d.); and "The Peacemaker taught us about the Seven Generations. He said, when you sit in council for the welfare of the people, you must not think of yourself or of your family, not even of your generation. He said, make your decisions on behalf of the seven generations coming, so that they may enjoy what you have today," Oren Lyons (Seneca), Faithkeeper, Onondaga Nation (PBS, n.d.).
10 The US had subscribed to this tenet. Michael Walzer (1977) provides a history of this development.
11 He introduced the concept in *Odysseus in America: Combat Trauma and the Trials of Homecoming* (2002) and *Achilles in Vietnam: Combat Trauma and the Undoing of Character* (2010). See also Litz et al. (2009), who argue that the individual who commits the objectionable act(s) may incur moral injury.
12 The eradication of conceptualizing negotiations in terms of "zero-sum games" has recently become a standard tenet of business and military curricula.

References

Arkin, J. (2014). Briefing the President but keeping the public in the dark. Center for Public Integrity, August 14. Retrieved from http://www.truth-out.org/news/item/25569-briefing-the-president-but-keeping-the-public-in-the-dark (accessed September 11, 2015).

Blood, M. (2014). Expert calls for closure of California nuclear power plant. Associated Press, August 25. Retrieved from http://www.staradvertiser.com/news/breaking/20140825_Expert_calls_for_closure_of_California_nuclear_power_plant.html?id=272574721 (accessed September 11, 2015).

Bohn, R.E. (1994). Measuring and managing technical knowledge. *Sloan Management Review*, 36(1), 61–73.

Catton, W.R. Jr. and El Dunlap, R. (1980). A new ecological paradigm for post-exuberant sociology. *American Behavioral Scientist*, 24(1), 15–47.

Caufield, C. (1989). *Multiple Exposures: Chronicles of the Radiation Age*. Chicago: University of Chicago Press.

Dyer, C.L. (2002). Punctuated entropy as culture-induced change: The case of the Exxon Valdez oil spill. In S.M. Hoffman and A. Oliver-Smith (eds), *Catastrophe and Culture: The*

Anthropology of Disaster (pp. 159–185). Santa Fe, NM: School of American Research Press and Oxford: James Currey.

Festinger, L. (1957). *A Theory of Cognitive Dissonance*. Stanford, CA: Stanford University Press.

——. (1959). Some attitudinal consequences of forced decisions. *Acta Psychologica*, 15, 389–390.

——. (ed.) (1964). *Conflict, Decision, and Dissonance*. Stanford, CA: Stanford University Press.

Festinger, L. and Carlsmith, J.M. (1959). Cognitive consequences of forced compliance. *Journal of Abnormal and Social Psychology*, 58(2), 203–210.

Hewitt, K. (1997). *Regions of Risk: A Geographical Introduction to Disasters*. London: Addison Wesley Longman.

Hoffman, S.M. and Oliver-Smith, A. (eds) (2002). *Catastrophe and Culture: The Anthropology of Disaster*. Santa Fe, NM: School of American Research Press and Oxford: James Currey.

Janis, I.L. (1962). Psychological effects of warning. In G.W. Baker and D.W. Chapman (eds), *Man and Society in Disaster* (pp. 55–92). New York: Basic Books.

Litz, B.T., Stein, N., Delaney, E., Lebowitz, L., Nash, W.P., Silva, C., and Maguen, S. (2009). Moral injury and moral repair in war veterans. *Clinical Psychology Review*, 29(8), 695–706.

Miller, M. (2012). Terrible knowledge and tertiary trauma, part I: Teaching about Japanese nuclear trauma and resistance to the atomic bomb. *The Clearing House: A Journal of Educational Strategies, Issues and Ideas*, 86(5), 157–163.

——. (in preparation). Aesthetics of the person: Atomic and nuclear disfigurement.

Oliver-Smith, A. (2002). Theorizing disasters: Nature, power, and culture. In S.M. Hoffman and A. Oliver-Smith (eds), *Catastrophe and Culture: The Anthropology of Disaster* (pp. 23–47). Santa Fe, NM: School of American Research Press and Oxford: James Currey.

Paine, R. (2002). Danger and the no-risk thesis. In S.M. Hoffman and A. Oliver-Smith (eds), *Catastrophe and Culture: The Anthropology of Disaster* (67–88). Santa Fe, NM: School of American Research Press and Oxford: James Currey.

PBS (n.d.). Ely Parker 1844–1865. Retrieved from: http://www.pbs.org/warrior/content/timeline/opendoor/roleOfChief.html (accessed September 11, 2015).

Rajan, S.R. (2002). Missing expertise, categorical politics, and chronic disasters: The case of Bhopal. In S.M. Hoffman and A. Oliver-Smith (eds), *Catastrophe and Culture: The Anthropology of Disaster* (pp. 237–258). Santa Fe, NM: School of American Research Press and Oxford: James Currey.

Shay, J. (2002). *Odysseus in America: Combat Trauma and the Trials of Homecoming*. New York: Scribner.

——. (2010). *Achilles in Vietnam: Combat Trauma and the Undoing of Character*. New York: Simon & Schuster.

Stephens, S. (2002). Bounding uncertainty: The post-Chernobyl culture of radiation protection experts. In S.M. Hoffman and A. Oliver-Smith (eds), *Catastrophe and Culture: The Anthropology of Disaster* (pp. 91–112). Santa Fe, NM: School of American Research Press and Oxford: James Currey.

Union of Concerned Scientists (n.d.). Nuclear power. Safety first. Now. Retrieved from http://www.ucsusa.org/nuclear_power (accessed September 11, 2015).

Walzer, M. (1977). *Just and Unjust Wars: A Moral Argument with Historical Illustrations*. New York: Basic Books.

Chapter 9

The human–computer relationship
Who shall survive?

Philip D. Carter

Introduction

As part of the effort to understand the dynamics between technology and humans, it is useful to look at the evolution of human consciousness. By appreciating the profound shifts that created the conditions for invention, technology may be liberated from a narrow utilitarian identity. It was fascination with the inner world of the mind – the dreams, wishes, aspirations, and imaginings – that inspired and informed invention. Similarly, our current collective dreams and imaginings give us glimpses of the future. It will be useful to look at these not so much through the rose-tinted lenses of the techno-evangelists or the warp of science-fiction writers, but more through the sensibilities of ordinary people.

We will consider how these insights can inform us in order to make useful decisions and direct our efforts with technology to create a more humane world. It would be useful to have a vision that is both practical and inspirational, so that in the face of real difficulties, we will not lose nerve. There are many underlying dynamics of evolutionary significance that have a determining influence on our design and use of technology, including: creating a workable way for both individual liberties and the wellbeing of the group to co-exist; integrating thinking with conscience; and developing a sober and realistic attitude to living in a universe that is complex, uncertain, and uncontrollable.

Technology and consciousness

Technology is typically considered to be a tool that has some operation of control over something. The beginning of technology is imagined as the epiphany of some clever ape smashing things with a stick. However, technology's birth was far more interesting:

> The critical moment was man's discovery of his own many-faceted mind, and his fascination with what he found there. Images that were independent of those that his eyes saw, rhythmic and repetitive body movements that served no immediate function but gratified him, remembered actions he could repeat more perfectly in fantasy and then after many rehearsals carry out.
>
> (Mumford, 1966, p. 45)

Apes still bash sticks, but none of them have concocted a screw or a knitting needle. They have been standing up, walking around with thumbed hands and free mouths for a long time. It was not the cunning of the hands or looseness of tongue that inspired and drove the stupendous cascade of human invention. Lewis Mumford made a sustained and detailed inquiry into the development of technology and offers multiple illustrations of how:

> Technics has been deeply modified at every stage of its development by dreams, wishes, impulses, religious motives that spring directly, not from the practical needs of daily life, but from the recesses of man's unconscious . . . It was initially through the fabrication of the mind, through dream and symbol, not alone through the cunning of his hands, that man learned to command his own bodily organs, to communicate and cooperate with his kind, and to master so much of the natural environment as would serve his actual needs and ideal purposes.
>
> (Mumford, 1970, pp. 415–416)

Seeing the intimate relationship between technology and the inner worlds of the mind can help free up technology from being equated with utility and control, and have it ready for the broader identity and role it will have for creating a more organic and humane society. However, this is no small thing. Liberation will require a shift in consciousness which was set up 5,000 years ago and is now the ground on which we approach thinking and seek understanding, the material we use to shape our identity.

Five thousand years ago, all things were considered and experienced as having an innate spiritual essence. Deities were part of an organic being of a living universe, agents of various cycles, like supervisors administering things that they had neither created nor controlled. Then there was the entrance of an omnipotent god, controlling nature, sending down floods, and delivering punishments. This god created humans in his own image, also having freedom of will:

> Along with – and as a consequence of – this loss of essential identity with the organic divine being of a living universe, man has been given, or rather has won for himself, release to an existence of his own, endued with a certain freedom of will. And he has been set thereby in relationship to a deity, apart from himself, who also enjoys free will.
>
> (Campbell, 1972, p. 76)

The Egyptian variety was the sun god, a deity of power, progress, and prestige. In an extraordinary feat, the Egyptians assembled a mega-machine to construct the pyramids. Modern institutions and bureaucracies can find their ancestor there. Change was an urgent value, progress was considered ordained by heaven, and to retard it was to go against nature (Mumford, 1970). Immense concentration was given to exploration and conquest. Later, this worldview was reinvigorated with modern science. Copernicus reasserted the sun as the central source and Newton fixed in absolutism; a mechanical universe where order was beauty. Christianity was infiltrated and easy adjustments were made to its narrative to emphasize the God-given right to have dominion over the material earth while waiting for entrance to the true home in heaven. The narrative of power, prestige, profit, and progress is deeply ingrained through centuries of sustained practice. It penetrates our thinking and works without us giving conscious attention to it.

Even to speak in the manner I am is a kindred approach which has not escaped the presiding narrative. In this chapter I am proposing a liberation from a mechanistic and power complex out into an organic and humane one, yet the writing and arguments have the same old familiar characteristics: that there is a problem or a crisis that must be solved and progress made. I could protest that I am relating to an evolving universe within a meta-context of learning, but I am not sure. I cannot align all my thoughts and descriptions into a neat thesis. And, in seeing that, I relax. Being in the unknown with an attitude of curiosity and inquiry is the very evidence I would expect if I am really coming up with something novel, something that is not saturated with the surety and narcissism that characterizes the prevailing mindset. My intent is telling. Or will be. That is, I will see clearer in time what my intent is. And I will better know in reflection to what extent I have indulged in selective inattention and whether the message is arrogant or over-cautious. I do have a strong commitment to questioning myself and updating on the presentation of new evidence, and, in that, I feel encouraged to continue to question other things, even our cherished ideas of progress and choice.

First, let us look at the idea that survival is the main mechanism of evolution. This is limited. The appearance of warm-blooded beasts suckling their young and the spread of flowers over the earth cannot be explained away as purely survival (Eiseley, 1946). If safety and surety were so central, then why would life have crept out of the primeval ooze? There would only have to be one thing, whatever it was; that would be it. No conflict or threat need ever arise. But there was differentiation. This is something very close and known to us, and was also a profound mystery.

Relationship

A central insight that provoked Darwin's theory of evolution was that everything in nature exists and grows within a relationship. Even time and space can be seen to be the result of a relationship (Buber, 1958). This can be appreciated by contemplating the dynamics between the earth and the sun and how they create the sequence of events on which we conceptualize time. If time is a product of the relationship, then the earth–sun "time" is just one of the many relational fields in which we find ourselves. Our immediate relationships offer different spreads of experience. When one is facing impending death in an accident, the passing of things can be slow. After one has been "in the flow," that is, totally immersed in an enjoyable activity, there is surprise at how much "real" time has passed. It should not be surprising (but it is) to also discover that the individual brain is fundamentally relational. The interpersonal neurobiologists (Badenoch and Cox, 2010; Siegel, 1999) are finding that there is a socially constructed schema in the brain and that this social self is not formed out of reason, language, or a self-identity, but *pre-dates* them: "It appears that mutual recognition and identification are the progenitors of reason, self-consciousness, and culture rather than vice-versa. This understanding overturns the cherished assumption that social behavior results mainly from a learning process mediated by a formal language" (Schermer, 2010, p. 492).

Further contemplation of the dynamics between relationship, time, and space will reward us with a fresh understanding of the deep structure of the universe, particularly if we factor in the operation of a spontaneity force that is non-conservable and non-causal. In the meantime, while interested minds ponder this, let us consider what we already know about the practical aspects of relationship dynamics: the qualities that revive us, uplift our spirits, inform our actions, and provoke new experiences. These are the immediate things that we can work with to have a positive impact on our design and use of technology.

Attitudes for work and daily life

Like two sets of ripples on a pond, things interpenetrate each other: individual and group, imagination and reality, agency and object, mind and brain, creator and created. This is no abstract idea; it is what we are in and it affects and involves our hearts and our emotions, our deepest feelings. The reflection of the moon on water, the leaves of a tree in the breeze, a bird in flight: appreciation of these things uplifts the spirit and gladdens the heart. It can be called grace, in that it comes free and unearned.

Appreciating these things evokes calmness: a humble and sober attitude that brings spaciousness to our experiences. One can make a commitment or dedication to being mindful of these things, of giving attention to this experience when it arises. There will be an amplification of positive effects in our dealings with the world. It becomes an attitude to life that has the qualities of devotion without being dependent on some external locus of authority.

In another effort of maturity, we can be accountable and self-responsible, yet at the same time responsive and in relation to the other, a mutual taking in of the other, without being subsumed or dominated. We can make a commitment to developing cooperative working relationships. This will revitalize our institutions, independent of their political structure. Reciprocity does not mean the parties have to be equal in power. It does not mean that everyone has to agree with or even understand the other. This is not something that can be itemized into a list or manual, but is an attitude of care with a default assumption of respect that is the beating heart and essential engine of any institution.

A small example of building cooperation is our experience in developing a system usability lab. We found that we did not need expensive equipment or elaborate processes of analysis. By getting alongside users, we could develop a simple co-inquiry into the user's experience while they were still situated in the use of the artifact. We called this situated co-inquiry (Carter, 2007). Engaging with a user during their use of a computer system was considered to be interfering. However, we found by developing a cooperative working relationship and tuning into the user's warm-up, the user could sustain his or her experience. The bulk of the analytical work could be done *in vivo*, with clarification from the user where necessary. Situated co-inquiry also became a useful method for collaborative design.

Laws and policy and their enforcement can inflate beyond their scope of usefulness when there is a vacuum of adequate family and organizational relationships, when insufficient emphasis and work is put into building professional practice. No matter how appropriate a law or policy, without the commitment and practice of reciprocity and personal responsibility, it can end up harming the people it intends to protect.

When we are accompanied, there is a calming affect. We need not react to every bit of bad news as some catastrophic error requiring an additional measure of bureaucratic control. Participation and appreciation can be like a rolling force building on its own successes. When people make contributions they are not required to do, goodwill spreads. The imagination prospers under such conditions of friendliness. There is a spaciousness for the generation of ideas to face new challenges.

The universe is complex, uncertain, and uncontrollable. The unknown can be embraced as the place where movement and learning occur. In the adventure into the unknown, life arises. Becoming interested in learning to live in the unknown requires vulnerability, a letting go of seeking simplistic and premature solutions. It is a step up into maturity and taking responsibility, to differentiate, and to be an individual. The alternative is an escalation of resignation, helplessness, and fright, which creates the vacuum in which institutions turn mean, dictators relish, and totalitarian regimes flourish.

Difficulties are anticipated. We could consider them as opportunities. Such things as invisibility and lack of appreciation are but great opportunities to practice humbleness, inquisitiveness, and tenacity. Surrender may be practiced, in the sense of a letting go of the ego and narcissistic assertions. There is the coming into a sensitivity to the experience of the self and the actual situation. Pain and uncertainty are certain and life cannot be lived free of them. Practice in living with pain will build resilience independent of what conditions arise in the future: deferring to authority and abdicating responsibility will diminish; ideologies will not inflate out of control; bureaucracies will not harden into being bullies. Our attention and energy turn to working with things exactly as they are, building on what we have, expanding our experiences. Chances of success in our endeavors increase. So too does the likelihood of technologies being designed to enhance human consciousness and experience.

As an experiment, we could shift our primary focus from objects to the act. We could see that the value of a work of art is in its ability to evoke further acts of creativity. Intelligence can be defined as the ability to act appropriately. Knowledge can be considered an act rather than a thing (Fromm, 1957). The emphasis moves from dogma to transformation. Mistakes are responded to from a learning perspective, not a punitive one. Learning is an act of getting to know something that was not known, not as memorization and repetition. New experience is realized as more satisfying than new things. The experiential can replace materialism. Love is not an abstract idea but an act. The goal is not to think right, but to act right.

Such a paradigm shift will release computer systems from being designed as though knowledge exists in things. It will prepare designers to appreciate process and workflow, and how technology can benefit and add to these processes. This will be in myriad ways, following formal and informal lines, in obvious and unexpected ways. For example, a system designed for clinical handover in a hospital will do well to recognize the skill of a highly experienced doctor as she uses the particular presenting situation of a patient to give junior doctors training, even though such training is not considered to be part of the handover. A system designed to streamline getting new patient information in hospital admissions will benefit by factoring in the urologist with 30 years of experience who is particularly adept at prompting elderly patients to remember and identify relevant things.

An appropriate design for a new system with a clear description of user requirements will never result solely from a manual or a checklist; there are too many nuances and exceptions in every human endeavor. Successful design will be assisted considerably by the development of certain abilities, such as astute observation, fluidity in changing perspectives, and a deep understanding of systems and their dynamics. Perhaps of most use, and always a go-to and recovery, is curiosity.

In our own image

The deed has been done – the computer is born. We have done a god act and created in our own image, as symbol creators and manipulators. The computer is a different order of thing from the knitting needle, the pipe, the screw, watches, lathes, or even the printing press. It is mechanized logic, an astonishing synthesis of engineering with symbol. We have taken abstraction itself and made it into an extraordinary machine.

It must now be up to us. We can no longer be under the illusion that anything or anybody else can save us or rectify the damage we have already done. We must do all we can so that technology is set up within a wider caring to create wellbeing for all. There is no choice.

Mumford did not blame technology and our absorption in it for our loneliness and unnatural plight. He regarded technology as a formative part of human culture as a whole. Technology was a reflection of our imaginative capacities, intimately integrated within the creative and humane elements of civilization:

> a broad streak of irrationality that runs all through human history, counter to man's sensible, functionally rational animal inheritance. As compared even with other anthropoids, we might refer without irony to man's superior irrationality. Certainly human development exhibits a chronic disposition to error, mischief, disordered fantasy, hallucination, "original sin," and even socially organized and sanctified mis-behavior, such as the practice of human sacrifice and legalized torture. In escaping organic fixations, man forfeited the innate humility and mental stability of less adventurous species. Yet some of his most erratic departures have opened up valuable areas that purely organic evolution, over billions of years, had never explored.
>
> (Mumford, 1966, pp. 10–11)

Mumford (1970, p. 423) visualized a certain detachment and withdrawal that could "lead to the assemblage of an organic world picture, in which the human personality in all its dimensions will have primacy over its biological needs and technological pressures." He did not say it was to be simple: "To describe even in the barest outline the multitude of changes necessary to turn the power complex into an organic complex, and a money economy into a life economy, lies beyond the capacities of any individual mind" (p. 423).

This will not be through the efforts of any one person, but will require a combined effort of many people doing the different things in line with their expertise and sensibilities. Our challenges are multiple: to integrate the power of ideas and ideals with heart and conscience; to be individuated and self-determined, no longer emotionally dependent, propped up by deferring to authority and avoiding responsibility; to enter into a relationship with each other and the universe with mutuality and reciprocity; and to become match-fit in living under conditions of uncertainty. This is the universe in which each moment is a new moment, the sum of all things that have come before, a deep interpenetration of intent and action in an ongoing unfolding of astonishing magnificence and horror.

Building collegiality and a commitment to reciprocity are highly effective in facing these challenges with nerve and imagination. When there are acts of kindness that are not earned or deserved, the spirit is uplifted, the group is heartened, and an atmosphere of goodwill permeates all relations. We are then much better placed to be in touch with things as they are. We are much better placed to come up with a response that will be effective. Perhaps our nature to be unnatural, to be nature's wild card, the force that breaks boundaries, that teases and torments the remaining gods, that tries the outrageous can be seen as an addition rather than a detriment. Apparently, we will not take the sensible approach to safety and survival, but must ride the edge of insanity as though we had a choice in the matter.

The future?

> You must give birth to your images
> They are the future waiting to be born
> Fear not the strangeness that you feel
> The future must enter you long before it happens.
>
> R.M. Rilke

New technologies get talked up; extraordinary claims are made for transformation and empowerment in a brave new world. This hype is keenly suffered by many professionals in the IT industry who have been repeatedly set up with unrealizable expectations. At the other pessimistic end, movie scriptwriters and novelists look into the future and see scenarios that are typically more hell than heaven. These stories we have about the future are important if only because creative endeavor tends to get channeled their ways. What then are the stories ordinary people have about the machine? What collective form is coagulating around our individual experiences, fears, dreams, and aspirations? What is the collective will and intent that will be shaping our future with the machine?

I assembled several groups and used the unscripted action methods of psychodrama to tap into a cross-section of ordinary people (Carter, 2010). Psychodrama is a discipline dedicated to evoking spontaneity through experiential dramatic means. Spontaneity is seen as a catalyst for creativity, enthusing the emotions and the intellect. In the 100 years since J.L. Moreno (1953, 1983, 1985) first conceptualized psychodrama, a rich body of knowledge and theory has been built up and applied across different domains (see www.pdbib.org).

In our inquiry, group members were invited to lay out their "truth" about "the machine," whatever that might mean to them: their experiences, reflections, dreams, fears, and aspirations. This was a collective production. One group member would enact a role and another would take a role in response to that. In this way, the different dynamics emerged. The group took moments to pause and to reflect, to see if anything was missing, to experiment with a new element, or to have one role encounter another. Our intention was to tune into what was significant, what was emerging, what had energy in order to create an accurate representation of our experiences and our imaginings. In an unusual move for psychodrama, I took some of the common elements across the different group enactments – the metaphors, images, actions, and characters – and scripted a story somewhat in the style of a fairytale or fable. Let us call it "The Picnic." In the spirit of ongoing creation, I have refined what was presented in Carter (2010).

A family was in a car going to a picnic.

"Look, what was that?" Dad asked. "Was it a Porsche? Maybe a Jag?"

But Daughter was texting and Son was playing a computer game.

"What?" Dad said. "Aren't you interested in cars? When I was young, we used to have so much fun in the car. We'd guess the brands of cars. Were Morris Minors the most popular or Volkswagens? Some thought Cadillacs were the best. In my day we had great times in the car. We used to sing songs and squabble."

They went off the main road onto a country road. Mother saw a bird in a tree.

"You don't have cars like you used to. They used to have character back then," said Father. "Now they're all the same."

"Sometimes I think you love cars more than me," said Mother.

He turned to look at her; the car went off the road and hit a rock. It wouldn't start again. They all got out. Father walked around the car.

"Fix it then," Mother said.

But he couldn't. He called for help. It wasn't going to come until the next day. That night they slept in the car as best they could. The next morning the sun came up. They wound down the windows but it was still very hot.

A Repairman came. He put his toolbox down three steps in front of the car. He paced around the car. He brought out a large piece of paper and opened it out. "This is not the car that has been scheduled to be fixed."

"Can't you fix it anyway?" Father looked at the toolbox.

The Repairman shook his head.

"It's a long way to come out," said Father.

"Exactly." He folded his schedule and put it in his toolbox.

"What about us?" said Mother.

"We can't take responsibility for you." He picked up his toolbox and left.

The next morning, the sun came up like a very large eye. Another Repairman came. He put his toolbox down three steps in front of the car. He paced around the car. He brought out the schedule and opened it out. "What happened?"

"It won't start," said Father.

"But it has not ended its warranty. It cannot be a problem of the car but a problem of the way it was used."

"We hit a rock," said Son.

"A-ha," said the Second Repairman. He folded up his schedule and picked up his toolbox.

"But you can't go," said Mother.

"I cannot fix a car that isn't broken."

"That's ridiculous," said Father.

"Do I look happy?" said the Second Repairman. "How do you think it is all on my own out here?"

"We have been here for two days," said Mother.

"Does the sun ever go down on the machine? Does a machine ever complain? We have no right to be weak; we must grit our teeth and do our duty."

"The machine is to serve us," said Mother, "to help us with the washing, to get us to picnics."

"To make us go fast," said Father.

But there was no way to convince the Second Repairman to stay and fix the car. There was not a cloud in the sky. He left. It was very hot and dry. The next morning, the sun came up, bigger and hotter and drier. A man came. He had a rope.

"What's the rope for?" asked Daughter.

"It's a comfort thing." The Man had the rope around his foot like a sling. "It keeps me amused."

"Can I use it for a clothesline?" asked Mother.

"Sure," said Ropeman.

"Can you repair cars?" asked Father.

"Yes, but I need oil."

"I have a liter in the back."

"Very good."

"You can have my Son as an Apprentice," said Father. "He isn't good with words. He's not gifted as a guard, he doesn't want to be a doctor, let him learn how to fix the machine. What other kind of work is there?"

"Machines give me comfort; to fix them is worship."

"Then fix ours."

"We have to synchronize the gears. We must work out how to mesh the gears. Can you help me? Can you humor me? Could you become the different parts of the car?"

"I don't know," said Mother, but she did anyway.

One person was a rod, another a gear, someone else a wheel, someone a piston. They jostled and poked, turned and moved around. They laughed a lot and almost fell in a heap. This was what Father had in mind for the picnic all the time. Even Mother was having a good time.

"Even you are having a good time," Father said.

"Yes, so strange. I feel free," said Mother.

A Researcher appeared with a questionnaire on service satisfaction. He made them read the consent forms and he told them they always had a choice; they didn't have to contribute to knowledge and human progress if they didn't want to. They signed the consent forms and filled in the questionnaire.

"I will be recommending improvements," said the Researcher. "Do you know they are developing an engine that speaks to you: an engine that can fix itself. Imagine that!"

"We want it to work for us now," said Mother.

"It is our tools that have made us great," said the Researcher. "If we can, then we must."

"We just want to get to the beach for a picnic," Mother said.

"Oh, don't you know?" The Researcher picked up a rock. "This is the beach."

"Where's the water?" said Daughter.

"It's been split into fuel and burnt. Unfortunate."

"The planet has been bled?" said Father.

"What about the fish and everything?" said Daughter.

"We're the last things left."

Father fell to his knees and cried. "We should have listened. We should have paid attention to the signs."

"All I've tried to do is look after everyone and make them safe," said Mother.

"Nothing left?" said Daughter. "Not even crabs?"

"Crabs," said Son who was piling rocks into a pile.

And that gave Ropeman a new idea. He whistled while he worked to give this thing he was making a body and legs. He put it down on the dried-out beach.

"Look!" said Son. "A crab."

And Daughter laughed and played with it too.

Father was standing with his head and arms raised to the whole round world. "We have got to get into relationship."

The children started played with the crab because eternity is a very long time.

There are many interesting dynamics presented in the story. One surprising finding in the groups was that the people enacting the machine in the dramas (vending machine, intelligent ticketing system, car) had a lot more energy and spontaneity than those people enacting the people in the scenarios (the user, the repairman, the helpdesk operator). One participant said:

> I was so surprised when I became the vending machine. It was fun. I didn't expect that because normally I don't like machines but I had such fun. It was like a holiday. I didn't have to think or prove anything. I could have gone on like that for a long time. There was no fatigue.

Reflecting on these experiences, we recognized that there was a tremendous relief when enacting the machine because there was no moral burden. There was a freedom and liberation from being human, a freedom from self-consciousness. Perhaps this indicates that technology per se is not equated with isolation from nature, domination, or destruction of life. This is good news for those working to integrate technology within a larger, more organic, and humane approach to life.

The future may be brighter than what we expect, for reasons other than what we think. Openness, naïvety, and curiosity all have extraordinary power to uplift the spirit, evoke spontaneity, and encourage collegiality, learning, and adventure. These are necessary sensibilities for the psychodrama producer. The empty stage is faced with a readiness for the unknown, a conviction that new things will happen, that the truth is not to be predetermined.

In IT, analysts of existing systems and designers of new ones do very well to inculcate such sensibilities. This may be a challenge given that they are considered the experts. Willingness to be honest and have integrity puts us on the path to face up to our own prejudices and assumptions, and thereby have an opportunity not to be a slave to them. Curiosity and naïve inquiry of another tends to warm them up to be accompanied in a co-inquiry. They are less likely to be defensive and feel shame when facing things that may not reflect so positively on them or how they operate in an organization. The systems analyst gathering user requirements will then have a much better chance to perceive the formal and informal channels of authority and workflow in the organization. The ability to design a system based on the actual reality of a group is increased and the work to cultivate the necessary buy-in to the new system is already initiated. Fluidity in movement between naïve inquiry and analysis can be practiced and developed. How psychodramatists train in these attitudes is illustrated by Clayton and Carter (2004), which may be accessible to others if they can tolerate the psychodrama jargon.

The motivation for collegiality arises, the commitment to reciprocity builds, we become involved, our collective and individual efforts of will and imagination gather momentum. Let us hope so. A more sober analysis of our chances of doing what is required, of growing up into the maturity needed to liberate ourselves, would have to reveal that they are slim. We have consistently indulged in childish ways, denying reality and avoiding responsibility. Little has changed save one thing: our technologies have the potential to wreak far greater damage than ever before. This must create the conditions in which we will wake up. It has to.

It will take an extraordinary provocation to initiate a movement from the power complex to an organic one. It will take a sustained participation by all manner of people in myriad ways. The motivator may well end up being love. The cherishing of the things we deeply care about might be the only thing strong enough that can turn us from our habitual self-absorption and impel us forward into the acts of service, guardianship, and creativity that are now required.

Perhaps, in taking that challenge up fully with no guarantee of success, we will earn for ourselves the self-esteem that we have only given the gods the rights to confer. We might settle into being, even if failure appears likely. We may come to dwell in this world in a manner that we have dreamt of for a very long time. We will do it because it is impossible.

Conclusions, reflection and critical thinking

1   It is the fascination with the inner world of the mind that has evoked technology and invention, more so than what was initiated by the hands or survival needs.
2   Technology per se need not be equated with isolation from nature, domination, or destruction of life.
3   With the computer, we have done a god act and created in our own image: that is, as symbol makers and manipulators.
4   The stories we are making up about the future are indicative of the actual future if only because our current creative efforts are being directed that way.
5   Explicit focus on self-responsibility and reciprocity will encourage companionship and a collective approach. This will moderate our fears and thereby weaken the grounds on which ideologies can oscillate out of control, institutions can act unethically, and technology can be used inappropriately.
6   We may prosper in a universe that is complex, uncertain, and uncontrollable.
7   Loving care for what we cherish will provide the fuel and liberation for the impossible acts required to move from a power complex to an organic one.

References

Badenoch, B. and Cox, P. (2010). Integrating interpersonal neurobiology with group psychotherapy. *International Journal of Group Psychotherapy*, 60(4), 463–481.
Buber, M. (1958). *For the Sake of Heaven*, L. Lewisohn (trans.). New York: Meridian Books.
Campbell, J. (1972). *Myths to Live by*. New York: Penguin Compass.
Carter, P. (2007). Liberating usability testing. *Interactions*, 14(2), 18–22.
——. (2010). The emerging story of the machine. *International Journal of Technology and Human Interaction*, 6(2), 1–12.
Clayton, G.M. and Carter, P.D. (2004). *The Living Spirit of the Psychodramatic Method*. Auckland: Resource Books.
Eiseley, L. (1946). *The Immense Journey*. New York: Vintage.
Fromme, E. (1957). *The Art of Loving*. London: Unwin.
Moreno, J.L. (1953). *Who Shall Survive?* New York: Beacon House.
——. (1983). *The Theatre of Spontaneity*. New York: Beacon House. (Original work published 1924.)
——. (1985). *Psychodrama*, Vol. 1, 4th edn. New York: Beacon House. (Original work published 1946).
Mumford, L. (1966). *The Myth of the Machine: Volume One: Technics and Human Development*. New York: Harcourt.

Mumford, L. (1970). *The Myth of the Machine: Volume Two: The Pentagon of Power*. New York: Harcourt.

Schermer, V.L. (2010). Mirror neurons: Their implications for group psychotherapy. *International Journal of Group Psychotherapy*, 60(4), 487–513.

Siegel, D.J. (1999). *The Developing Mind: How Relationships and the Brain Interact to Shape Who We are*. New York: Guilford.

Chapter 10

Academic ethos

Embracing a culture of practical wisdom in higher education

*Alex E. McDaniel, Michael A. Erskine,
and Diane R. Watkins*

Introduction

Technologies have always presented a disruptive force in education and this will undoubtedly continue as the evolution of technology accelerates. The ubiquity of technology in the hands of learners is undisputed. From the papyrus of antiquity to the smartphone of today, technology has often caused disruption in education. Such disruption is perceived both positively and negatively as it progresses through the hype cycle that accompanies technological advancements (Clegg et al., 2003). Empirical research shows that learning may be enhanced (Parker and Chao, 2007) or hindered (Fried, 2008) through technology. For example, historically, researching answers during an exam may have been considered a breach of academic integrity. Yet, in contemporary society, not utilizing technological advances to solve a problem may be considered a significant disadvantage. Is it wise for higher education to hide behind the shield of academic integrity in order to avoid dealing with the various undefined issues that accompany innovative technologies?

Just as the adoption of the calculator changed the way in which mathematics is taught, all disciplines must pragmatically embrace technological advancements (Plowman, 2000). It is essential to be mindful of academic outcomes and adjust the practices of teaching to incorporate phronesis at its core. Such action is essential to adapt to the reality of contemporary learning. Instead of prohibiting technology and access to the wealth of information that is available to learners, we need to evaluate ways to make the incorporation of technology into the learning process less punitive and more beneficial.

This chapter explores academic ethos as higher education's commitment to implement and sustain a culture of practical wisdom. Practical wisdom is the ability to accurately perceive any situation, discern multiple viewpoints regarding the situation, reflect, think dialectically and dialogically about the situation, formulate appropriate responses, and act accordingly (Schwartz and Sharpe, 2010). As rapid technological change presents a challenge towards achieving academic ethos, we argue the importance of imparting practical wisdom to learners. With the ease of access to information, the role of an educator has changed to being a guide, helping to navigate and interpret the over-abundance of information. By imparting practical wisdom, students learn to discern information relevance, credibility, and applicability. The process of judiciously applying what is learned is the core of practical wisdom and is a necessary skill in today's society.

Higher education presents immense challenges, but by using the principle of academic ethos, educators can approach the challenges produced by rapidly changing and emergent technologies with inclusivity toward such advances. Academic ethos is a philosophical standpoint allowing educators and educational institutions to embrace rapid technological advancements while maintaining the fundamental principles of imparting knowledge and cultivating wisdom. It takes higher education beyond preparing students simply to be a "more competitive item of human capital" (Clegg et al., 2003, p. 51) to being independent thinkers with the practical wisdom to morally inform and influence society in positive ways. Academic ethos is about giving opportunities to others so that they may have the freedom to make wise choices. It is about helping students to acquire the knowledge, skills, and moral values that they need to live safe and fulfilled lives, as contributing citizens, in a multi-cultural world; it is about developing enquiring and ethical minds, as well as the desire to help create a sustainable and more peaceful world (Rüegg, 1986).

While this chapter addresses the impact of technology on the academic ethos, the findings also apply to governmental, non-profit, and for-profit organizations. As disruptive technologies are introduced within organizations, it is essential to cultivate the respective ethos of the organization through the application of practical wisdom. To highlight these principles in a way that is easily translated and familiar to all, the remainder of this chapter continues to explore this phenomenon through the domain of higher education.

The role of academic ethos in higher education's integration of technology

Throughout recorded human history, technology has been one of the disruptive forces in the zeitgeist, or intellectual, moral, and cultural climate of each era. The notion of technology's disruptive nature on both culture and the practices of teaching and learning is in no way a novel concept. The cycle of reforming academic ethos repeats during times of large technological advances; thus, now that the issue has once again become contemporary, the balance between academic ethos and technology must be revisited.

The history of academic ethos

Academic ethos has been described as an unwritten code of conduct, much like the Hippocratic Oath, that should guide the behavior of those in the academic profession as they pursue the mission of the university as a social institution (Ashby, 1968; Rüegg, 1986; Shils, 1978). This multi-faceted mission centers on the acquisition, expansion, and transmission of knowledge, and the preparation of students to be professionals in an ever-changing world (Rüegg, 1986; Shils, 1978). Just as the world is ever-changing, the mission of the university, and thus the academic ethos that guides it, must be dynamic and flexible in order to effectively accommodate the zeitgeist (Rüegg, 1986).

Several disruptive technologies that have changed history and drastically affected the balance of academic ethos in each era of modern education include the transition to the written word and the adoption of the modern printing press, and continue with today's cutting-edge, often controversial, scientific research. Although there have been many technologies that have changed history, these three had a particularly dramatic impact on the academic ethos of the day; thus, they are described in detail.

The struggle to maintain the status quo of institutional practices far pre-dates writing itself. A notable example of the dichotomy between the benefits of emerging technologies and their downfalls is found in the narrative of *The Phaedrus*. The dialogue between Socrates and Phaedrus, as reported by Plato in approximately 360 BCE, describes Socrates' disdain for writing as a primary means of teaching and learning. Moreover, Socrates regarded written knowledge as false knowledge from his standpoint of classical wisdom (Swaine, 1998). Socrates described a conversation in which Thamus, the King of Egypt, chastises Theuth, a god who brought reading and writing to his people, about the shortcomings of his invention. Specifically, Thamus explains that someone who invents a technology is too closely invested and tied to the technology to see anything but how wonderful it is and the positive impacts that it brings. As Socrates continues his narrative, he reveals the specific arguments that Thamus makes against the adoption of writing as a means of learning:

> If men learn this, it will implant forgetfulness in their souls: they will cease to exercise memory because they rely on that which is written, calling things to remembrance no longer from within themselves, but by means of external marks; what you have discovered is a recipe not for memory, but for reminder. And it is no true wisdom that you offer your disciples, but only its semblance; for by telling them of many things without teaching them you will make them seem to know much, while for the most part they know nothing and as men filled, not with wisdom, but with the conceit of wisdom, they will be a burden to their fellows.
> (Hackforth, 1952, p. 157)

Socrates argued that the written word is not capable of transferring the same level of quality as knowledge attainable through first-hand experience, or through interactive and thought-provoking conversations. The ability to question one another in interactive dialogue is a critical element in what Socrates believed to be the acquisition of valid knowledge. This is to say that the scent of an orange can be described in writing, but a reader might not be able to fully comprehend the fullness of the aroma. On the other hand, someone who has experienced the joy of peeling back the skin of an orange and has savored the spray of citrus will be reminded of the scent, allowing them to recall the unwritten details. Socrates suggests that without prior knowledge or experience, writing is insufficient to impart true knowledge to the reader. His contention is that the reader is left with a false knowledge, a danger that represents the reader as learned and wise, but full of foundational holes that make his or her knowledge weak at best. However, the written word ultimately became the de facto method for acquiring, storing, and sharing knowledge. While early writing was primitive and scarce, the opportunity provided by the written word was gradually recognized and adapted by scholars and institutions of that era.

The power of the written word continued to evolve through the efforts of King Charlemagne, who was largely illiterate but embraced the value of writing later in his life. He believed that to control his vast empire, which encompassed most of what is now known as Western Europe, a standard form of writing would need to be developed, including a legible font and punctuation to indicate cadence (Butt, 2002; Daniels and

Bright, 1996). This was because during the Dark Ages, one of the dimmest periods of European history, few people were educated and even fewer were literate. Interestingly, many of the monks, whose primary responsibility it was to copy manuscripts, could not actually read or understand what they were transferring onto new pages. Recognizing the power of the knowledge contained in various writings, particularly the Bible and the Benedictine Rule, Charlemagne set out to unify his empire under one church, with one written language (Dutton, 2004). Perhaps the most lasting impact made by Charlemagne was the revival of learning and the efforts put forth into the perfection of the written word. This development, in part, led to the Carolingian Renaissance (Butt, 2002; Daniels and Bright, 1996).

With the vision of standardizing the culture within his expanded realm, Charlemagne approached the wise Alcuin, a respected scholar and theologian. Alcuin embraced the motto "learn in order to teach" (*disce ut doceas*) and was a driving force behind the creation of what we recognize as the original liberal arts (*trivium*), including grammar, rhetoric, logic, as well as the more practical fields (*quadrivium*) of mathematics, geometry, arithmetic, astronomy, and music (Burns, 1907). The end result was a unified empire that embraced a common language and base of knowledge from which to grow.

While the Carolingian Renaissance brought about efficiencies for scribes who copied manuscripts and scholars who interpreted them, a subsequent disruptive technology was the modern printing press, with movable type, which gradually replaced scribes and handwritten manuscripts. Such printing allowed the written word to become accessible to commoners. While initially scholars were concerned that commoners would lack the practical wisdom to interpret what they read without scholarly guidance, the modern printing press has been credited with leading to the Reformation, the Renaissance, and the Scientific Revolution (Dewar, 2000).

In the age of scribes, information was indexed in a scribe's memory or using various techniques such as "ingenious bookmarks, lists of chapter headings, concordances, marginal glosses, arcane symbols, numbered lines and columns, alphabetically arranged epitomes" according to Reeds (1984, p. 331, as cited in Dewar, 2000, para. 80). In the late 15th century, printers offered indexes, title pages, and section breaks, and effectively created a standard template for printed works (Dewar, 2000). In addition to the technical changes of writing, the practice of learning changed significantly. While in the age of scribes manuscripts were read or lectured about, the age of printed text empowered the auto-didactic learner:

> Possibly no social revolution in European history is as fundamental as that which saw book learning (previously assigned to old men and monks) gradually become the focus of daily life during childhood, adolescence and early manhood . . . As a consumer of printed materials geared to a sequence of learning stages, the growing child was subjected to a different developmental process than was the medieval apprentice, ploughboy, novice or page.
>
> (Eisenstein, 1980, p. 432)

Identical copies of manuscripts provided scholars with the capability to refine knowledge by providing feedback, allowing the correction and expansion of subsequent editions. This was a precursor to the common practice of peer-reviewing scholarly works. While many cultures greatly benefited from the widespread use of the modern printing press, cultures that censored its use were, and still are, disadvantaged today (Dewar, 2000).

The academic ethos was also threatened in the mid-20th century when the original assumption that only good could result from scientific discoveries was dissolved. For example, the invention of the nuclear bomb and the widespread use of pesticides revealed a dark side to scientific discovery (Shils, 1978). Applying genetic engineering to humans also introduced apprehension about the dangers of the misuse of scientific research and knowledge. From these developments, the academic ethos was reformed to include the authoritative monitoring of using human subjects for scientific research. These scientific discoveries and the resulting moral and ethical quandaries they exposed also revealed the need for wise decision making in academic research (Shils, 1978).

The disruptive nature of technology

As the previous historical examples demonstrate, technological advances may not be readily accepted by scholars, but often lead to dramatic progress for humanity. Socrates begrudged the widespread use of reading and writing as a legitimate form of knowledge acquisition, storing, and sharing; however, he could not foretell how this technology would ultimately affect modern society. Charlemagne leveraged the power of the written word to control an enormous empire comprised of disparate cultures and ultimately sparked the Carolingian Renaissance (Dutton, 2004). To that end, many of the works and knowledge of that era were maintained, whereas they could have been lost if they had only been stored within the minds of the scholars. The significance of such losses cannot be estimated. Similarly, the Gutenberg printing press troubled scholars, who feared that intellectual pursuits would be undermined by the widespread availability of printed books to common people. Again, scholars were hesitant to accept a technology that ultimately brought greater good to society.

Perhaps the historical scholars' apprehensions toward technology were not unwarranted as scientific discoveries do not always benefit the common good. Recent examples of this are the advances in genetic engineering and atomic weaponry, which were rapidly introduced without first fully discerning all of the negative repercussions that these technologies would bring. What was needed in each of these cases was practical wisdom. Practical wisdom encourages the accurate perception of a situation, thoughtful consideration of multiple viewpoints, and self-reflection in order to wisely respond and act toward the common good (Schwartz and Sharpe, 2010). In these cases, practical wisdom would have allowed these cutting-edge technologies to be adopted conscientiously and methodically in order to balance the benefits and drawbacks.

In today's technologically saturated society, an understanding of such historical examples is crucial. Contemporary technological advances brought about through networked and ubiquitous computing have led to significant changes in the way humans collect, analyze, share, and process information. For instance, the majority of Americans now choose the Internet as their leading knowledge source when learning about specific scientific issues (National Science Foundation, 2010). The massive quantity of information that is now available requires individuals to possess the ability to synthesize information into meaningful and applicable knowledge, which is at the core of practical wisdom.

Interestingly, humans have adapted to functioning in an information-abundant society. For instance, contemporary researchers prefer to skim articles for relevant information and quickly jump from possible sources frequently without repeating a previous visit. This is also true for the average person, who has adapted to reading quickly and efficiently while weaving together meaning from disparate bits of information (National Science Foundation, 2010; Williams and Rowlands, 2010). However, it is essential that practical wisdom be applied to ensure that such derived meaning is accurate, reliable, and valid. In the *Nicomachean Ethics*, Aristotle suggested that "practical wisdom must be cultivated by the major institutions in which we practice" (Schwartz and Sharpe, 2010, p. 8). Thus, academia, guided by an academic ethos, should use technology to foster practical wisdom in society.

Using technology in academia to foster practical wisdom: a balancing act

The technological advances of the Digital Age have introduced a number of imbalances that we believe are related to our discussion. One imbalance is between the vast amount of information available through digital technologies versus the wisdom to effectively acquire, evaluate, and use the information. Another imbalance is between the inconceivable number of choices people must make versus their ability to wisely choose between the various options available to them (Schwartz, 2004). The third imbalance is between the characteristics of what Prensky (2009) terms a *digital native* and those of a wise person.

The immense amount of information available on the Internet, along with the many ways in which people have to access that information at any time and from anywhere using a myriad of technology tools, is unprecedented in human history. This has created an imbalance between the amount of information available and the ability to evaluate that information in order to use it to make informed and wise choices. Individuals need practical wisdom to be able to select reliable sources of information, incorporate the new information into their current knowledge, and use the information to make choices that not only benefit themselves, but also support the common good.

Further, the enormous number of options available to decision makers leads to an incredible number of choices and decisions to make daily (Schwartz, 2004). However, an abundance of choices can render decisions even more difficult to make. In fact, it can lead to decision overload and cause less satisfaction with the choices that are actually made (Haynes, 2009; Schwartz, 2004). Not only the everyday choices of what to eat and what to wear, but life-changing choices such as whom to have relationships with, and what school and career path to choose are just a few of the choices that individuals need to make. Technological advances may have actually complicated these decisions. For example, with the advent of online social networks, the number of tools and choices for communicating with people is astonishing. In many ways, these tools have changed the way in which social and professional relationships are formed and maintained. People communicate and form relationships with others from around the world, creating a global neighborhood. This freedom of communication has many benefits; however, the anonymity of the virtual sphere, as well as the number of people available to communicate with, also increases the chances of coming into contact with dangerous individuals. Students need the practical wisdom to discern the feelings and intentions of strangers that they only know online while determining how much contact to allow.

Technology not only influences the number of choices humans have every day, but also the way that *digital natives*, or those who have grown up using digital devices, consume digital content, interact within the virtual sphere, think, and process information (Prensky, 2009). Contrasting the characteristics of a digital native with the characteristics of a wise person highlights the necessity to teach practical wisdom. For instance, a digital native is a rapid information consumer, who multi-tasks and seeks immediate gratification (Prensky, 2009), while a wise person considers perspectives other than their own, examines the social context of a situation, and uses both intuition and emotions to enhance intellectual reason (Schwartz and Sharpe, 2010).

The characteristics of the digital native and the immediacy with which they like to interact with information seem to contradict the insightful and contemplative qualities that make a person wise. Thus, crafting engaging learning experiences that allow students to practice practical wisdom helps students develop wisdom that can be applied in their personal and professional lives to benefit themselves and the others with whom they interact.

The current state of academic ethos

In addition to maintaining and balancing academic ethos, tertiary institutions should also include practical wisdom in their curricula. To become responsible members of society, students would greatly benefit from understanding the importance of applying practical wisdom in their personal and professional lives. The best way to teach practical wisdom is to allow students to witness, study, and practice wise decision making (Sternberg et al., 2009). The foundation for this is to develop teaching strategies that incorporate the modeling, exploration, and application of wise decision making. Technology tools can help support this teaching, but the instructional strategies are the core element.

Historically, higher education has continued to use a slightly modified practice of pedagogy for its instructional strategies. As pedagogy is designed for a different group of learners, this approach is not sustainable with the disruptions being brought forth by easy access to information through emerging technologies. It is important to investigate higher education's approach to instruction and the transfer of knowledge to learners.

At its outset, pedagogy was the science involved with teaching children (Watkins and Mortimore, 1999). The word itself stems from the Greek words *paidos* (child) and *agogos* (leader). The pedagogical philosophy of instruction purports that the learner is dependent on the educator for learning, who is directly responsible for deciding what and how things are learned. Learners are directed and informed by what they will learn, the specific standards they must meet for progression, and are primarily motivated by external factors (instructor evaluation, grades, etc.). In a strict hierarchical instructional environment, this approach can yield satisfactory results among learners who bring limited experience and knowledge to the table at the beginning of instruction. Unfortunately, this approach loses its appeal and efficiency when applied to today's adult learners who bring a wealth of background experience, knowledge, and virtually limitless access to even the most complex forms of information.

Whereas the pedagogical approach to teaching and learning puts the instructor at the center of the stage, an andragogical approach shifts the focal point more towards the learners. The name itself describes the different philosophical standpoint of andragogy, as it is built from the Greek words *anere* (adult) and *agogos* (leader). The term "andragogy" was created to draw attention to the differences between self-directed and instructor-led learners well after pedagogy became the established instructional philosophy (Delahaye et al., 1994).

Andragogy shifts the focus of learning from the strategies employed by the instructor, and places the focus on the needs and strategies of the learner. The motivations for adult learners can be summarized with six basic assumptions: 1) adult/self-directed learners need to know why they are learning; 2) experience provides the basic building blocks for learning (active learning including failure); 3) adult/self-directed learners must be responsible for their educational decisions and play a critical role in both their planning and evaluation of instruction; 4) immediate relevance (either professionally or personally) of what they are learning is essential; 5) learning should be problem-based and not content-based; and 6) adult/self-directed learners are primarily motivated by internal factors (Knowles et al., 2012).

Moving from pedagogy to andragogy shifts the center of attention from the instructor to the learner, but retains the instructor as a critical element, responsible for providing information and resources to the learner. However, an alternative teaching methodology is evolving in which the instructor focuses on being a facilitator of learning, collaboratively defining learning outcomes and methods with the students. This approach, known as heutagogy, is one in which the students learn, for the most part, independently (Hase and Kenyon, 2000). Through heutagogy, the instructor prepares the learners by helping them to understand how to select relevant and reliable resources. Rather than being the primary source of information, the instructor teaches the students not *what* to learn, but instead *how* to learn, and encourages them to pursue self-efficacy (Ashton and Newman, 2006). Using a heutagogical methodology, learning may not necessarily follow a linear or prescribed path, but rather follows whatever path is necessary for the learner to achieve their learning goals. Through this approach, learners acquire skills to effectively utilize and synthesize a variety of resources, such as their peers, instructors, past experiences, and new information. This type of learning allows for the practice of real-world decision making, emulating situations that students will likely encounter in their chosen careers.

The infusion of practical wisdom into the teaching and learning paradigm will help inspire future learners toward their individual goals and will in turn influence the wisdom of the communities in which they live and practice. Recognizing that learners are creative, independent, and capable of great achievements introduces the beginning elements of balance back into how we collectively perceive the science of instruction. Practical wisdom compels us to embrace heutagogy as a possible solution toward bridging the gaps that have become imminent through the ubiquity of technology and information. Heutagogical practices create wise learners who are capable of self-managing the continuing flood of information.

Immediate steps

There are numerous technologies currently used by educators to foster practical wisdom which improves the pragmatism of existing teaching practices and significantly enhances the student learning experience. Table 10.1 describes the *Sixteen Principles of Teaching for Wisdom* derived from *the Balance Theory of Wisdom* (Sternberg, 1998, 2001) and provides example teaching methods and supportive technologies for teaching practical wisdom.

Table 10.1 Sixteen principles of teaching for wisdom (derived from the balance theory of wisdom) along with teaching methods and supportive technologies

General guidelines for teaching wisdom	Teaching method	Supportive technologies
Explore the importance of wisdom for life satisfaction	Demonstration, role playing, discussions	Video, multimedia-enhanced case studies, primary sources, simulation, interactive text
Demonstrate importance of wisdom for life satisfaction	Demonstration	Video, multimedia-enhanced case studies, simulations, interactive text
Explore the usefulness of interdependence	Peer projects, discussions	Simulations, synchronous and asynchronous communication
Role-model wisdom	Demonstration, peer projects	Simulation, games, primary sources
Read about wise judgments and decision making	Framing, literature, critical evaluation	Primary sources, interactive text, short messaging, open content
Discern self-interest as well as the interests of others	Reflective analysis, learning communities, project-based learning, framing	Videos, short messaging, synchronous and asynchronous communication, portfolio development
Balance competing intrapersonal, interpersonal, and extrapersonal interests	Reflective analysis, learning communities, project-based learning, framing	Videos, short messaging, synchronous and asynchronous communication, blogs, online journaling, portfolio development
Explore the importance of the path toward an outcome	Role playing, inquiry-based learning	Videos, simulations, games, primary sources
Balancing roles	Role playing, experimental learning, peer projects, case studies	Games, simulations, primary sources

General guidelines for teaching wisdom	Teaching method	Supportive technologies
Encourage students to explore, evaluate, and integrate their values into their thoughts and actions	Reflective analysis	Short messaging, online journaling, digital storytelling
Encourage dialectical thinking	Learning communities, reflective practices, framing	Synchronous and asynchronous communication, short messaging, digital storytelling, primary sources
Encourage dialogical thinking	Learning communities, project-based learning, framing	Social networking environments, synchronous and asynchronous communication, primary sources
Demonstrate the value of having the common good be the goal	Learning communities, project-based learning, service learning	Social networking environments, synchronous and asynchronous communication, primary sources, video
Encourage and reward wisdom	Role playing, experiential learning	Achievements, badges, practical simulations, games
Encourage self-reflection about their lives and thought processes	Reflective analysis	Short messaging, online journals, digital storytelling
Demonstrate balancing self-interests and the common good	Demonstration, critical evaluation	Primary sources, open content

Sources: Sternberg 1998, 2001; Sternberg et al., 2009

Reflective analysis using synchronous/asynchronous communication and online journaling

An essential part of teaching practical wisdom is both reflection and self-reflection. Traditionally, these have been accomplished through journaling and essays. The interactive nature of contemporary online journaling enhances "student and teacher relationships, active learning, higher order thinking, and greater flexibility in teaching and learning more generally" (Ferdig and Trammell, 2004, p. 13). Reflection supports the comparison of differing ideas to form a synthesis of the recently acquired information with a newly ascribed meaning helping to shape relevance for the learner (Boud et al., 2013). Contemporary synchronous and asynchronous communication technologies allow such reflection to occur without temporal and physical boundaries. Unlike the unidirectional self-reflection that occurs in isolation, modern self-reflection through communication technologies also allows for inclusiveness and open participation from peers and mentors.

Problem-based learning using multimedia-enhanced case studies, simulation, games, and achievements

Problem-based learning, traditionally defined as a student-centered approach in which students solve problems to gain a greater understanding of a subject, allows students to explore the importance of navigating the path towards an effective and appropriate outcome (Hmelo-Silver, 2004). Furthermore, case studies provide a foundation for simultaneously addressing memory, analytical, creative, and practical skills (Sternberg et al., 2009). Multimedia-enhanced case studies that leverage audio, video, and inter-activity for enhanced authenticity allow learners to make realistic connections, explore differing outcomes, and ultimately attain a deeper understanding of the impact of a decision-making process. These case studies can help develop empathy toward others, which is a necessary component of practical wisdom (Sullivan and Rosin, 2008).

Immersive and imaginative simulations help learners to develop knowledge through experience, which leads to learning (Kolb, 1983). Immersion in a simulated environment allows students to actively experiment in a safe environment with time for reflection by encouraging the inclusion of emotional and intellectual processing (Le Rossignol, 2009; Lindquist and Long, 2011; Silberman, 2007). Providing interactivity also allows students to experience different outcomes based on their choices. Problem-based learning, games, and simulations enable students to "participate in new worlds. They let players think, talk, and act in new ways. Indeed, players come to *inhabit* roles that are otherwise inaccessible to them" (Williamson et al., 2005, p. 105). Achievements, in the form of digital badges and other rewards, motivate learners to achieve increasingly higher levels of mastery. "In the future, more sophisticated simulation algorithms will allow humans to exercise their imaginative capacity in ever-more complex what-if constructions, allowing for more thorough exploration of possibilities and, in turn, wiser decisions." (Prensky, 2009, p. 4).

Demonstration using video, interactive text, and primary sources

Practical wisdom teaches us to embrace valid, classic methodologies, regardless of form, and to augment them with technology only when it will enhance learning. The classical method of demonstration allows learners to observe a modeled behavior which they strive to emulate or evaluate, so it is critical not to discard proven methodologies, like demonstration, that continue to have a beneficial impact on learners (Zimmerman and Jaffe, 1977). Technological innovations that allow more rapid and effective delivery and consumption of video, interactive text, and digitized primary sources can facilitate and enhance classical demonstration.

The study of history also has direct implications for teaching practical wisdom. For example, Wineburg (2001) describes the process an educator uses to explore the evolving nature of history rather than only the historical facts. This is achieved by first introducing students to the thinking of philosophers, revolutionaries, and tyrants. This theory of human nature then works as a framework for future learning about the historical events and the various human choices that were made in order for those events to occur. The learning experience is then supported by the students analyzing primary sources about specific events and culminates with them re-enacting specific aspects of those events. This experience provides students with a better understanding of the various perspectives of the historical events (Lindquist and Long, 2011; Wineburg, 2001), which helps them to develop the ability to decipher various facets of a situation, see the world from the perspective of others, and develop empathy, which are facets of practical wisdom (Wineburg, 2001).

As all academic disciplines carry a rich history, discipline-specific primary sources can facilitate the exploration of the development of the discipline *gestalt* in order to provide context for the students. "Context, from the Latin *contexere*, means to weave together, to engage in an active process of connecting things in a pattern" (Wineburg, 2001, p. 21). This context, supported by the exploration of primary sources, allows students to create new understanding and provides the foundation for future learning in their academic pursuits. This also supports the development of practical wisdom within their academic domain as they prepare to make wise decisions within their future profession. Studying history in an analytical way using primary sources highlights the importance of the many choices that humans make. "The making of history is a dynamic process. What happened in the past wasn't fated or meant to be. It occurred because human actors shaped their destinies by the choices they made, just as people today shape their futures by the choices they make" (Wineburg, 2001, pp. 160–161).

Peer projects and learning communities through online social networks

Online social networks are easy-to-use tools that support group communication and collaboration. Such networks can be used for practicing dialogical and dialectical thinking. Students can share their perspectives, read and consider the perspectives of their peers, and work together to integrate the varying viewpoints to create a synthesis of the perspectives. This helps them practice framing a situation to find a solution that meets the needs of all parties involved. By creating social capital, it also helps build a sustainable and collaborative learning community that reaches beyond the physical and temporal boundaries of formal education environments.

Critical evaluation using open content

Critical evaluation of content is an important aspect of practical wisdom and can be nurtured through the regular use of open knowledge repositories. For example, Wikipedia, an online encyclopedia that fosters the social and participatory construction of knowledge, is an ideal tool to help students develop practical wisdom. Unlike traditional encyclopedias, Wikipedia uses a "more open, less hierarchical approach to collaborative knowledge construction" (Eijkman, 2010, p. 174). Knowledge repositories such as Wikipedia present "a distinct shift in the balance of power towards 'the people'" (Lipczynska, 2005, as cited in Eijkman, 2010, p. 182), in that the knowledge is readily accessible to anyone with Internet access and is available in multiple languages and dialects. Not only can educators teach how to critically assess the reliability of information, they could also use Wikipedia as an editing tool by teaching students to become effective contributors of shared knowledge (Wannemacher, 2011).

Wikipedia and similar shared open-content repositories also represent a fundamental shift in the concept of intellectual property and ownership by supporting the creation of content that is developed in a collaborative, anonymous, and non-proprietary manner. This is reminiscent of changes that occurred during the era of the printing press, when most scribed manuscripts did not state an author. This changed following the spread of capitalism and individualism, which placed an emphasis on the notion of content ownership (Dewar, 2000; Eisenstein, 1980).

Framing through short messaging

Short messaging, or the public sharing of highly condensed information, has become a popular method for quickly and succinctly communicating. The utilization of such technologies allows students to assess, evaluate, and concisely frame information. To accurately and concisely frame a situation into a short message, students must go through a process of understanding and contextualizing, which is an essential step toward making a wise decision. Based on the context of the situation and the reason for the decision, it is essential to develop the right frame to make an appropriate decision (Schwartz, 2004; Schwartz and Sharpe, 2010).

Future technologies

The disruptive nature of technology is frequently masked by the direct digitization of analog teaching techniques. Specifically, emerging technologies often penetrate into teaching and learning as *digital doppelgangers* of existing tools and methods. This is apparent when we observe digital technologies being implemented to replace analog practices, such as transitioning from handwritten papers to printed editions, and eventually electronic versions. Another example might be the introduction of electronic student response systems, which are merely digital replications of the feedback received from student hand-raising. However, when a disruptive technology, not merely a digital duplication, is introduced, institutions of higher education have generally resisted the integration of such paradigm-altering technologies.

The debate concerning the benefits and risks of technological shifts is ever-present. However, when a critical mass of technological development and adoption is reached, societal shifts are imminent regardless of value judgments. Instead of investing valuable resources in an attempt to resist the inevitable technological change, this is an opportunity for institutions of higher education to lead such revolutions and to rebalance the academic ethos. Furthermore, developing practical wisdom in learners should become a goal of higher education.

Potential academic outcomes of practical wisdom

Pursuing an aggressive agenda of incorporating practical wisdom in higher education delivers positive individual, institutional, and community outcomes. Wise learners understand that the value of their judgments increases with deliberate mindfulness, which leads to an enhanced community (Sternberg et al., 2009). Individuals, institutions of higher education, and communities imbued with practical wisdom will benefit from knowing how to make wise decisions in an increasingly complex world.

Individual outcomes

Individuals who embrace practical wisdom are able to achieve satisfaction and happiness along with developing the ability to include deliberate values into their judgments. Furthermore, students of practical wisdom are flexible and able to understand differing perspectives, weaving them together to create deeper levels of understanding. Learning practical wisdom is important because knowledge alone does not necessarily lead to a happy and satisfied life (Aristotle, 2014; Sternberg et al., 2009). Alternatively, wisdom provides a balance of individual values with those of the community, allowing learners to make optimal decisions that benefit the common good. This balance creates harmonious relationships and fosters an overall better world.

Institutional outcomes

Reforming the academic ethos to strategically embrace technology will allow academic institutions to more effectively teach practical wisdom to the modern learner as well as ensuring that such learners can discern information in our complex world. "Aristotle focuses our attention on something critically important: character and practical wisdom must be cultivated by the major institutions in which we practice" (Schwartz and Sharpe, 2010, p. 7). In an age where knowledge is ubiquitous and universally integrated into daily life, it is essential that higher education adapts in order to stay relevant and applicable. Higher education must differentiate itself by adding value through the development of wise learners who can do more than just access information, but also interpret, assess, and correctly apply knowledge. In order to continue their respective missions, institutions of higher education must once again embrace the practice of imparting practical wisdom as a mechanism that enables learners to excel in an age of ever-changing technology. The principles of academic ethos will guide higher education toward producing learners that are competitive, self-guiding, and capable of thriving in a global society.

Community outcomes

A community reflects the aggregate qualities of its members, so a community comprising wise members will lead to a wise community. Communities greatly benefit from a balanced academic ethos that integrates technology at its core and generates students who embody practical wisdom. Students who are taught to be self-sufficient and wise problem solvers will provide value to their communities well before completing their studies. Strong, effective, and diverse pillars of a community reflect the quality and values of its members. Ultimately, wise individuals and academic institutions that embrace a balanced academic ethos lead to successful, sustainable, and thriving communities.

Conclusion

In contrast to the way in which early scholars under-estimated the power of the written word, it is crucial that contemporary scholars accept that current and future technological advances will forever alter the way humans teach and learn. Ubiquitous and instantaneous access to knowledge provides the foundation on which the modern forms of pedagogy, andragogy, and heutagogy should be expanded. Regardless of the teaching methodology or academic discipline, educators should guide students to become wise navigators of knowledge and information. Doing so will ensure that students can critically examine and discern information relevance, credibility, and applicability. In addition, educators should integrate practical wisdom into their curricula to teach students how to accurately perceive any situation, to discern multiple viewpoints, to reflect, to think dialectically and dialogically, and to act accordingly by making wise decisions. Institutions should be mindful that providing students with the skills to make wise decisions may also help them have happier, more satisfying lives (Aristotle, 2014).

It is important for higher education to recognize that the students of today will soon be professionals in a rapidly changing and more complex global community. The problems they will be faced with, such as global warming, political unrest, and social injustice, will require practical wisdom to be adequately addressed in order to find the common good. What greater calling could there be for institutions of higher education than to impart not only knowledge, but also the practical wisdom that students need to become wise leaders in their personal lives, their chosen professions, as well as in the ever-expanding global community? By modernizing the academic ethos to accept and embrace technologies in order to harness their power to teach practical wisdom, institutions of higher education have the opportunity to change the world for the better, one student at a time.

Reflection and critical thinking

1   Through technology, students have ubiquitous exposure to an ever-expanding volume of information. What would be the consequences of producing students who lack the ability to critically evaluate the relevance and authenticity of information through the lens of practical wisdom?
2   Although many disruptive technologies ultimately provided immense benefits to societies, institutions were often initially hesitant to embrace them. What are some of the possible outcomes of not maintaining a balanced ethos when confronted with ambiguous and perilous issues such as world hunger, political unrest, and natural disasters?
3   Imagine that you are an executive faced with introducing a disruptive technology into an established industry to ensure a competitive advantage. What considerations might you face regarding the decision to adopt the technology? How would you use practical wisdom to guide your decision-making process?
4   Disruptions such as the printing press caused institutions to reevaluate and revise their ethos. Which disruptive technologies were introduced in your lifetime and how did the contemporary institutions respond? Considering the various technologies in your personal life, how can you use practical wisdom as a guide to maintain a balanced life ethos?
5   Heutagogical approaches are becoming more prominent for teaching and learning. What are some of the possible advantages and disadvantages, as well as their potential impacts, on academic ethos?
6   Aristotle suggests that knowledge alone does not necessarily lead to happiness. How does practical wisdom help people live happier, more satisfying lives?
7   Traits of digital natives may contradict with the traits of a wise individual. How can digital natives use technology to become wise individuals?

References

Aristotle (2014). *Nicomachean Ethics*, C.D.C. Reeve (trans.). Indianapolis: Hackett Publishing Company.

Ashby, E. (1968). A Hippocratic oath for the academic profession. *Minerva*, 7(1), 64–66.

Ashton, J. and Newman, L. (2006). An unfinished symphony: 21st century teacher education using knowledge creating heutagogies. *British Journal of Educational Technology*, 37(6), 825–840.

Boud, D., Keogh, R., and Walker, D. (2013). Promoting reflection in learning: A model. In R. Edwards, A. Hanson, and P. Raggatt (eds), *Boundaries of Adult Learning* (pp. 32–56). London: Routledge/Open University Press.

Burns, J. (1907). *Alcuin. The Catholic Encyclopedia*, vol. 1. New York: Robert Appleton Company.

Butt, J.J. (2002). *Daily Life in the Age of Charlemagne*. Westport, CT: Greenwood Publishing Group.

Clegg, S., Hudson, A., and Steel, J. (2003). The emperor's new clothes: Globalization and e-learning in higher education. *British Journal of Sociology of Education*, 24(1), 39–53.

Daniels, P.T., and Bright, W. (eds) (1996). *The World's Writing Systems*. New York: Oxford University Press.

Delahaye, B.L., Limerick, D.C., and Hearn, G. (1994). The relationship between andragogical and pedagogical orientations and the implications for adult learning. *Adult Education Quarterly*, 44(4), 187–200.

Dewar, J.A. (2000). The information age and the printing press: Looking backward to see ahead. *Ubiquity: An ACM Magazine and Forum* (August), Article 8.

Dutton, P.E. (2004). *Charlemagne's Mustache and Other Cultural Clusters of a Dark Age*. New York: Palgrave Macmillan.

Eijkman, H. (2010). Academics and Wikipedia: Reframing Web 2.0+ as a disruptor of traditional academic power–knowledge arrangements. *Campus-Wide Information Systems*, 27(3), 173–185.

Eisenstein, E.L. (1980). *The Printing Press as an Agent of Change*, vol. 1. Cambridge: Cambridge University Press.

Ferdig, R.E. and Trammell, K.D. (2004). Content delivery in the "blogosphere." *The Journal*, 31(7), 12–20.

Fried, C.B. (2008). In-class laptop use and its effects on student learning. *Computers and Education*, 50(3), 906–914.

Hackforth, R. (ed.) (1952). *Plato: Phaedrus*, vol. 119. Cambridge: Cambridge University Press.

Hase, S. and Kenyon, C. (2000). From andragogy to heutagogy. *Ultibase Articles*, 5(3), 1–10.

Haynes, G.A. (2009). Testing the boundaries of the choice overload phenomenon: The effect of number of options and time pressure on decision difficulty and satisfaction. *Psychology and Marketing*, 26(3), 204–212.

Hmelo-Silver, C.E. (2004). Problem-based learning: what and how do students learn? *Educational Psychology Review*, 16(3), 235–266.

Knowles, M.S., Holton III, E.F., and Swanson, R.A. (2012). *The Adult Learner*. London: Routledge.

Kolb, D.A. (1983). *Experiential Learning: Experience as the Source of Learning and Development*. Englewood Cliffs, NJ: Prentice Hall.

Le Rossignol, K. (2009). Designing blended learning in higher education: the neomillenial learner and mediated immersion. *International Journal of the Humanities*, 6(10), 53–60.

Lindquist, T. and Long, H. (2011). How can educational technology facilitate student engagement with online primary sources?: A user needs assessment. *Library Hi Tech*, 29(2), 224–241.

Lipczynska, S. (2005). Power to the people: The case for Wikipedia. *Reference Reviews*, 19(2), 6–7.

National Science Foundation (2010). Science and technology: Public attitudes and understanding. Retrieved from http://www.nsf.gov/statistics/seind10/c7/c7h.htm (accessed September 14, 2015).

Parker, K. and Chao, J. (2007). Wiki as a teaching tool. *Interdisciplinary Journal of E-Learning and Learning Objects*, 3(1), 57–72.

Plowman, T.S. (2000). Academic integrity and informational technology. *TechTrends*, 44(1), 24–30.

Prensky, M. (2009). H. sapiens digital: from digital immigrants and digital natives to digital wisdom. *Innovate: Journal of Online Education*, 5(3). Retrieved from http://www.wisdom-page.com/Prensky01.html (accessed September 14, 2015).

Reeds, M. (1984). Recent books on the history of the book. *Scholarly Publishing*, 15(4), 331.

Rüegg, W. (1986). The academic ethos. *Minerva*, 24(4), 393–412.

Schwartz, B. (2004). *The Paradox of Choice*. New York: HarperCollins.

Schwartz, B. and Sharpe, K. (2010). *Practical Wisdom: The Right Way to Do the Right Thing*. New York: Penguin.

Shils, E. (1978). The academic ethos. *The American Scholar*, 47(2), 165–190.

Silberman, M.L. (Ed.) (2007). *The Handbook of Experiential Learning*. Hoboken, NJ: John Wiley & Sons.

Sternberg, R.J. (1998). A balance theory of wisdom. *Review of General Psychology*, 2(4), 347–365.

——. (2001). Why schools should teach for wisdom: The balance theory of wisdom in educational settings. *Educational Psychologist*, 36(4), 227–245.

Sternberg, R.J., Jarvin, L., and Grigorenko, E.L. (2009) *Teaching for Wisdom, Intelligence, Creativity, and Success*. Thousand Oaks, CA: Corwin.

Sullivan, W.M. and Rosin, M.S. (2008). *A New Agenda for Higher Education: Shaping a Life of the Mind for Practice*, vol. 14. Hoboken, NJ: John Wiley & Sons.

Swaine, L.A. (1998). A paradox reconsidered: Written lessons from Plato's Phaedrus. *Educational Philosophy and Theory*, 30(3), 259–273.

Watkins, C. and Mortimore, P. (1999). Pedagogy: What do we know? In P. Mortimore (ed.), *Understanding Pedagogy and its Impact on Learning* (pp. 1–19). London: Paul Chapman.

Wannemacher, K. (2011). Experiences and perspectives of Wikipedia use in higher education. *International Journal of Management in Education*, 5(1), 79–92.

Williams, P. and Rowlands, I. (2010). *Information Behaviour of the Researcher of the Future*. London: British Library/Joint Information Systems Committee.

Williamson, D., Squire, K., Halverson, R., and Gee, J.P. (2005). Video games and the future of learning. *Phi Delta Kappan*, 87(2), 104–111.

Wineburg, S. (2001). *Historical Thinking and Other Unnatural Acts: Charting the Future of Teaching the Past*. Philadelphia: Temple University Press.

Zimmerman, B.J. and Jaffe, A. (1977). Teaching through demonstration: The effects of structuring, imitation, and age. *Journal of Educational Psychology*, 69(6), 773–778.

Chapter 11

Can scientific method help us create a wiser world?

Nicholas Maxwell

Introduction

Two great problems of learning confront humanity: (1) learning about the universe, and about ourselves and other living things as a part of the universe; and (2) learning how to make progress toward as good a world as possible. We solved the first problem in the 17th century when we created modern science. That is not to say that we know everything that there is to be known, but rather that we have discovered a method which enables us progressively to improve our knowledge and understanding – the empirical method of science. But we have not yet solved the second problem. And that combination of solving the first problem and failing to solve the second one puts us in a situation of unprecedented danger. Increasing our scientific knowledge and technological know-how enormously increases our power to act. Often, of course, this has magnificent outcomes. Modern science and technology have made the modern world possible, with all its immense benefits. But in the absence of the solution to the second problem, our enhanced powers to act have also led to all our current global crises: global warming, explosive population growth, destruction of natural habitats and rapid extinction of species, depletion of finite natural resources, vast inequalities of wealth and power around the globe, pollution of earth, sea, and air, the lethal character of modern war, the menace of modern armaments, even the AIDS epidemic (AIDS being spread by modern travel). All these have come about, paradoxically, because of our successes, our enhanced powers to act bequeathed to us by modern science and technology, via modern industry, agriculture, medicine, hygiene, transport, and the technology of war. They have come about because of our immensely increased powers to act without an accompanying increase in our power to act *wisely*.

Many blame science for our problems. But that is entirely to miss the point. Rather, what we need to do is *learn* from our solution to the first great problem of learning how to go about solving the second problem. We need to *learn* from scientific progress how to achieve social progress toward a good world.

The Enlightenment

This was the basic idea of the 18th-century Enlightenment, especially the French Enlightenment (see Gay, 1973). Unfortunately, in developing this profoundly important idea, the *philosophes* of the Enlightenment made a series of blunders, and it is the defective version of the Enlightenment program which emerged as a result that we built into the institutions of academia in the early 20th century when we created departments and disciplines of social science. The outcome is a kind of inquiry devoted, in the first instance, to the acquisition of knowledge – *knowledge-inquiry* as I shall call it. This holds that, first, knowledge is to be acquired; once acquired, it can be applied to help solve social problems. It is this that we are still suffering from today (see Maxwell, 1984, Chapters 2, 3, and 6).

In order to implement properly the profound Enlightenment idea of learning from the solution to the first great problem of learning how to go about solving the second one, there are three crucial steps that we need to get right:

1   The progress-achieving methods of science need to be correctly identified. These methods need to be correctly generalized so that they become fruitfully applicable to any worthwhile, problematic human endeavor, whatever its aims may be, and not just applicable to the endeavor of improving knowledge.
2   These correctly generalized progress-achieving methods then need to be exploited correctly in the great human endeavor of trying to make social progress toward as good a world as possible.

Unfortunately, the *philosophes* got all three steps wrong. They misconstrued the nature of the progress-achieving methods of natural science; they failed to generalize the methods of science properly; and, most disastrously of all, they made the entirely wrong application of these methods. They applied these methods to developing *social science*, to the task of improving *knowledge* of the social world, whereas they ought to have applied the properly generalized progress-achieving methods of science directly to *social life*, to the *social world itself*. Instead of seeking to make *social progress toward an enlightened world*, the *philosophes* ended up seeking to make no more than intellectual progress in *knowledge* about the social world.

Academic inquiry as it exists by and large today – knowledge-inquiry – still embodies these ancient blunders. As a result, academia as we know it today is a botched attempt to create institutions of learning designed to help us solve the second great problem of learning. In order to create what we so urgently need, a kind of inquiry rationally designed to help us make progress toward as good a world as possible, we need to modify academia as it exists today just sufficiently to correct the three blunders we have inherited from the past. The outcome would be a new kind of academic enterprise that I shall call *wisdom-inquiry*. Wisdom-inquiry is designed to enable us to learn from our solution to the first great problem of learning how to go about solving the second problem. Here is what we need to do to create wisdom-inquiry.

Correcting the first blunder: scientific method

First, we need to correct current orthodox ideas about the nature of the progress-achieving methods of science. From D'Alembert in the 18th century to Karl Popper in the 20th, the widely held view, amongst both scientists and philosophers, has been (and continues to be) that science proceeds by assessing theories impartially in the light of evidence, *no permanent assumption being accepted by science about the universe independently of evidence* (see Maxwell, 1998, pp. 36–45). Preference may be given to simple, unified, or explanatory theories, but not in such a way that nature herself is, in effect, assumed to be simple, unified, or comprehensible.

This orthodox view, which may be called *standard empiricism*, is, however, untenable. If taken literally, it would instantly bring science to a standstill. For, given any accepted fundamental theory of physics, T—Newtonian theory say, or quantum theory – it will always be possible to concoct endlessly many empirically more successful rivals which agree with T about observed phenomena, but which disagree arbitrarily about some unobserved phenomena, and which successfully predict phenomena, in an ad hoc way, that T makes false predictions about, or no predictions. Physics would be drowned in an ocean of such empirically more successful rival theories (see Maxwell, 1974; 1984, Chapter 9; 1998, Chapter 2; 1999; 2000; 2004, Chapters 1 and 2; 2005; 2010, Chapter 5; 2011).

In practice, these rivals are excluded because they are disastrously disunified. *Two* considerations govern acceptance of theories in physics: empirical success and unity. In demanding unity, we demand of a fundamental physical theory that it ascribes *the same* dynamical laws to the phenomena to which the theory applies.[1] But in persistently accepting unified theories, to the extent of rejecting disunified rivals that are just as, or even more, empirically successful, physics makes a big persistent assumption about the universe. The universe is such that all disunified theories are false. It has some kind of unified dynamic structure. It is physically comprehensible in the sense that explanations for phenomena exist to be discovered.

But this untestable (and thus metaphysical) assumption that the universe is physically comprehensible is profoundly problematic. Science is obliged to assume, but does not know, that the universe is comprehensible. Much less does it know that the universe is comprehensible in a particular way. A glance at the history of physics reveals that ideas have changed dramatically over time. In the 17th century, there was the idea that the universe consists of corpuscles, minute billiard balls, which interact only by contact. This gave way to the idea that the universe consists of point-particles surrounded by rigid, spherically symmetrical fields of force, which in turn gave way to the idea that there is one unified self-interacting field, varying smoothly throughout space and time. Nowadays we have the idea that everything is made up of minute quantum strings embedded in 10 or 11 dimensions of space-time. Some kind of assumption along these lines must be made, but, given the historical record and that any such assumption concerns the ultimate nature of the universe, that of which we are most ignorant, it is only reasonable to conclude that it is almost bound to be false.

The way to overcome this fundamental dilemma inherent in the scientific enterprise is to construe physics as making a hierarchy of metaphysical assumptions concerning the comprehensibility and knowability of the universe, these assumptions asserting less and less as one goes up the hierarchy, and thus becoming more and more likely to be true, and more nearly such that their truth is required for science, or the pursuit of knowledge, to be possible at all. In this way, a framework of relatively insubstantial, unproblematic, fixed assumptions and associated methods is created within which much more substantial and problematic assumptions and associated methods can be changed, and indeed improved, as scientific knowledge improves. In other words, a framework of relatively unspecific, unproblematic, fixed *aims* and methods is created within which much more specific and problematic aims and methods evolve as scientific knowledge evolves. There is positive feedback between improving knowledge, and improving aims-and-methods, improving knowledge-about-how-to-improve-knowledge. This is the nub of scientific rationality, the methodological key to the unprecedented success of science. Science adapts its nature to what it discovers about the nature of the universe (see Maxwell, 1974; 1984, Chapter 9; 1993; 1998, Chapter 2; 1999; 2000; 2002; 2004, Chapters 1 and 2; 2005; 2007, Chapters 9 and 12; 2010, Chapter 5; 2006a; 2011).

This hierarchical conception of physics, which may be called *aim-oriented empiricism*, is depicted in Figure 11.1. At level 7, there is the assumption that the universe is such that we can acquire some knowledge of our local circumstances. If this minimal assumption is false, we have had it whatever we assume. It can never be in our interests to abandon this assumption. At level 6, we have the more substantial and risky assumption that the universe is such that we can learn how to improve methods for improving knowledge. This promises to be too fruitful for progress in knowledge not to be accepted. At level 5, there is the assumption that the universe is comprehensible in some way or other – it being such that something exists which provides in principle one kind of explanation for all phenomena. At level 4, there is the even more substantial assumption that the universe is *physically* comprehensible, there being some kind of invariant physical entity, pervading all phenomena which (together with instantaneous states of affairs) determines (perhaps probabilistically) how events unfold in space and time. In other words, the universe is such that the true physical "theory of everything" is unified or physically comprehensible. At level 3, there is the even more substantial assumption that the universe is physically comprehensible in some more or less specific way. Superstring theory, or M-theory, might be this assumption today. At level 2, we have currently accepted fundamental theories of physics: at present, the standard model, and general relativity. At level 1, we have accepted empirical data.

As we descend this hierarchy, we go from an assumption at the top that is almost certain to be true to an assumption, at level 3, that is almost bound to be false. The hope is that we can keep falsity confined to assumptions as low down in the hierarchy as possible. The idea is to concentrate criticism where it is most likely to be fruitful – low down in the hierarchy. We need to try to modify ideas here so that they are compatible with assumptions higher up in the hierarchy, and at the same time accord best with empirical progress at levels 1 and 2 – or promise to promote empirically progressive research programs at these levels (Maxwell, 1984, Chapter 9; 1998; 2002; 2004, Chapters 1, 2, and Appendix; 2005; 2006a; 2011).

Thus, physics seeks not truth per se, but rather truth *presupposed to be explanatory*. Yet science does not just seek explanatory truth; more generally, it seeks valuable truth – if anything, even more problematic. And it seeks truth to be used by people, and by institutions, in one way or another, if anything even more problematic. There are, in short, highly problematic assumptions concerning metaphysics, values, and human use implicit in the aims and priorities of scientific research. These need to be made explicit within science, and subjected to sustained imaginative and critical scrutiny, by scientists and non-scientists alike, in an attempt to improve aims so that they come to represent the best interests of humanity (see Maxwell, 1977; 1984, Chapter 5; 2004, pp. 51–67; 2008). The aim-oriented empiricist conception of the methods of physics depicted in Figure 11.1 can readily be generalized to take into account problematic assumptions associated

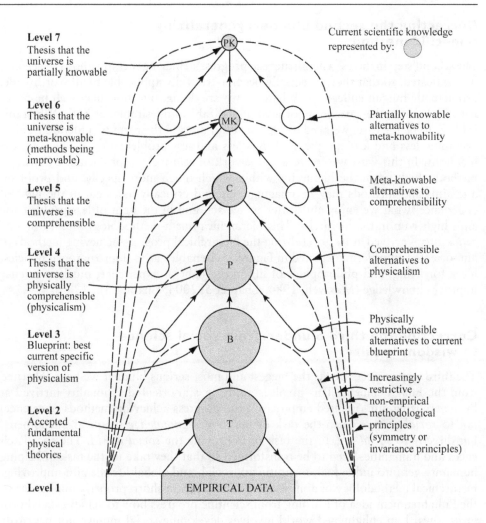

Level 7
Thesis that the universe is partially knowable

Level 6
Thesis that the universe is meta-knowable (methods being improvable)

Level 5
Thesis that the universe is comprehensible

Level 4
Thesis that the universe is physically comprehensible (physicalism)

Level 3
Blueprint: best current specific version of physicalism

Level 2
Accepted fundamental physical theories

Level 1

Current scientific knowledge represented by:

Partially knowable alternatives to meta-knowability

Meta-knowable alternatives to comprehensibility

Comprehensible alternatives to physicalism

Physically comprehensible alternatives to current blueprint

Increasingly restrictive non-empirical methodological principles (symmetry or invariance principles)

EMPIRICAL DATA

Figure 11.1 Aim-oriented empiricism

with the aims of science having to do with *values*, and the *social uses* or *applications* of science. It can be generalized so as to apply to the different branches of natural science. Different sciences have different specific aims, and thus different specific methods, although throughout natural science there is the common meta-methodology of aim-oriented empiricism (see Maxwell, 2004, pp. 39–47).

So much for the first blunder of the traditional Enlightenment and how to put it right. It is important to correct this blunder not only for science, but also because it is only when this has been done that scientific method becomes especially helpful, indeed, vitally necessary – when generalized – in enabling us to make progress toward as good a world as possible, as we shall see.

Correcting the second blunder: generalizing scientific method

The second step involves generalizing the progress-achieving meta-methods of science, just indicated, so that they potentially become fruitfully applicable to all worthwhile, problematic human endeavors. Whatever we are doing, our aims may well be problematic, because they are (more or less) unrealizable, undesirable, or both. When this is likely to be the case, we need to represent our aims in the form of a hierarchy, aims becoming less and less specific, and thus less and less problematic, as we go up the hierarchy. In this way, we create a framework of relatively unproblematic aims and methods, high up in the hierarchy, within which much more specific and problematic aims and methods may be imaginatively and critically assessed, in the light of experience, what we enjoy and suffer, as we act, and in the light of less problematic aims higher up in the hierarchy. This hierarchical meta-methodology – *aim-oriented rationality* – arrived at by generalizing the hierarchical progress-achieving methods of aim-oriented empiricism depicted in Figure 11.1 enables us to improve social policies, ideas for living, and philosophies of life in the light of experience, much as science improves knowledge (Maxwell, 1984, Chapter 5; 2004, Chapter 3).

Correcting the third blunder: from social science to wisdom-inquiry

The third step corrects by far the biggest and most serious blunder we have inherited from the Enlightenment. This involves applying aim-oriented rationality (arrived at by generalizing aim-oriented empiricism, the progress-achieving methods of science) not to *social science* or to the task of improving *knowledge* of social phenomena, but directly to *social life*, to the task of improving the *social world*. The social sciences and humanities need to be transformed so that they take up the task of helping humanity get into individual, institutional, social, and global life the aim-improving, hierarchical methodology of aim-oriented rationality. In short, properly implemented, the Enlightenment idea of learning from scientific progress how to achieve social progress toward an enlightened world involves developing social inquiry not primarily as social *science*, but rather as social *methodology* or social *philosophy*. The basic task of social inquiry and the humanities would be to help people tackle problems of living in increasingly cooperatively rational ways so that what is of value in life may be attained. Somewhat similar to the way in which natural science, in the pursuit of knowledge, proposes and attempts to falsify conjectured solutions to problems of knowledge, so social inquiry and the humanities, in order to help people achieve what is of value in life, would propose and critically assess conjectured solutions to problems of living – possible social actions, policies, political programs, new social arrangements and institutions, ways of living, and philosophies of life. Social inquiry and the humanities would have the task too, of course, of actively promoting cooperatively rational tackling of problems of living in the social world. And again, somewhat similar to the way in which natural science ought to put aim-oriented empiricism into scientific practice, so too a basic task of social inquiry and the humanities would be to get into personal and social life, and into other institutions besides that of science – into government, industry, agriculture, commerce, the media, law, education, international relations – the progress-achieving methods of aim-oriented rationality (designed to improve problematic aims) arrived at by generalizing the methods of science (see Barnett and Maxwell, 2008; Longuet-Higgins, 1984; Maxwell, 1976; 1980; 1984; 2004, Chapters 3 and 4; 2006b; 2007; 2012; 2014; McHenry, 2009).

It is exactly this that the *philosophes* failed to do. Instead of applying aim-oriented rationality to *social life*, the *philosophes* sought to apply a seriously defective conception of scientific method to *social science*, to the task of making progress toward not a *better world*, but better *knowledge* of social phenomena. And this ancient blunder, developed throughout the 19th century by J.S. Mill, Karl Marx and many others, and built into academia in the early 20th century with the creation of the diverse branches of the social sciences in universities all over the world, is still built into the institutional and intellectual structure of academia today, and is inherent in the current character of social science (see Aron, 1968; 1970; Farganis, 1993; Hayek, 1979; Maxwell, 1984, Chapter 6).

The upshot of correcting the three blunders of the Enlightenment would be a revolution in academia. Instead of academia being devoted, in the first instance, to the pursuit of knowledge – knowledge-inquiry as I have called it – we would have a new kind of academic enterprise devoted to the pursuit of wisdom: wisdom-inquiry as I have called it. Wisdom is to be understood here as the capacity and the active endeavor to realize what is of value in life, for oneself and others ("realize" meaning both "apprehend" and "make real" or "create"), wisdom in this sense including knowledge, technological know-how and understanding, but much else besides. Wisdom-inquiry puts problems of living at the heart of the academic enterprise. It strives to help humanity tackle problems of living – especially the grave global problems indicated above – in increasingly cooperatively rational ways, and strives, too, to help humanity put aim-oriented rationality into practice in its diverse endeavors, above all the endeavor to make progress toward as good a world as possible.

Adverse consequences

So far, we have failed to correct the three blunders of the Enlightenment. We have failed to transform knowledge-inquiry so that it becomes wisdom-inquiry. We have failed to get the aim-improving meta-methodology of aim-oriented rationality into the fabric of social life, into our diverse institutions and social endeavors. Even worse, we have not as yet had the idea that this urgently needs to be done. The idea has been around for decades, but it has been ignored.

The consequences of these blunders have been dire indeed. Almost all our current global crises have arisen because we have successfully pursued aims that seemed inherently desirable, but which have subsequently turned out to have adverse repercussions. We strive to achieve progress – economic, industrial, and social – and, as a result, along with much that is good, we bring about global warming, pollution, depletion of natural resources. We strive to cure and prevent disease, and usher in rapid population growth. We promote modern agriculture, and destroy natural habitats and bring about the extinction of species. We pursue wealth and plunge the world into debt. We seek security, build up our armies and armaments in defense, prompt others to do likewise, and provoke war. Traditional ideas about what constitutes a good world and how to achieve it, from both right and left, have had such damaging consequences when attempts have been made to put them into practice that the whole idea of making progress toward a good world has become discredited.

In order to avoid these adverse consequences of our actions, it is vital that we put aim-oriented rationality into practice so that we may discover unsuspected drawbacks in the aims we pursue early on, and so that we may develop social and political *muscle* able to modify our aims, our actions, in the light of what we discover. It is this that we have singularly failed to do. Indeed, we have not even seen the need to make the attempt. Current conceptions of rationality, from Bayesianism to critical rationalism, fail to stress the vital need to improve aims as we act. Social inquiry, instead of actively

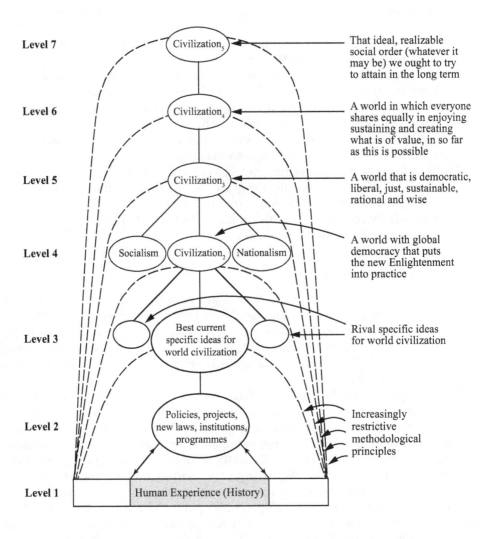

Figure 11.2 Aim-oriented rationality applied to creating civilization

helping humanity build aim-oriented rationality into social life, has instead concentrated on acquiring *knowledge* of social phenomena.

It is above all when we come to the immense and profoundly problematic enterprise of making social progress toward an enlightened, wise world that it is vital to put aim-oriented rationality into practice. The aim of such an enterprise is notoriously problematic. For all sorts of reasons, what constitutes a good world, an enlightened, wise or civilized world, attainable and genuinely desirable, must be inherently and permanently problematic. Only the effective social and political implementation of aim-oriented rationality could hope to empower us to make progress toward such a highly problematic goal as a genuinely good world. Figure 11.2, formally analogous to Figure11.1, indicates what might be involved.

Our failure to correct the three blunders we have inherited from the Enlightenment has meant that we have failed to exploit – even recognize – the full resources of the progress-achieving methods of science which, when generalized, promise to provide the vital assistance we need in order to make social progress toward a genuinely civilized, enlightened world. *Aim-oriented rationality is not sufficient, but it is necessary.*

Technology and practical wisdom

Once upon a time, technological discovery and development seemed to be the key to progress toward a better world. Medical technology enhanced health and longevity; agricultural technology vastly increased the production of food; technology in transport, communications, power production, architecture, entertainment, and indeed in every aspect of life, enhanced the quality of life in a multitude of ways.

But in the last few decades, as we have seen, a darker side to all this technological and human progress has become all too apparent. Modern medicine and hygiene have led to the population explosion; there may be as many as 11 billion people on earth by the end of this century, many more than our planet can comfortably sustain. Technologically-enhanced modern agriculture has just about kept pace with the growing human population, but at the expense of the natural world. It has led to the destruction of tropical rainforests and other natural habitats, and the rapid extinction of species. We are living in an age of mass extinction of unprecedented rapidity caused by us. There is the technology of war, which has vastly increased our power to maim and kill – to the extent that we now even have the power to destroy our world by means of nuclear war. Something like 12 million people were killed in wars in the 19th century, whereas in the 20th century, over 100 million people died as a result of war – and we are not doing too well in the 21st century so far. Once upon a time, we relied on spears and arrows; now we have the technology of conventional, nuclear, chemical, and biological armaments. Perhaps most serious of all, there are the impending disasters of climate change, engendered by the technology of power production and transport that pumps carbon dioxide into the atmosphere (aided by aspects of agriculture and forest destruction). These global problems have an impact on and intensify each other. Population growth intensifies problems of food production at the same time as climate change sabotages agriculture; as vast areas of the earth, in north Africa, Asia, and elsewhere, become uninhabitable, those who have lived there will try to flee to neighboring lands, already under stress, and will be repulsed – just the conditions for war.

The root of the problem is the one I have already identified. We once thought – and our universities are organized as if we still think – that the key to human progress consisted of this: *first*, we need to acquire scientific knowledge and technological know-how; then, *second*, this knowledge and know-how can be applied to help solve social problems. But this traditional procedure, inherited from the Enlightenment, is an intellectual disaster and a recipe for human disasters – as our modern world reveals all too clearly. If our concern is to make progress toward as good a world as possible, then the problems that fundamentally require our attention and concern are not problems of knowledge or technology, but our *problems of living* – problems we encounter as we live our lives, and problems we and our children will encounter in the future if we go on as we are and present trends continue. Problems of living are resolved by *what we do* or what we refrain from doing. Even when new knowledge and technology are required – as they are in connection with medicine and agriculture, for example – it is always what this knowledge and technology enables us to *do*, or *refrain* from doing, that solves the problem, not the knowledge and technology in itself.

At the heart of our thinking, whether in life or in universities, we need to put our problems of living and what we need to do about them, at all levels, from the personal, the social, and the institutional to the international and global. We need to develop in our culture, our social world, traditions of serious, imaginative, critical exploration of what our problems are and what we might do about them. We need to try to transform our social world so that it comes to encourage and facilitate cooperatively rational tackling of problems of living. Schools and universities need to engage with and promote such cooperatively rational tackling of problems of living. And we, the public, need to do this too. Technology without practical wisdom can be, as we have seen, a menace.

There is, however, a gulf between the problems of living we encounter at the personal level as we live our lives and the problems of living encountered by humanity as a whole – our global problems indicated above. Individually we strive to earn a living, find love, bring up children, achieve success – or perhaps just get enough to eat from day to day. We may be aware of looming global crises: rapid population growth, climate change, devastating loss of natural habitats, disappearance of wild animals and species, wars, tyrannies, pollution of earth, sea and air. Some of us are more aware of these global problems than others. These global crises arise, of course, as a result of the combined actions of humanity. And yet, as far as most of us are concerned, our personal contribution to the creation, maintenance, or intensification of these global problems is minute. There is this massive disconnect between the global problems that confront humanity and the personal problems that confront each one of us in our personal lives.

This is, above all, why we so urgently need to bring wisdom-inquiry into existence. It would be a primary task of wisdom-inquiry to help us bridge the gulf that exists at present between our personal problems of living and our common global problems confronting all of us together, humanity as a whole. A basic task of wisdom-inquiry would be to help us discover how we can act with others to get the powers that be – governments, multi-nationals, industry, banks, economic systems, and media outlets – to change their ways so that we all begin to do what needs to be done in order to start to resolve the immense and grave problems that confront us all. We need wisdom-inquiry to help us discover how we can begin to take charge of our future intelligently, rationally, humanely – that is, *wisely*.

The crises we face have been made possible by the astonishing successes of modern science and technological research. This prompts some to condemn science and technology. However, we have seen that this is the wrong thing to do. We need to learn from our immense success in solving the first great problem of learning how to go about solving the second problem. The methods employed in solving the first problem – that is, the progress-achieving methods of natural science – when properly understood, properly generalized, and, above all, properly implemented, become profoundly relevant to resolving those problems of living, from the personal to the global, that we need to solve in order to make progress toward an enlightened, civilized world. The methods of science hold the key to the practical wisdom we need to acquire to create global civilization.

Conclusion

The upshot of correcting the three Enlightenment blunders, which are still built into the intellectual/institutional structure of academia today, is a new kind of inquiry – wisdom-inquiry – rationally organized and devoted to helping us solve the second great problem of learning, making progress toward as good a world as possible. The scientific task of improving knowledge and understanding of nature becomes a part of the broader task of improving global wisdom – wisdom being the capacity to realize what is of value in life, for oneself and others, and thus including knowledge and technological know-how, but much else besides ("realize" here means both "apprehend" or "experience," and "make real" or "create").

Universities as currently constituted betray both reason and humanity. We urgently need to bring about a revolution in our universities and other institutions of learning so that they take up the task of helping us solve the second great problem of learning, making progress toward a better, wiser world.

What needs to be done to transform knowledge-inquiry into wisdom-inquiry

1 There needs to be a change in the basic intellectual *aim* of inquiry, from the growth of knowledge to the growth of wisdom – wisdom being taken to be the capacity to realize what is of value in life, for oneself and others, and thus including knowledge, understanding, and technological know-how (but much else besides).

2 There needs to be a change in the nature of academic *problems* so that problems of living are included as well as problems of knowledge – the former being treated as intellectually more fundamental than the latter.

3 There needs to be a change in the nature of academic *ideas* so that proposals for action are included as well as claims to knowledge – the former, again, being treated as intellectually more fundamental than the latter.

4 There needs to be a change in what constitutes intellectual *progress* so that progress-in-ideas-relevant-to-achieving-a-more-civilized-world is included as well as progress in knowledge, the former being indeed intellectually fundamental.

5 There needs to be a change in the idea as to where inquiry, at its most fundamental level, is located. It is not esoteric theoretical physics, but rather the thinking we engage in as we seek to achieve what is of value in life. Academic thought is a (vital) adjunct to what really matters: personal and social thought active in life.

6 There needs to be a dramatic change in the nature of social inquiry (reflecting points 1–5 above). Economics, politics, sociology, etc. are not fundamentally *sciences* and do not fundamentally have the task of improving knowledge about social phenomena. Instead, their task is threefold. First, it is to articulate problems of living, and propose and critically assess possible solutions, possible actions, or policies, from the standpoint of their capacity, if implemented, to promote wiser ways of living. Second, it is to promote such cooperatively rational tackling of problems of living throughout the social world. And, third, at a more basic and long-term level, it is to help build the hierarchical structure of aims and methods of aim-oriented rationality into personal, institutional, and global life, thus creating frameworks within which the progressive improvement of personal and social life aims-and-methods becomes possible. These three tasks are undertaken in order to promote cooperative tackling of problems of living, but also in order to enhance empathic or "personalistic" understanding between people as something of value in its own right. Acquiring knowledge of social phenomena is a vital but subordinate activity, which is engaged in to facilitate the above three fundamental pursuits.

7 Natural science needs to change so that it includes at least three levels of discussion: evidence, theory, and research aims. Discussion of aims needs to bring together scientific, metaphysical, and evaluative consideration in an attempt to discover the most desirable and realizable research aims. It needs to influence, and be influenced by, the exploration of problems of living undertaken by social inquiry and the humanities, and the public.

8 There needs to be a dramatic change in the relationship between social inquiry and natural science so that social inquiry becomes intellectually more fundamental from the standpoint of tackling problems of living, promoting wisdom. Social inquiry influences choice of research aims for the natural and technological sciences, and is, of course, in turn influenced by the results of such research. (Social inquiry also, of course, conducts empirical research in order to improve our understanding of what our problems of living are and in order to assess policy ideas whenever possible.)

9 The current emphasis on specialized research needs to change so that the sustained discussion and tackling of broad, global problems that cut across academic specialties are included, both influencing and being influenced by specialized research.

10 Academia needs to include sustained imaginative and critical exploration of possible futures, for each country, and for humanity as a whole, policy and research implications being discussed as well.

11 The way in which academic inquiry as a whole is related to the rest of the human world needs to change dramatically. Instead of being intellectually dissociated from the rest of society, academic inquiry needs to be communicating with, learning from, teaching, and arguing with the rest of society in such a way as to promote cooperative rationality and social wisdom. Academia needs to have just enough power to retain its independence from the pressures of government, industry, the

military, and public opinion, but no more. Academia becomes a kind of civil service for the public, doing openly and independently what actual civil services are supposed to do in secret for governments.

12 There needs to be a change in the role that political and religious ideas, works of art, expressions of feelings, desires, and values have within rational inquiry. Instead of being excluded, they need to be explicitly included and critically assessed, as possible indications and revelations of what is of value, and as unmasking of fraudulent values in satire and parody, vital ingredients of wisdom.

13 There need to be changes in education so that, for example, seminars devoted to the cooperative, imaginative, and critical discussion of problems of living are at the heart of all education from five-year-olds onwards. Politics, which cannot be taught by knowledge-inquiry, becomes central to wisdom-inquiry, political creeds and actions being subjected to imaginative and critical scrutiny.

14 There need to be changes in the aims, priorities, and character of pure science and scholarship so that it is the curiosity, the seeing and searching, the knowing and understanding of individual people that ultimately matters, the more impersonal, esoteric, purely intellectual aspects of science and scholarship being means to this end. Social inquiry needs to give intellectual priority to helping empathic understanding between people to flourish (as indicated in point 6 above).

15 There need to be changes in the way in which mathematics is understood, pursued, and taught. Mathematics is not a branch of knowledge at all; rather, it is concerned with exploring problematic *possibilities* and developing, systematizing, and unifying problem-solving methods.

16 Literature needs to be put close to the heart of rational inquiry, in that it explores imaginatively our most profound problems of living and aids personalistic understanding in life by enhancing our ability to enter imaginatively into the problems and lives of others.

17 Philosophy needs to change so that it ceases to be just another specialized discipline and becomes instead that aspect of inquiry as a whole that is concerned with our most general and fundamental problems – those problems that cut across all disciplinary boundaries. Philosophy needs to become again what it was for Socrates: the attempt to devote reason to the growth of wisdom in life.

18 Academic contributions need to be written in as simple, lucid, and jargon-free a way as possible so that academic work is as accessible as possible across specialties and to non-academics.

19 There needs to be a change in views about what constitute academic contributions so that publications which promote (or have the potential to promote) public understanding as to what our problems of living are and what we need to do about them are included, in addition to contributions addressed primarily to the academic community.

In addition, the following four institutional innovations also ought to be made to help wisdom-inquiry to flourish:

1 Natural science needs to create committees, in the public eye, and comprising scientists and non-scientists alike, concerned with highlighting and discussing failures of the priorities of research to respond to the interests of those whose needs

are the greatest – the poor of the earth – as a result of the inevitable tendency of research priorities to reflect the interests of those who pay for science and the interests of scientists themselves.

2   Each university needs to create a seminar or symposium devoted to the sustained discussion of fundamental problems that cut across all conventional academic boundaries, global problems of living being included as well as problems of knowledge and understanding.

3   Each national university system needs to include a national shadow government, seeking to do virtually, free of the constraints of power, what the actual national government ought to be doing. The hope would be that virtual and actual governments would learn from each other.

4   The world's universities need to include a virtual world government which seeks to do what an actual elected world government ought to do if it existed. The virtual world government would also have the task of working out how an actual democratically elected world government might be created.

Note

1 For a detailed account of what it means to assert of a physical theory that it is unified, including a procedure for grading degrees of unity, see Maxwell (1984, pp. 373–386; 1998, Chapter 4; 2004, pp. 160–174).

References

Aron, R. (1968). *Main Currents in Sociological Thought*, vol. 1. Harmondsworth: Penguin.
——. (1970). *Main Currents in Sociological Thought*, vol. 2. Harmondsworth: Penguin.
Barnett, R. and Maxwell, N. (eds) (2008). *Wisdom in the University*. London: Routledge.
Farganis, J. (1993). Introduction. In J. Farganis (ed.), *Readings in Social Theory: The Classic Tradition to Post-modernism* (pp. 1–25). New York: McGraw-Hill.
Gay, P. (1973). *The Enlightenment: An Interpretation*. London: Wildwood House.
Hayek, F. (1979). *The Counter-revolution of Science*. Indianapolis: Liberty Press.
Longuet-Higgins, C. (1984). For goodness sake. *Nature*, 312(5991), 204.
Maxwell, N. (1974). The rationality of scientific discovery. *Philosophy of Science*, 41(2), 123–153.
——. (1976). *What's Wrong with Science?* Hayes: Bran's Head Books.
——. (1977). Articulating the aims of science. *Nature*, 265(5589), 2.
——. (1980). Science, reason, knowledge and wisdom: A critique of specialism. *Inquiry*, 23(1), 19–81.
——. (1984). *From Knowledge to Wisdom*. Oxford: Blackwell – ——. (1993). Induction and scientific realism: Einstein versus van Fraassen. *British Journal for the Philosophy of Science*, 44(1), 61–79, 81–101, (2), 275–305.
——. (1998). *The Comprehensibility of the Universe: A New Conception of Science*. Oxford: Oxford University Press.
——. (1999). Has science established that the universe is comprehensible? *Cogito*, 13(2), 139–145.
——. (2000). A new conception of science. *Physics World*, 13(8), 17–18.
——. (2002). The need for a revolution in the philosophy of science. *Journal for General Philosophy of Science*, 33(2), 381–408.

——. (2004). *Is Science Neurotic?* London: Imperial College Press.

——. (2005). Popper, Kuhn, Lakatos and aim-oriented empiricism. *Philosophia*, 32(1–4), 181–239.

——. (2006a). Practical certainty and cosmological conjectures. In M. Rahenfeld, (ed.), *Gibt es sicheres wissen?* (pp. 44–59). Leipzig: Leipziger Universitätsverlag.

——. (2006b). The Enlightenment programme and Karl Popper. In I. Jarvie, K. Milford, and D. Miller (eds), *Karl Popper: A Centenary Assessment. Volume 1: Life and Times, Values in a World of Facts* (pp. 177–190). Aldershot: Ashgate.

——. (2007). From knowledge to wisdom. *London Review of Education*, 5(2), 97–115.

——. (2008). Do we need a scientific revolution? *Journal for Biological Physics and Chemistry*, 8(3), 95–105.

——. (2010). *Cutting God in Half – and Putting the Pieces Together Again: A New Approach to Philosophy*. London: Pentire Press.

——. (2011). A priori conjectural knowledge in physics. In M. Shaffer and M. Veber (eds), *What Place for the a Priori?* (pp. 211–240). La Salle, IL: Open Court.

——. (2012). How universities can help humanity learn how to resolve the crises of our times – from knowledge to wisdom: The University College London experience. In G. Heam, T. Katlelle, and D. Rooney (eds), *Handbook on the Knowledge Economy*, vol. 2 (pp. 158–179). Cheltenham: Edward Elgar.

——. (2014). *How Universities Can Help Create a Wiser World: The Urgent Need for an Academic Revolution*. Exeter: Imprint Academic.

McHenry, L. (ed.) (2009). *Science and the Pursuit of Wisdom: Studies in the Philosophy of Nicholas Maxwell*. Frankfurt: Ontos Verlag.

Index